MW01611190

THE
LEADERSHIP
REVOLUTION

"Change makes things different. While Transformation makes us different."

And your work is helping to transform the world, Kevin!

Brian

THE
LEADERSHIP
REVOLUTION

Because Evolution Takes Too Long

BRIAN CUNNINGHAM

Curious Human
PUBLICATIONS

Published 2018 by Curious Human Publications LLC

Copyright © 2017 by Curious Human Publications LLC

All rights reserved. No part of this book may be reproduced, stored, or transmitted by any means—whether auditory, graphic, mechanical, or electronic—without written permission of the publisher except in the case of brief excerpts used in critical articles and reviews. For more information contact: curioushumanpublications@gmail.com

ISBN: 978-1-7322507-0-3 (Paperback)
978-1-7322507-2-7 (Ebook)

Cover image credits: Gold design bar adapted from Shutterstock © Hakinmhan, evolution illustration silhouette adapted from Shutterstock © Uncle Leo, and butterfly by Michael Rohani.

Book design by DesignForBooks.com

Printed in the U.S.A.

Dedicated to
the courageous Leaders and Followers everywhere,
who show up every day in service to others.

Contents

Part 1

"The Separation"
The Hero's Journey and
The Call to Action   7

Part 2

"The Initiation"
Crossing the Threshold and Exploring a New Possibility (the journey into extra-ordinary Leadership)   129

Part 3

"The Return"
Integrating OUR Experiences and Sharing OUR Leadership Mastery (extraordinary Leadership in action)   305

Acknowledgments

It is people that inspire me to do so many of the things I do. And it is the following people who have very positively contributed to my experience in Leadership and in life, and in such a way that it has ultimately been reflected in the following pages.

Although this list of people could not possibly include everyone who has impacted me related to this work, I thank you all! I thank you from the bottom of my heart.

Thank you and much love to Tom Evans, my fourth-grade teacher, who in that one year, impacted me for the rest of my life. This is the value that our teachers can bring to the world.

Thank you and much love to Phil Maldonato, for demonstrating to me our real potential, when we commit to becoming a serious student in the dojo and in life.

Thank you and much love to Mike Leyh, my brother, for our early morning, pre-work meditation sessions and our deep discussions that started in the workplace many years ago, and that continue to this day.

Thank you and much love to David Dibble (author of the New Agreements in the Workplace), for everything you shared with me about real Leadership. And thank you for helping me to more clearly "see" the systems that surround us, and for helping to further unleash my spirit in the workplace. Much of the work that I have committed to, including this book, are a continuation of my time of study and exploration with you.

Thank you and much love to Linda Dibble, Christine Ho, John Rossfeld, John Madrid, Mike Harris, Dan Otero, Ellen Schweigert, Lillian Gallindo, Holley Hudgins Martinez, Howie Morales . . . "Love always wins." Nothing could be more true.

Thank you and much love to Jed Rudd, Ashleigh Garcia and Liana Ryan . . . and Charles, Peggy, Carrie, Kari, Joe, Pat, Tammy, Wayne, David, Robert, Ray, Ryan, Adam, and Cari and Elizabeth, and Peter and Autumn and Danielle!

Thank you and much love to everyone else who impacted me deeply, along the way!

Thank you and much love to all of the authors and creators of the presentations and books and workshops and videos and articles and blogs that I have read and studied and learned and grown from over the years.

And finally, thank you so much my dear wife, Deborah, and my son, Lee! Deborah has carried so much on her back, and for so long. I, we, our family, would not be where we are, without her love and commitment to us. I love you, Deborah. And Lee, you have inspired me since day one.

Introduction
Why are we here?

Clearly, we must go much further in our
explorations if we are to discover the deeper
realities and possibilities of Leadership . . .

Welcome to what may be the most extraordinary and valuable Leadership development exploration that we have ever been a part of. I do not say that for dramatic effect. The journey that we are about to embark on here is both unique and innovative within Leadership development circles. There is so much more available to us from a Leadership perspective! And we are going to take this journey all the way! This exploration will finally position us to understand, experience and express the full possibility of Leadership. This model of Leadership understanding and development is proven to significantly transform the performance and impact of individual Leaders, groups and teams in the here and now of the challenges we all face together. This is the Leadership journey that so many of us have been, not so patiently, waiting for.

For far too long we have been faced with the challenge of sorting through the maze of Leadership development material, while trying to make sense of how it all fits together. And yet, through our efforts and our commitment, we have actually improved our Leadership performance in many areas. However, the deeper possibilities of Leadership have continued to elude us, while we wait for the present Leadership development approaches to somehow complete their slow, *Evolutionary* process of transforming into something that more effectively works for us and for those we serve. But we don't have time to wait anymore! The complexity around us continues to increase exponentially, as do the challenges we face. Meanwhile, our groups and teams and organizations and customers and citizens everywhere continue to struggle unnecessarily, due to the clear and present insufficiency of far too many Leaders in far too many places.

Because of the rapid innovations of our technology and the amount of information we have access to, and the ongoing evolution of our expectations as customers and stakeholders, Leaders have been increasingly challenged to serve others and our organizations in a way that addresses these multiple types of issues. The gap between what is needed from Leaders in this day and age and what many Leaders are delivering, has continued to grow.

I will not waste our time with pointing out the numerous examples and results of questionable Leadership out there. If we simply look around, we can see far too many examples of unnecessary dysfunction and blatant *Leadership Malpractice*. While we are looking around, we may also find a few examples of great Leadership. It's just that these examples of great Leadership are too few and too far between. And there is no longer any reason why these examples of great Leadership should not be more a part of our daily experience.

My purpose in writing this book is to help to expedite, in a very real way, the next *Revolutionary* leap in Leadership understanding, development and practice. This book is for Leaders, and Followers, everywhere. It is for advanced Leaders as well as for beginning or aspiring Leaders, and for every kind of Leader in between. It is for those who are inspired by Leadership and also for those who may have become more than a little critical or cynical about Leadership, due to the many examples of just plain poor Leadership performance out there. This book is also for the Leaders who are already clearly committed to and on a path to moving deeper into their potential, in service to others.

Now let's get very clear from the beginning as to what I'm talking about when I refer to the *Leadership Revolution*. I AM NOT referring to any kind of activity that would create anger or negativity toward others. There is already too much of that out there. What I am referring to, however, is a *Revolution* in the way we think about Leadership, talk about Leadership, and interact as Leaders; what we expect from Leaders and the way we transform or grow as Leaders ourselves. I am referring to the more rapid development of Leaders that our organizations, governments, teams and families deserve, and have long waited for. I am talking about a *Revolutionary* shift in the level of *Awareness, Attention* and *Focus*, and the honesty, integrity, courage and performance of Leaders everywhere, and with those working hard and coming up soon to serve others as exceptional Leaders. I am talking here about a *Revolutionary* shift in how Leaders think and see and perform each and every day. *This is the Leadership Revolution that I am talking about!*

This book is not meant to simply add to the already voluminous collection of written material on the topic of Leadership. This book is meant to more directly provide the foundational means to deeply understand the possibility of Leadership, and in a way that is both accessible and applicable to the complexity of real-world Leadership. It is meant as a call to action for Leaders everywhere to take FULL responsibility for the privilege of Leading others, while providing us with a proven framework to do just that. This book is meant to help create a new and functional paradigm for Leaders everywhere, including those who hire these Leaders and are responsible for keeping them on board.

We will accomplish all of this through a clear and focused exploration of the foundational challenges of Leadership, the foundational elements of extraordinary Leadership, as well as through the exploration of a comprehensive, functional model or framework for Leadership development to help us understand the full progression and possibility of Leadership. The unique and innovative model for Leadership development that we will be exploring together is called the **AQ Model** (AQ = Awareness Quotient). Our experience in life starts and ends with our awareness. Therefore, the boundaries of our understanding and performance as leaders are directly tied to the depth and breadth of our awareness, or our Awareness Quotient.

Clearly, we must explore much further and deeper and wider in our awareness if we are to discover the deeper realities and possibilities of Leadership, and to be able to genuinely express these within the complexities of our daily lives. The uniqueness of the AQ Model lies in its ability to clearly illuminate, connect and integrate the full progression of Leadership development, from more well-known and common approaches to Leadership, up through much more advanced and deeply impactful approaches to our Leadership. The AQ Model is structured in a way that clearly maps out a natural progression of Leadership development and, just as importantly, includes a practical process of "up-leveling" the Leadership performance of ourselves and others, in real time! This latter component is one of the true missing links in Leadership development practice.

The material we are about to explore has a purposeful rhythm to it, a flow to it, a repetition to it, and a structure to it that is supportive of accelerating our genuine understanding and growth as Leaders. It is presented in a way that pulls us along as we absorb and integrate our discoveries. We will be guided through an exploration of the full progression of our Leadership expression, with all of its extraordinary possibilities. And although we will start in somewhat familiar territory, be assured that we will steadily move into higher and higher levels of insight, understanding and expression of the real possibilities of our Leadership performance. We will take this journey all the way, and then back around to reconnect us with where it all started. This is the Leadership journey that we have been waiting for!

And if you are one of the many Leaders out there who also desires to connect more deeply with a real expression of your "Leadership Purpose," then this book will also speak to you very directly. When understood more deeply, the workplace is actually an incredible tool for personal, organizational, community, and planetary transformation (thank you for that one and so much more, David Dibble). And on an even deeper level, Leadership is an incredibly valuable tool and path to deeper levels of self-awareness and self-actualization. *This is the Leadership Revolution that I am talking about!*

This Leadership journey that we are about to embark on, will come alive for us as we explore, in a functional way, the potential and possibility of Leadership. The purpose of this book is to support this process in the here and now of the challenges we face as Leaders. The AQ Model serves to further clarify our commitment to excellence as Leaders, while supporting our expression of this much more consistently! This book is about you and me and us, stepping more fully into our duty and responsibility as Leaders, in service to others. I am confident that this exploration will take us on an inspiring Leadership journey, one that has the potential to transform our teams, our organizations, our communities, and our lives. We have no more time for anything less! And since the complex challenges we face continue to come at us, even as we read these words, what is clearly needed is a *Leadership Revolution, Because Evolution Takes Too Long.*

I have organized this book, this journey, into three parts. Part 1 illuminates the key, foundational elements of genuine Leadership as well as the first two levels or the "status quo" of Leadership. Part 2 takes us into our Leadership purpose and on an extra-ordinary Leadership journey far beyond the status quo, through our exploration of levels 3–7. And Part 3 takes us even higher and farther and deeper into the genuine possibilities of Leadership with a focus on Leadership levels 8, 9 and 10. Along the way, we will explore a number of key pieces of the BIG, complex puzzle of Leadership. All together, these three parts take us on an experiential journey into the depth of real Leadership, the expression of Leadership that our groups and teams and organizations need and deserve.

This work could have been broken up into three separate smaller books, as more than one publisher recommended to me. However, it was important to me to include all of the key information necessary for the full Leadership journey in one place. We no longer need to pick through various books or sources of information out there to put together the full progression of Leadership possibility, now that we have a complete map of the terrain we must cover. And this map has the capability of taking us all the way. Enjoy the journey!

Part 1

"The Separation"
The Hero's Journey and
The Call to Action

One of the overarching themes of the exploration that we are about to go on through the pages of this book is "The Hero's Journey," as popularized through the brilliant and inspiring work of Joseph Campbell, an American educator, lecturer and writer, best known for his work with exploring the human experience through comparative mythology. Campbell illuminated the similarity of the hero stories that are characteristic of many cultures and religions and developed a model for the "Hero's Journey" that describes the key elements of this progression as expressed through these stories. The three main phases of Campbell's Hero's Journey are, in summary:

1. *The Separation* – making the decision or "responding to the call to adventure"; to cross the threshold and to move well beyond the status quo.

2. *The Initiation* – jumping into an extra-ordinary journey and committing to the work, while enduring the trials and tribulations necessary for us to grow

significantly as human beings to achieve a much higher level of understanding and personal mastery.

3. *The Return* – crossing the threshold back into the world of the ordinary while keeping one foot in each world (the world of the ordinary and the world of the extraordinary); to serve as an inspiring model and an effective guide for others.

As a key theme for our incredibly challenging and rewarding exploration as Leaders, the Hero's Journey has many parallels that I hope will speak to you and support you, as they have me and many others. Our Leadership journeys can be extremely challenging, and they can have a significant impact, positively or negatively, on everyone we interact with. Therefore, we must step into this extraordinary journey with the courage necessary to withstand the challenges that will surely come to us, or we risk being pulled back again into the status quo of Leadership. Connecting with the archetype of the Hero's Journey can provide us with the inspired perspective that we may very much need to survive and thrive on this journey of service to others.

In Part 1 of this book, we begin our journey of "*Separation*" from the status quo of Leadership by exploring and coming to a deeper understanding of the foundational drivers of extraordinary Leadership, and the all-too-common expression of the status quo of Leadership (Leadership levels 1 and 2). This sets the stage for us as we prepare to *respond to the call to adventure* and cross the threshold to move well beyond the status quo while helping others do the same. And as one of my dear friends, who is also an extra-ordinary Leader on the Hero's Journey, is fond of saying, "buckle up, we are going for a ride!"

CHAPTER 1

The Root Cause

It all starts and ends with Awareness.

Let's begin our journey at the beginning, by first clarifying the deeper, root cause of the problem we all face related to the practice of Leadership. Let's begin to understand and prepare to steel ourselves for the reality of what we face together as Leaders. The root cause of the problem with Leadership everywhere is not the performance and results of our organizations, although there are certainly significant opportunities to achieve even higher-level results and to increase the ease with which these results are achieved. And the root cause of the problem with Leadership is also not our Leader's ability, or lack thereof, to engage with and to support and unleash the potential of those in the workplace, although there are certainly significant opportunities in this area. These issues are important to our Leadership responsibilities but they are still just symptoms of a deeper Leadership problem. The real problem of Leadership goes much deeper.

The root cause of the planet's Leadership challenges actually lies in the insufficient *Awareness, Attention* and *Focus* of too many Leaders, related to the levels of complexity and possibility in which we are all involved. Please think about that for a second.

We do not suffer from a lack of Leadership information, so much as from an insufficient *clarity of perception* (*Awareness*), *directional discrimination* (*Attention*) and *spatial concentration* (*Focus*) with the foundations and possibilities of Leadership.

There is an enormous amount of valuable Leadership experience, research, education and training available in schools and universities across the planet. There is a vast amount of valuable Leadership information available through books, magazines, blogs, seminars, and podcasts. And yet, we still suffer unnecessarily, as a result of ineffective and often harmful Leadership approaches, since much of the information out there does not directly address the root cause of the Leadership challenge.

Many books on the topic of Leadership focus are attempting to describe the main characteristics of "Great Leadership." And while a good start, this information is not typically enough to help us to deeply understand where these characteristics come from, or how to manifest them in the here and now of our Leadership experience. Other materials share the latest research on the topic of Leadership in an attempt to prove to us what a great Leader looks like and acts like. And some materials will profess their e-z secrets to achieving Leadership greatness. These approaches can be helpful on some level. But, if these well-intentioned, well-read sources really had the e-z secrets to great Leadership, our organizations, communities, country and the planet would be teeming with great Leaders by now. We would see great Leaders everywhere! But that is clearly not the case.

And so, while there are certainly many great books and a lot of informative material available on various aspects of Leadership and on the various pieces of the puzzle of Leadership, this book will help us, perhaps for the first time, to really understand:

WHAT the deeper foundations and higher levels of Leadership are actually made up of, and how they are connected;

WHY it is critically important for us to understand the full picture of Leadership in order to move beyond the status quo of Leadership;

WHERE we and others are presently *grounded* as Leaders, along with where it is possible for us to progress to; And perhaps most importantly

HOW we can take some definitive steps towards *up-leveling* and *grounding* ourselves in higher levels of Leadership in order to perform as extraordinary Leaders. The kind of extraordinary Leaders that we are committed to *Being* and the kind of extraordinary Leaders that others deserve to be served by. Additionally, this book will illuminate how to significantly *up-level* the performance of other Leaders (and Followers), in real time.

We have no more time to waste with vague concepts or even with well-researched Leadership frameworks that do not lead to immediate and significant improvements in our genuine Leadership performance. We are facing too many serious issues within our groups, organizations, industries and governments to continue with Leadership information or theories that sound great, or make for good presentations or books, but, in the end, just don't work to the degree we all need today!

What we will NOT get from this book is more well-meaning Leadership information or research that, in the end, doesn't move us forward in the here and now. Research is a great place to start, and I have enjoyed and benefitted from countless hours of it. But unless our research is meticulously explored and tested within the context of the realities of our present-day challenges, then all we are typically left with is an interesting theory. What we will get instead through the exploration of the AQ Model is a comprehensive and straight-forward, reality-tested model of Leadership development that reflects the depth of what is really possible for us as Leaders within our complex workplaces. What we will get is, finally, a clear and systematic understanding of functional Leadership that has the potential to more immediately and more positively impact our performance as Leaders. The AQ Model will be illuminated and explored while providing us with a clear road map and process to grow our Leadership *Awareness, Attention and Focus*, to manifest our real potential as Leaders.

It is time to stop pretending that we are serving our organizations as fully responsible Leaders when we are too often falling far short of our potential. It is time to more consistently deliver what many really needed from us as Leaders, which is quite frankly, what we are being paid to do. It is time to take all that we have learned and understand how it fits together within the BIG, complex puzzle of Leadership, so that we can actually move forward into a level of Leadership that truly serves the needs of our teams, companies, communities, families, governments and the planet. It is time for a personal, group, local, regional, national and world-wide *Leadership Revolution*. That is our challenge and our responsibility as Leaders.

Now, let's jump into this mission-critical exploration related to our achieving extraordinary levels of Leadership performance. It all starts and ends with *Awareness*. That is simply a universal principle. It all starts and ends with *Awareness*, including Leadership. Without *Awareness*, there can be no comprehension of stimuli, or clarity of perspective within an experience. And with limited *Awareness*, we get only limited comprehension and perspective.

A challenge in these types of discussions, however, is that there isn't a common understanding of what *Awareness* is. Additionally, interrelated words like **Consciousness, Awareness, Attention**, and **Focus**, are often times used interchangeably, creating even further confusion around these critical elements of Leadership.

Although these concepts are mission-critical to our growth and development as Leaders and human beings, very few people really understand how these concepts function and how they relate to and influence each other. Few have a real *working* knowledge of these somewhat obscure concepts, especially as related to Leadership. So, let's fix that right now.

The model we will explore here is based on the exploration and experience with how these elements function within our unfolding experience in life. There are certainly other perspectives on these terms and we are obviously free to adopt those or to create our own. What is most important here is the interrelatedness of these four elements, rather than what we call them. So, let's address this issue, simply and clearly, to create a common understanding and dialogue around these interrelated concepts, as these concepts are such critically important aspects of Leadership and our lives.

In order to create a more functional understanding around the critical concepts of *Consciousness, Awareness, Attention* and *Focus*, I would like to explore a fairly simple model or map. Hang in there with me on this one! The interrelatedness of these concepts should become very clear as we go along. And also remember, **the map is never the terrain**. In other words, maps or models or frameworks are just tools to view and gain some degree of understanding about a set of interrelated variables, or the "terrain." Looking at a mountain on a map does not compare to climbing the mountain and experiencing it for ourselves. And just as this book represents a map or a model for extraordinary Leadership, our real purpose is to support each other in stepping into this map and stepping into and experiencing the realm of extraordinary Leadership for ourselves.

That being said, I would like to map out these four important and interrelated, foundational concepts for our Leadership growth. Let's start at the macro level and then move down to the micro. We will start with the concept of *Consciousness*. Now as stated previously, this is a word that can take on different definitions or meanings, depending on where we look and who we are talking to. And since there are no governing bodies on these kinds of things, let's create and explore our own model of these concepts, so that we can at least create a common dialogue and understanding related to our current exploration.

Let's look at it this way. **Consciousness** is BIG. One way to think about it is that it represents the totality of everything we can potentially perceive and experience as humans. It includes the entirety of life, incorporating all of the phenomenon universally available to all of us. So, *Consciousness* is BIG, REALLY BIG. Think of it as a REALLY BIG BALL that contains within it a nearly endless number of small bubbles. And these bubbles represent anything and everything that we are potentially able to perceive, and therefore experience, as humans. There is a lot more going on in this field of *Consciousness* but, for the sake of our current exploration, this should begin to give us a functional understanding of what *Consciousness* is, and how to more purposefully access it and play in it.

Now, inside this REALLY BIG BALL of *Consciousness*, there is another ball, only much smaller. And this ball is our individual ball of *Awareness*. To be more accurate, it's actually shaped like an amoeba, with tentacles reaching out in every direction. Remember that picture of the amoeba from grade school biology? And, no two people's amoebas are exactly the same shape or size. Our *Awareness* represents a key element of our uniqueness as a human being. And since our *Awareness* sits inside the REALLY BIG BALL of *Consciousness*, which is filled with all those bubbles of possible perception and experience that I spoke about earlier, then any of these bubbles contained within our ball or amoeba of *Awareness* represent the perceptions and experiences that we have access to as an individual. Picture this in our minds for a second. Imagine a BIG BALL (*Consciousness*) filled with bubbles and a smaller ball (*Awareness*) inside the BIG BALL, and this smaller ball contains only a portion of the bubbles within the BIG BALL. That should clarify the model a little more so far.

So now, picture this ball or amoeba of our *Awareness* sitting in the BIG BALL of *Consciousness*, and this amoeba of *Awareness* is constantly undulating and expanding or contracting. Its tentacles have the ability to reach out in any direction, and this can happen consciously or unconsciously. Our *Awareness* can stretch outward to encompass even more of the individual or groups of bubbles, which represent additional perceptions and experiences available to us. At this point, this model or map should help us to clearly see and understand how these two elements (*Consciousness and Awareness*) relate to each other.

As stated earlier in this chapter, *Awareness* is the place within which our active experience in life starts, unfolds and ends (if there is such a thing), and the place that significantly influences our experience throughout life. *Awareness*, or our growing *Awareness*, is also then one of the keys for our growth as Leaders. *Awareness* could be described as the amount and

type of access we have at any given moment, to the numerous perceptions and experiences (bubbles) available within
the REALLY BIG BALL of *Consciousness*. *Awareness* is our
individual ability to see and know and experience a portion
of the perceptions and experiences available to us within the
field of *Consciousness*. In other words, it is our level, or degree,
or more accurately, the three-dimensional shape of our *Awareness*, that allows us to access and operate or play in the field of
Consciousness. More or greater *Awareness* allows us to access a
greater degree (a greater portion of the bubbles) of *Consciousness*, or more of what's inside the REALLY BIG BALL and all
the possibilities available to us there.

Another point that I would like to make here before moving
on is that the size of the REALLY BIG BALL (*Consciousness*)
is most probably outside our ability to directly manipulate.
The field of *Consciousness* is what it is, or more accurately, it
is what it continues to become. However, the size, or level,
or degree, or shape of our *Awareness* is most certainly within
our field of influence. And this is really important since, as we
increase our *Awareness*, we are able to perceive more and experience more, and do more as a result. This is critical to us from
a Leadership standpoint. Our ability to Lead exceptionally is
based on our ability to perceive and understand the depth of
the **what** and **why** and **where** and **how** of our Leadership, and
this ability comes from our level of *Awareness* of all of this.

And here is another BIG KEY related to *Awareness*. As
our *Awareness* increases, so does our degree of choice. Our
ability to choose is one of the BIG KEYS to our growth and
effectiveness as a Leader and as a human being. As we may
know by our experiences in life so far, not everyone has access
to the same number or types of choices. Some react (usually
out of fear) based on a more limited number of choices, while

others appear to have access to more and better choices within the same situation. This access to more and better choices is not necessarily an IQ (Intelligence Quotient) thing, or even an EQ (Emotional Quotient) thing. It is more of an AQ (*Awareness Quotient*) thing. Think about that one for a bit!

To summarize at this point, we have the REALLY BIG BALL of *Consciousness*, filled with bubbles. And inside of this, sits a much smaller ball (amoeba) of *Awareness*, which contains only a portion of the bubbles within the REALLY BIG BALL of *Consciousness*. And the ball of *Awareness* actually expands and contracts based on many factors, which is another exploration that we will briefly touch on towards the end of this chapter. And as our individual ball of *Awareness* expands or reaches out with its tentacles, we have access to more and better choices, which can lead to more and better Leadership performance. As our ball of *Awareness* contracts, we have access to fewer and more limited choices, which leads to lesser and more limited Leadership performance. It goes without saying, but I will say it anyway. We should clearly focus on things that help to expand our ball of *Awareness* and do less of or avoid the things that contract our ball of *Awareness*.

Well, that was interesting and fun but we are not done with this model yet. Next comes the concept of **Attention**. Think of *Attention* as an even smaller ball or, more accurately, an amoeba again. And our ball of *Attention* sits inside of our ball of *Awareness*, which sits inside the REALLY BIG BALL of *Consciousness*. *Attention* could be described as our *video camera*, which we can theoretically point in any direction we choose, towards any of the bubbles of perception and experience, or "scenery" within our *Awareness*. And with some practice, we can point our video camera in multiple directions at the same time. And this is really important, and another BIG KEY. Where we place or point our *Attention* (our video camera) dictates, to a large degree, what we will see and experience in our lives. Obviously, right?

Where we point our *Attention* (our video camera) is actually dictated by our individual ability or power to choose. And once again, our ability to choose is based on our level of *Awareness*. So, our level of *Awareness* directly impacts our *Attention*, or our ability to point our video camera where we choose. Point our video camera at inspiring things and we and others are inspired. Point it at garbage or illusions and we get just that. So, we should choose wisely, where we place our *Attention*. We should "pay attention" to the direction of our vision and deeper purpose, as much as possible. The term, "paying attention" actually indicates that there is some kind of energy exchange happening here and indeed there is. Just as we would pay with money in exchange for goods or services, we must pay or purposefully exert some energy to guide our *Attention* to where we choose. Otherwise, our *Attention* just goes where it goes or where it has been programmed to go. And then, we get what we usually get. Simple!

Now moving right along to the concept of *Focus*. You can probably guess where we are going next with this Ball analogy. Think of *Focus* as an even smaller ball (amoeba) that sits inside the ball of *Attention*, which sits inside the ball of *Awareness*, which sits inside the REALLY BIG BALL of *Consciousness*. So, at this point, we have a ball inside a ball, inside a ball, inside a REALLY BIG BALL. It's sort of like one of those Russian nesting dolls.

Focus could be described in our unfolding analogy as a combination magnifying, telephoto and wide-angle view *lens* for our video camera (*Attention*) that we can control to varying degrees. And what we *Focus* on, which specific bubbles of perception and experience, is obviously partially dependent on what we are pointing our video camera (*Attention*) towards. Are we seeing another of the KEY relationships or interdependencies here? Each ball interacts with and influences the ball inside of it. And guess what else? Each ball also influences the bigger ball that it sits in. That is important because we can actually recalibrate, readjust or align any of the three smaller balls that are within our direct control (*Awareness, Attention* and *Focus*) by using any of the other balls. Get that? By orienting ourselves towards any one of these areas, we can have an impact on the others. This principle will become quite valuable as we begin to explore the *how* of extraordinary Leadership.

Focus operates much like a camera lens that allows us to see and hold great expanses of scenery and experience the full breadth of a situation or to dial down to a discreet, minute level of detail. And with practice, we can *Focus* to a degree on both at the same time. And here is one more interesting and valuable element of the interrelatedness between our *Focus* and *Attention* and *Awareness*. We can also *Focus* our *Attention* both inwardly and outwardly simultaneously, within our field of *Awareness*. With controlled *Focus*, we can actually look inward and see and experience and connect with our *Attention* and *Awareness* as we look outward and see and experience the effect of our *Attention* and *Awareness*. This maneuver can produce some interesting insights and it is entirely achievable, even by us mere mortals. Just play with that one a little and see what we see.

Our **Consciousness** could be viewed as all that we can potentially perceive or experience as a human being, while our **Awareness** incorporates everything that an individual currently has access to perceive and experience. Our **Attention** is reflected by what an individual is currently oriented towards and perceiving and experiencing right now. And finally, our

Focus represents the depth or breadth and clarity of what an individual is actually perceiving and experiencing right now. The field of *Consciousness* could be described as our shared playground as human beings, while it is our individual level or degree of *Awareness*, *Attention* and *Focus* that largely influences our distinct perspective, experience and performance within this shared field of *Consciousness*.

Hmmm, maybe I should have just stated all that in the beginning, but I hope that the ball analogy and exploration helped to anchor these concepts more deeply. And here is one more KEY that I mentioned earlier in the chapter. In general, "acceptance" increases our *Awareness*, while "resistance" decreases our *Awareness*, and also our *Attention* and *Focus*. Think about that one. Think about all of the various forms of acceptance or resistance that we experience!

And why is all of this so important? Well, our individual *Awareness*, *Attention* and *Focus* are foundational to our growth and performance as a Leader! This is where it all starts and this is where it all ends. So, we should start here. However, many Leadership development models start somewhere else. Many focus on attempting to acquire various Leadership "tools" or "skills," or they will focus on attempting to adopt various and well-researched Leadership "traits," such as integrity or courage or compassion. And, of course, there is some value in this type of exploration. But since these methods are approaching the concept of Leadership development from the middle or the end of the progression, or from somewhere downstream, the results they provide may still be sub-optimal or unnecessarily challenging and disconnected.

Why start somewhere downstream and then have to swim back against the current, when we can start at the foundation, at the "headwaters," and develop our Leadership potential as a participant in the more natural flow of things? Our Leadership performance and potential starts with, and is anchored in, our individual *Awareness, Attention* and *Focus*. That is why the AQ Model of Leadership development starts with and puts so much *Attention* on this foundation throughout this book. Leadership traits flow out of our individual *Awareness, Attention* and *Focus*, and NOT the other way around, typically. That is one of the reasons why methods that have us focus first on Leadership traits can have such variable results.

And now, to be very clear and to bring this exploration to a practical level, the AQ Model is designed around the experiential exploration and application of these foundational drivers of extraordinary Leadership (*Awareness, Attention* and *Focus*). The Leadership progression that follows, quite naturally introduces us to more expanded states of *clarity of perception* (*Awareness*). This can help us, in a very real way, to better understand the deeper reality of whatever situation we find ourselves in as a Leader. This is critical to our effectiveness and while most Leaders might believe that they are already operating at a high level of *Awareness* and with a deep understanding of reality, the blatant truth is that we are operating far below our potential in this area. Many of us can't even imagine how marginally we are performing in this critical area when compared with our potential. As a result, we often fall far short of our potential as Leaders, and our groups, teams and organizations and customers pay the price. But the good news is that we are all well on our way to addressing this issue in the here and now.

Secondly, the Leadership progression that follows, also quite naturally, introduces us to more expanded states of *directional discrimination* (*Attention*). This can help us, in a very real way, to better control where we orient our vision and expression of Leadership. This is a critical factor in maintaining our commitment as an extraordinary Leader, while also supporting the growth, development and performance of those we are responsible to. Once again, while most Leaders would believe that they are already operating with a high level of *Attention* and with a consistent orientation to the most important elements of our role, the blatant truth is that we are also operating far below our potential in this area. We often fall far short of our potential in this area and our groups, teams and organizations and customers pay the price. But once again, we will be taking on this matter, very directly.

And thirdly, the Leadership progression that follows, also quite naturally, introduces us to more expanded states of *spatial concentration* (*Focus*). This can help us, in a very real way, to better see and hear and pick up on even the subtlest forms of stimuli or feedback that the environment is sharing with us. This is a critical factor in our ability to gather the information and perspective we need to understand and make the best decisions possible, and to provide the best support possible to others, during our work within a complex situation. And again, while most Leaders would believe that they are already operating with a high level of *Focus* and with a consistent ability to perceive the most important elements of a challenge, the blatant truth is that we are also operating far below our potential in this area. We often fall far short of our potential in this area, and our groups, teams and organizations and customers pay the price. And we will be approaching this opportunity, very purposefully.

And very importantly here, we should not be offended by the reality of statements directly above. Most of us have been doing our best, given the training and programing we have received up until now. The fact that we are operating far below our potential in these critical areas of our *Awareness, Attention* and *Focus*, should be exciting to us! To know that there is so much more within our potential as a Leader should inspire us to commit to this type of work, so that we can serve others and our organizations even better. Imagine, as well as we are doing now, we can do so much better and give so much more and serve in much more meaningful ways and achieve more sustainable results. We are capable of so much more as Leaders and recognizing our opportunities for further improvement is a key step on our journey into higher and higher levels of Leadership performance.

The progression that we will follow is designed to quite naturally expand our Leadership capability and capacity with our *Awareness, Attention* and *Focus*. By exploring and playing with the key elements of the AQ Model, we will quite naturally develop expanded abilities with these three foundational elements of extraordinary Leadership, and with so much more. We will position ourselves to express these expanded states in real time and during the reality of our challenging work environments. The results of this can be profound. That's just how it works! But please don't believe me. Just continue along on this journey, in earnest, and we will prove this to ourselves.

There is so much more we could explore here, and the implications of playing with this, consistently and in real time, are incredibly valuable. This understanding is critical for us as Leaders in our efforts to bring all aspects of ourselves to an issue, especially a complex Leadership situation. There is more to come on this as we move forward and build on this foundational element of extraordinary Leadership, as we continue on our Leadership journey.

Please see Figure 1 for a visual image of this simple but very functional model of the interrelatedness and interconnectedness between *Consciousness, Awareness, Attention & Focus.*

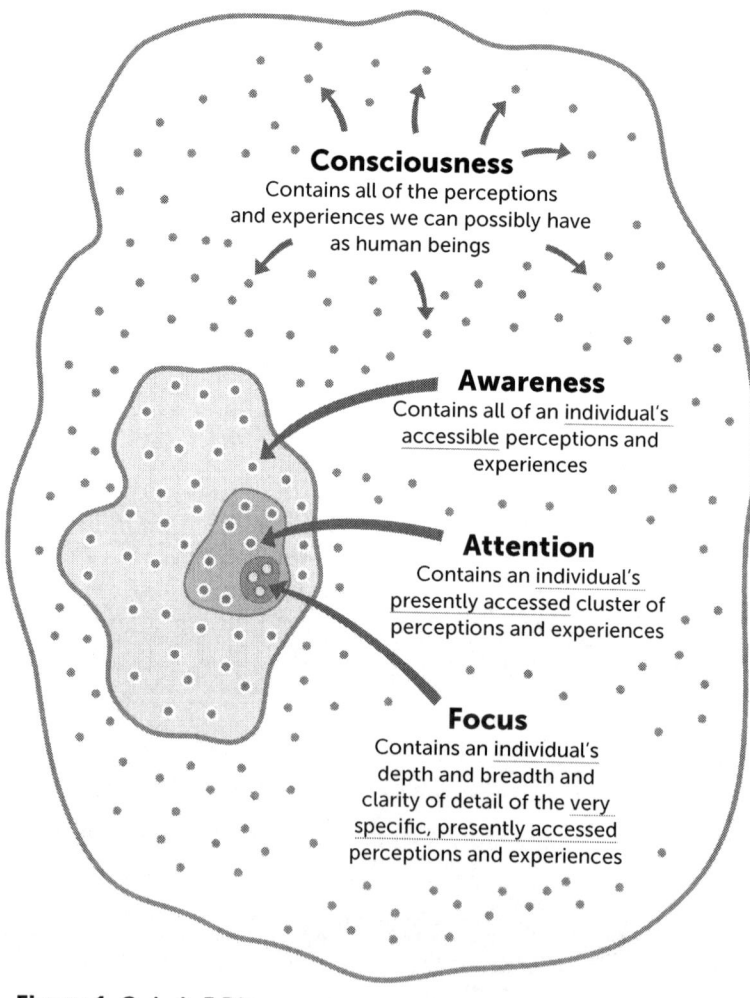

Consciousness
Contains all of the perceptions and experiences we can possibly have as human beings

Awareness
Contains all of an individual's accessible perceptions and experiences

Attention
Contains an individual's presently accessed cluster of perceptions and experiences

Focus
Contains an individual's depth and breadth and clarity of detail of the very specific, presently accessed perceptions and experiences

Figure 1. C, A, A, F Diagram

CHAPTER 2

The "Meaning" of Leadership

Leadership is simply, Love in Action.

While we are in the process of illuminating some of the key foundational challenges and opportunities with extraordinary Leadership, we must also explore and further clarify the often vague or overly confusing concept of "Leadership" itself. After all, how can we get really good at something if we are not crystal clear about what it really is, foundationally? We must be clear about what it looks like, and feels like, and smells like. There are many books available on Leadership and numerous definitions and quotes related to this topic. And many of them are quite good and inspiring. Yet there still seems to be an insufficient understanding of the more functional meaning of Leadership, one that helps us to more immediately "get it" or enables us to more immediately jump in and apply it! So, let's address that here and now.

The meaning of Leadership, as opposed to the definition, pertains to Leadership from an experiential perspective. Knowing the meaning of a concept is to understand the concept from an experiential standpoint. So, let's explore the meaning of

Leadership, rather than an arbitrary definition. When we more deeply explore the meaning of Leadership, as related to our best vision of ourselves in alignment with our true purpose as Leaders, we find at a foundational level that Leadership is simply, **Love in Action.**

Let's take a moment to clarify our terms here, as the word "Love," like the word "Leadership," is one of those terms that can be difficult to create a common understanding around. Let's clarify our terms, so that we can create the alignment that we need to more gracefully and clearly move forward. From the perspective of extraordinary Leadership:

> **Love** *is the experiential understanding of our connection as human beings; the deep appreciation and respect for our unique experiences, challenges and gifts, our humanness; and the deep desire to serve and support each other. This is a foundational element of our Leadership "Being."*

> **Action,** *in this case, refers to any movement that attempts to create a shift or change toward a more positive direction; a shift or change toward more productive thoughts, words, behaviors, paradigms, systems, processes, individuals, groups, organizations, communities, etc. This is a foundational element of our Leadership "Doing."*

Love creates "connection," and *Action* creates "movement." So, if we were to further explore the meaning of Leadership based on this perspective, it is fundamentally about *Connection and Movement*. It is about *Support and Growth*. Leadership is about *Acting in Service* to others, and ourselves. Leadership, or **Love in Action**, is the movement, the very deep movement, of who we are in service to others. Therefore, anything we do in alignment with these foundational principles is an expression of Leadership.

Without this clear understanding of Leadership, *grounded in Love* and *focused in Action*, we will not be able to *move ourselves*, or help others to *move themselves*, enough to create the deeper shifts or changes that we all long for; the shifts and changes that help others to rise above the *energetic threshold* required for them to step into their best selves and to passionately and consistently give their best effort.

Real Leadership can most certainly help to build better products or services and achieve various organizational goals and objectives. However, these are merely the outcomes manifested by doing what is really most important, which is helping ourselves and others to learn and grow and to be better people; better than we were the day before and better than our minds may believe we could be. As long as we are *Leading* or supporting ourselves or others in *moving* forward, with *Love*, then we are on the right track as a Leader. And when we lose sight of this, we become, at best, successful, and at worst, a tyrant.

At a foundational and functional level then, Leadership is *Love in Action*. It is the movement, *the deep movement of who we are in service to others*. It brings to bear all that we are on all levels. It holds nothing back. It is steadfast and transparent, and courageous and vulnerable, and subtle and powerful. Leadership is about relationship. It is about the positive, productive relationship with ourselves and those we serve. In its genuine form, it is a win-win relationship, where everyone gains from the interaction and the work. It can be expressed in every action, no matter how large or small. So, from now on, we should be able to describe the meaning of Leadership in just three simple words, **Love in Action**, and know what that really means. It's so simple!

And while we are at it, we should also briefly explore and clarify the flip side of the Leadership coin and that is the concept of "Followership." The meaning of Followership is NOT related to any version of the word "subordinate." Followership is actually the act of co-leading or co-creating with another Leader. Followership is about the active, engaged support of another, or of an activity or a cause, to help events to move forward in a desired direction.

No matter where our position sits within an organization, team or group, if we commit ourselves to actively engaging with and supporting the forward movement of an effort in a positive way (Love in Action), then based on the meaning of Leadership we explored above, we are also a Leader. We are always either Leading or Following, even if we happen to be in a more Senior or Executive level position. Leadership and Followership are just two sides of the same coin! Therefore, if we consider ourselves to be in a Follower role, we still have an incredible opportunity to take our commitment and performance to a much higher level, and to benefit so many others by doing so. As we read what follows, every time I use the word "Leader or Leadership," know that it applies equally to what others would consider "Follower or Followership." They are essentially two sides of the same coin.

When we are able to understand and connect with this foundational meaning of Leadership, our Leadership journey, our Hero's Journey, becomes infused with and supported by a principle and an energy that is virtually unlimited in its ability to support us and carry us along through the challenges and joys of Leadership, while we work to serve others in an extraordinary way! *This is the Leadership Revolution that I am talking about!*

CHAPTER 3

The Core Elements of the Foundation of Leadership
Being & Doing

Being is mostly internal work, while
Doing is mostly external work.

Now that we are becoming a little more grounded in the foundational elements of extraordinary Leadership, let's do some further exploration into some of the core elements within this foundation. This exploration should help us to understand and operationalize or implement and express our more foundational approach to Leadership. The core elements of our foundation of Leadership can then become a key driver of our efforts along our Leadership journey. These very real expressions of our deeper purpose as Leaders are most needed in our organizations today. This is what individuals everywhere have been crying out for, to finally fulfill the promise of Leadership.

Let's get right into the exploration of the core elements of our Leadership foundation, which are our *"Being"* and *"Doing."* These two key drivers of extraordinary Leadership can provide us with a direct strategy to more effectively move forward onto the path of a genuine Leader. In order to take our Leadership approach to significantly higher levels of service and effectiveness, we must clarify the key elements and expression of our Leadership *Being* and *Doing*. This represents very specifically, some of the key elements of the "what and why and where and how" of this higher level of Leadership.

As we may suspect by now, this book is not about merely pondering a bunch of Leadership terms or concepts. Pondering is a good place to start! However, this book is in our hands to serve as a "jumping in" point; jumping into our best expression of Leadership in order to fulfill our responsibility as a Leader, to others and ourselves. This book will help us to clarify What we are here to do as a Leader; Why we are here to serve as a Leader; Where this will take us and those we serve; and very specifically, How we are going to do this, on a daily basis. The *Leadership Revolution* has already started, and our personal contribution to this *Revolution* can begin right now!

Let's jump, momentarily, to the end of this exploration, so that we can catch a glimpse of where it is all going as we move through it. At the very core of performing as an exceptional Leader, we need only to focus on and accomplish two fundamental things. We need to be nice, and we need to move things forward. Let me say it another way. As a Leader, we need to *BE* genuinely supportive and professional, and we need to *Do* the right thing(s). That's fundamentally it! And when we can do those two fundamental things on a consistent basis, we are well on our way to serving as an extraordinary Leader.

If we can consistently do these two things, we will clearly separate ourselves from the status quo of Leadership. This courageous act can mark the important transition from the first phase of the Hero's Journey (The Separation), where we follow our inner call to adventure out beyond the status quo of

Leadership, to the second phase of the Hero's Journey (The Initiation). This is where we purposefully choose to jump into an extra-ordinary journey and commit to the work and the trials and tribulations necessary to grow significantly as a Leader, and to achieve a much higher level of understanding and personal Leadership mastery! It just doesn't get any more exciting than this for a Leader! Well, that is until the third phase of the Hero's Journey. But this first, huge step can inspire our daily Leadership practice and experience, and that of those we impact, with a very real and palpable missing piece of the vision for what is possible in the workplace.

The exploration of our Leadership *Being* and *Doing* should help us to understand where this journey is taking us and also how to get there. Now let's go back to where we started in this chapter and explore some of the important details of the core elements of the foundation of Leadership, *Being* and *Doing*.

Being relates to our consistent internal "Mindset," attitude, and perspective on life. It is represented by our "paradigm" or our core "programming," and significantly informs how we show up and perform and present ourselves to others. Our *Being* is incredibly important to our success in achieving an expression of extraordinary Leadership. Our *Being* as a Leader can be both an expression of our values and the values of the organization.

On a more fundamental level, our *Being* is actually a reflection of our *Awareness*, and this is important since Leadership has so much to do with understanding and addressing what is really needed by an organization or its employees and customers. That is why our *Being* is so critical to extra-ordinary Leadership and why it represents such a large part of our success as Leaders. We just can't progress too far on our journey into extra-ordinary Leadership, unless we earnestly explore and become crystal clear about our way of *Being*.

Now, let's move on to the concept of *Doing*. *Doing* relates to our consistent, formal and informal approach to moving things forward and getting things done in our increasingly complex work environment and in life. This is our consistent and purposeful approach to prioritizing and Leading ourselves and others in accomplishing key activities. This includes our personal and group accountability structures and tools, and our commitment to using them. It is our ability to effectively plan and to execute on a plan. We can see our *Doing* expressed though our "Skill Sets" and our "Tool Sets," which we will also explore soon.

As an extra-ordinary Leader, it is critically important to develop the ability to consistently identify the *right things* to do and then to work and support others to get these right things done. The good news here is that there are quite a few evidence-based methods that we can choose from to maximize our potential with becoming a high-level *Doer*. There is typically more focus and training available related to the *Doing* parts of our roles. Trainings on the *Doings* of Leadership are everywhere. Historically, there has not been as much focus on the *Being* side of this equation. However, this has begun to change more recently.

The key in our choice of *Doing* methods is that the approach we use must be continually assessed based on its *functionality* within our specific workplaces. In other words, IT MUST WORK, consistently and reliably. And that means that it must support and move us toward the achievement of our goals and objectives, while minimizing any wasted effort or resources. And MOST IMPORTANTLY, it must minimize the unnecessary frustration or drama that can occur and that is all too common when employees and teams are working to get something done. If our model for getting things done does not do these things consistently and well, then our approach needs to change.

Being is mostly internal work, while *Doing* is mostly external work. As I mentioned earlier, there are numerous trainings to help Leaders with their approach to *Doing*. These trainings can provide us, through an external teacher, information that we can then apply to a given situation. However, the development of our *Being* must come from within us. Certainly, others can talk to us about *Being* concepts or we can read about this from many sources, but we must then do the necessary internal exploration and work to develop and live out of our personal way of *Being*. It doesn't work any other way if we are committed to extraordinary Leadership.

Let's now explore this concept of *Being* and *Doing* from a more practical perspective to help us understand how it plays out in many of our workplaces. Let's do this by briefly looking at a few common scenarios related to the performance of our Leaders.

There are Leaders out there who are certainly very nice (*Being*), but for some reason, they just can't seem to consistently get things done (*Doing*). I guarantee that we have all worked with a Leader in this category. Other Leaders we know are real "work horses," and are high performers when it comes to getting things done (*Doing*). But for some reason, they are also consistently kind of a jerk about it (*Being*). What's up with that? This can take a significant toll on everyone around them, to the point that others may leave the organization because this Leader is allowed to consistently behave in this way. And then there is this third, most unfortunate but still all too common scenario, where a Leader is both a jerk (*Being*), and also incapable of consistently getting things done (*Doing*). This is clearly a major problem for an organization and its people, and yet there are still a number of these Leaders out there!

These three simple examples should help to bring to life just how this concept of *Being* and *Doing* plays out every day in workplaces everywhere. And unless these two core elements of the foundation of extraordinary Leadership are purposefully explored by us as Leaders, then things will continue to go where they go, and we will continue to get what we get, which is most often the status quo. But wait, let's look at one other possibility here related to Leadership. It is clearly possible for a Leader to do two things at the same time, especially a Leader who is committed to extraordinary Leadership. It is clearly possible for us as Leaders to consistently be nice (*Being*), while simultaneously and consistently working towards and supporting others in moving things forward (*Doing*). High-level integrity is evident when our *Doing* becomes a consistent expression of our *Being*. Extraordinary Leadership occurs at the intersection of these better versions of our *Being* and *Doing*. Please see Figure 2.

In summary, the core elements of the foundation of extraordinary Leadership are *Being* (our Leadership Mindset) and *Doing* (our Leadership Skill Sets and Tool Sets), and we must be crystal clear about what these elements mean to us as individual Leaders. And then we must apply them consistently in the real world. To make things really clear and simple, our fundamental duty and responsibility as an extraordinary Leader is to *be nice* and *do the right things*, often within incredibly complex and challenging situations. *Being* nice is an expression of real strength and deep *Awareness*. And *Doing* the right thing(s) is an expression of genuine commitment and a refined *Attention* and *Focus*.

When we do these things consistently, we will find ourselves moving beyond the status quo and in the company of a growing group of Leaders who have also made the courageous decision to move into more genuine, higher levels of Leadership performance. We will find ourselves firmly planted on the path to phase two of the Hero's Journey! This is the exciting and valuable training ground, where through our work and commitment and courage and passion for serving others as a Leader, we can seize the opportunity to transform ourselves and the experience of others! We will further explore the process of becoming crystal clear about our Leadership *Being* and *Doing,* when we clarify our personal "Leadership Purpose" in Part 2 of our journey. These are the *deeper explorations in Leadership Awareness* that we must commit to.

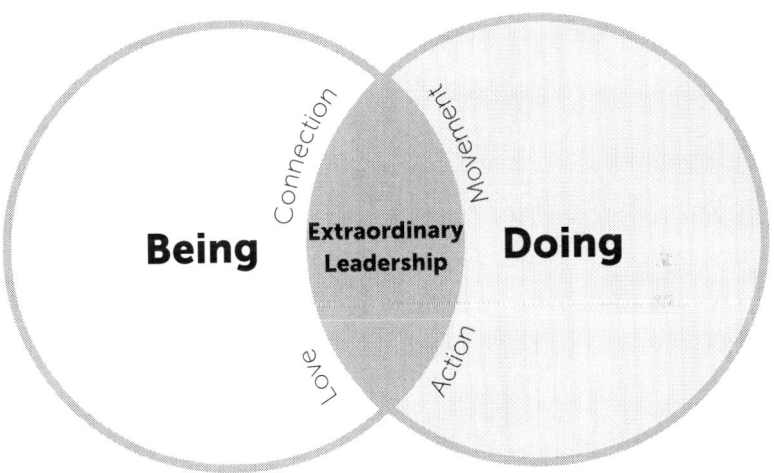

Figure 2. Being & Doing Model

CHAPTER 4

Tool Sets, Skill Sets, Mindsets & Meta-Mindsets

When we are able to create this level of alignment within ourselves and our teams and our organizations, extra-ordinary things happen.

This next exploration should be fairly straightforward. It will be focused on a basic model that is designed to clearly illuminate which specific areas of our performance, or that of others, may need attention. This may sound pretty basic and, in a way, it is, but it is amazing how often Leaders miss or skip over the basics and then wonder why their groups or teams or organizations continue to struggle and produce sub-optimal results.

Let's call this next model the T.S.M.M. Model, which stands for Tool Set, Skill Set, Mindset and Meta-Mindset. It is interesting that when results are sub-optimal, many Leaders still waste everyone's time by getting upset and broadcasting their frustrations in some way instead of doing the real work of Leadership, which is to assess and diagnose root causes to determine the reality impacting a situation, and then to address that reality, directly. There are probably many reasons for this dysfunctional approach. However, the focus of this chapter is to provide extra-ordinary Leaders with a simple diagnostic tool to identify areas of performance limitation, or performance excellence, to more productively support everyone's movement into higher levels of performance. This exploration will take us far beyond the common but limited Leadership perspective of, *"to achieve success, make sure the team has the equipment they need (tools), the training they need (skills), and that they understand our expectations (which are usually based on our particular programing)."*

Let's consider that our daily Leadership and workplace performance lies across several connected performance domains, consisting of our Tool Sets, Skill Sets, Mindset and Meta-Mindset (See Figure 3). Our Tool Set includes all of the "problem-solving gadgets" that we have access to. Examples include: a hammer, a saw, a pen, a spreadsheet or data set, a computer, a smart phone, a schedule, a standardized form, a planning document, a budget, process improvement methods such as LEAN/Six Sigma, etc.

This should clarify the domain of Tool Sets for us and differentiate it from the other domains. And yes, this is a basic yet critical understanding. We must constantly ensure (assess, question, determine and address) that our team has the appropriate tools available to get the job done and to achieve the results we need, especially in a rapidly changing, complex environment. If we don't ensure this, we should at least spare everyone our unnecessary frustration and upset when deliverables are not adequately produced. And as a question to us all, what Leadership Tools have we picked up and explored most recently? And, what Tools have we ensured that our team has access to recently?

The next performance domain is that of our Skill Sets. Our Skill Sets are directly related to our ability and level of effectiveness in utilizing problem-solving gadgets (Tools). Skill Sets are often developed through some degree of training with a tool and our experience with applying it in real-life situations. Our Skill Sets can also have a wide range or levels of ability, from "novice" through "expert" and even "master." Example Skill Sets could include: if our Tool is a hammer, then *hammering* would be part of our needed Skill Set; if our Tool is a spreadsheet, then *populating, and presenting the data on the spreadsheet* would be our needed Skill Set; if a work schedule is our Tool, then effective *scheduling* would be part of our needed Skill Set. Tools, for the most part, do nothing in and of themselves. It is our level of skill in choosing and utilizing various tools that creates much of what we are responsible for producing in life.

If a hammer is part of our required Tool Set, then developing an effective ability with hammering would be part of our essential Skill Set. Our ability with hammering will be critical to the outcome produced by our hammering and our overall success as an employee or as part of a team. If LEAN/Six Sigma Performance Improvement Methods are a key part of our Tool Set and a critical element of our job performance Skill Set, then understanding how and in which way to use and apply these tools will be critical to our and the organization's success. As a related side note, it is interesting to me as I have read and heard about many industry examples of performance improvement methods such as LEAN/Six Sigma, "failing." From the perspective of the T.S.M.M. Model, LEAN/Six Sigma cannot, in and of itself, fail. It is only a Tool. In this sense, a Tool cannot fail (unless it literally breaks). It is OUR ability to choose the right tool and to use it and to apply it effectively that creates the outcome, either failure or success. So, what has really failed in many of these problematic LEAN/Six Sigma implementations? Can we guess?

Skill Sets are developed through some form of ongoing education, training, practice, real world application, monitoring of ongoing performance, coaching to higher levels of skill, and/ or see one-do one-teach one types of approaches. Skill Set development is a critical, ongoing, purposeful activity to position ourselves and our teams to thrive in an environment of ever-increasing complexity. In too many instances, Leaders do not give this domain the critical, ongoing attention it needs, and yet still become frustrated when team performance is not at the level necessary to produce the appropriate outcomes. Skill Set development and the ability to continuously learn and grow are a core competency for extra-ordinary Leaders.

Let's review just this first part of the T.S.M.M. Model's simple but impactful utility. If, as a Leader, a deliverable or an issue was not addressed appropriately by our team, we must first ensure (assess, question, determine and address) that our team has the appropriate tools to do the job, and that they had received the appropriate level of education, training, coaching, return demonstration, etc., to develop the necessary skills for the job. We can ensure this by simply asking some very specific questions related to these variables. Any gaps or variances based on the answers received must then be addressed. Incidentally, this approach can and should be applied to ourselves and to our fellow Leaders.

Skipping or short-cutting these first two domains of performance are a common way that many Leaders attempt to cut costs. Yet, many times, these dysfunctional Leadership approaches actually cost much more! And these types of scenarios can occur at all levels of an organization, from the frontline to the boardroom. However, when we value these two performance domains, and place the required *Awareness*, *Attention* and *Focus* on even just these first two domains of the model, our team and organizational performance can improve significantly. This is clearly a key part of our responsibility as an extra-ordinary Leader. What Skill Set(s) have we developed or have we been working on for ourselves most recently, and what Skill Sets are we supporting others in developing?

Before we move to the next domain in this model, I would like to ground this T.S.M.M. Model in some of our previous explorations, since it is all connected. These first two domains of performance (Tool Sets and Skill Sets) are expressed through our *"Doing,"* right? While the next two domains of our performance in this model come out of our *"Being."* Remember, our *Being* and *Doing* represents the core of our foundation as an extra-ordinary Leader. We can now layer over these core foundational elements the understanding that our *Doing* is expressed through the Tool Sets that we have access to and the Skill Sets that we have developed through using these tools. And that our *Being* is informed by and expressed through our Mindset and our Meta-Mindset. This should provide us with another layer of understanding and alignment with the T.S.M.M. Model and to the overall approach within the AQ Model. It's another piece of the puzzle!

The next critical performance domain we will explore is that of our Mindset. We should consider our Mindset as a key driver of the development of our Skill Set(s), just as our Skill Set(s) and their degree of development are a key driver of our ability to effectively choose and utilize the elements in our Tool Set. Again, it's all connected. The depth and clarity of our Mindset (*Being*) provides us with the internal energy or motivation required to establish the foundation and consistency of our *Doing*. Our *Doing* flows out of our *Being*. It can be the driving force behind the things we choose to do in life and, therefore, the experiences we have and the results we achieve.

Our Mindset can be glimpsed through our consistent thoughts and beliefs or our paradigm. And our Mindset expresses itself through our typical characteristics or traits or personality as a Leader. These traits include things like our level of integrity, commitment, passion, engagement, vision, courage, compassion, respect, discipline, motivation, excellence, etc. Some version of these traits can also often be found in an organization's "Values."

Organizational Values typically come from the particular Mindset of an individual Leader or group of Leaders. The challenge then becomes to engage as many individuals as possible in the deep understanding of these values and in a genuine and consistent expression of them, in order to establish a group Mindset. A group Mindset then fuels the consistent *Doing* of the organization or group or team through their use of chosen tools and their developed skills with these tools. And it is this group *Being* and *Doing* that then forms the "culture" of an organization.

These Mindset traits are very often the subject of Leadership articles and books. Much of this material focuses on informing us which of these traits have been proven by some research to produce the best Leaders. This material then recommends that we should *Be* like this or *Be* like that as a Leader. Just *Be* more courageous. Just *Be* more compassionate, and visionary, and motivated, etc. Just *Be* it! The only problem with this approach is that without a clear understanding of the connection between our *Being* (Mindset and Meta-Mindset) and *Doing* (Tool Sets and Skill Sets), our efforts with genuinely connecting with and consistently expressing these well-researched Leadership traits can be, many times, sub-optimal. If only it was as simple as just doing some research on the best Leadership traits, and then adopting them and telling other Leaders to just *Be* like this or that. But it is not. There is a little more to it than that. There are a few more pieces of the Leadership puzzle that we need to understand with this process. That is where the T.S.M.M. Model comes in to support us.

It should be clear at this point how critical our Mindset is and how it is directly connected to and a driver of the Skill Sets that we develop and the Tool Sets we choose. Also, at this point, an additional question may have arisen in our minds. If our Mindset informs and drives the Skills we develop and the Tools we choose, then what informs and drives the development and growth of our Mindset? Good question! And the answer is our Meta-Mindset. The prefix "Meta" simply means "beyond." Therefore, this next performance domain is "beyond the Mind." If we were to explore another connection within the AQ Model, our Meta-Mindset is the product of our depth of and clarity of our *Awareness*, which then directly informs our *Attention* (Mindset) as to what is most important to us or to what is most needed at a given time. This is then expressed through our *Focus* on the use of the most appropriate Tool Sets and the development of the most appropriate Skill Sets. The pieces of the puzzle continue to come together! Look at them closely!

And now let's more specifically explore our Meta-Mindset. What do we actually find in this performance domain? Our Meta-Mindset includes our Emotional Intelligence (EI) or Emotional Quotient (EQ), which is basically our ability to understand and control our own emotional states; our ability to recognize the emotional states of others and modify our behaviors accordingly; and our ability to effectively manage social situations and groups. And as most of us in Leadership probably know on some level, our EQ is critical to our overall success as a Leader in these complex times. Much has been written on the topic of EQ, and an extra-ordinary Leader deeply explores this concept.

An additional key element of our Meta-Mindset, and the element that precedes and is connected to our Emotional

Quotient, is our Awareness Quotient (AQ). As indicated previously our AQ is represented by the depth and clarity of our *Awareness*. So, our Meta-Mindset is essentially made up of our AQ and our EQ. They are the connected and powerful drivers of much of what we think, believe, say and do.

To connect this domain of performance to our AQ Model, our Meta-Mindset is basically our field of *Awareness*. Remember our CAAF Model? Remember how our ball or amoeba of *Awareness* sits in the BIG BALL of *Consciousness*? And that our amoeba of *Awareness* has these tentacles that reach out in various directions within the BIG BALL of *Consciousness* to incorporate the perceptions and experiences that are available within its reach? And that the distinct size, shape and configuration of our amoeba of *Awareness* establishes our level of *Awareness* or the type and depth of perceptions and experiences that we presently have access to? So, our Meta-Mindset represents an important aspect of our individual level and depth and breadth of *Awareness, or our Awareness Quotient.*

With our understanding of the T.S.M.M. Model, we should now possess a more complete picture of our key domains of our performance and that of others. This might then be a valuable tool to assess any gaps in performance, and to then engage in more targeted, productive efforts. If all we need is a more appropriate tool, then let's focus there. In this situation, there is no need for frustration or judgement of ourselves or others. If the appropriate tools are available, then we should focus on ensuring that we have the appropriate education (including the objectives of an effort) and training to develop the required Skill Sets. Again, we can skip the upset and demoralizing lectures.

Once these two domains have been appropriately addressed, and if performance is still lacking, the T.S.M.M. Model then guides us to look deeper, to assess our own or another's Mindset, and once again to address this without any unnecessary drama. This is the domain of our thoughts and beliefs about a situation or about life in general. And how do we influence our own or another's Mindset? Well, as we explored earlier, it is not just a matter of telling ourselves or others to *Be* a certain way. This approach does not go deep enough. In order to impact our Mindset, we must work through our Meta-Mindset, which includes our ability to identify and understand the deeper reality of our purpose and connections as human beings. The higher levels of Leadership that we will soon be exploring include numerous approaches that work in and from our Meta-Mindset.

Another important consideration is that none of us has access to every Tool Set out there. And none of us is performing at the highest level with every Skill Set possible. Our Mindsets do not possess a complete understanding of every Leadership characteristic or trait. And our Meta-Mindsets do not incorporate the fullness of all possible perspectives and experiences available to us. So, as an extra-ordinary Leader, we should endeavor to align these performance domains, as much as possible, with the needs and possibilities within our current and future dynamics. And, we should endeavor to support others similarly. When we are able to create this level of alignment within ourselves and our teams and our organizations, extra-ordinary things happen. Our collective performance and results move more gracefully, from *ordinary to extra-ordinary*. This is why we are here! *This is the Leadership Revolution that I am talking about!*

Performance Domains (T.S.M.M. Model)

Doing		Being	
Tool Set (Macro Level)	**Skill Set** (Micro Level)	**Mindset** (Quantum Level)	**Meta-Mindset** (Boson Level)
1. Problem Solving "Gadgets" a. A Hammer b. A Planning Document c. A Work Plan d. PDCA (Plan, Do, Check, Act) e. and other process improvement methods f. Our Leadership Purpose Statement g. etc.	1. Ability and Level of Expertise with a Tool or Tool Set a. Hammering b. Planning c. Executing a Work Plan d. Managing a process improvement effort e. Implmenting our Leadership Purpose f. etc.	1. Belief System/Paradigm 2. Clarity of Purpose 3. Personal Values a. Excellence b. Courage c. Commitment d. Compassion e. Discipline f. Motivation g. etc.	1. Awareness Quotient (AQ) a. Degree of Awareness b. Intent c. Love 2. Emotional Quotient (EQ) a. Emotional Self-insight b. Insight with others c. Empathy d. Managing Social Situations
Examples	*Examples*	*Examples*	*Examples*
1. A Hammer	1. Hammering	1. The desire to build something well	1. The Awareness that we are here to create
2. A Plan	2. Planning	2. The desire to create an effective Plan	2. The Awareness that Plans connect things together
3. Speaking	3. Public Speaking	3. The desire to give a meaningful Speech	3. The depth of Awareness of our, "I have a dream..." Speech

Figure 3. T.S.M.M. Model

CHAPTER 5

The Energetic Threshold

*We must light our own fire every day to
be able to help others do the same.*

Let's do one more important exploration before we transition into the Leadership Levels of the AQ Model. I realize that we have covered a lot of ground and quite a few critical Leadership concepts in Part 1, but the material covered so far is *essential* to grounding us and preparing ourselves to step confidently out of the Leadership status quo and firmly onto the path of an extra-ordinary Leader. The material covered in Part 1 of this book is designed to deepen and anchor this foundational Leadership material within us, and also to introduce us to a more expanded perspective on Leadership. And hopefully, to cause us to question things a little more deeply.

The material covered in Part 1 is designed to serve as a springboard, to create the energy, and momentum needed for us to overcome the gravity of our old habits and our old programming that keeps us tethered to the status quo. It truly takes courageous effort to step onto the path of the extra-ordinary Leader and to remain committed here. This Leadership journey that we are on together, is a very real expression of The Hero's Journey.

Now, in order to create the momentum necessary for the learning, growth, and outcomes that we are committed to, let's begin to illuminate a specific Leadership issue that impacts our organizations and workplaces everywhere. This issue is critically important to understand in order for us to be able to effectively address it. This key foundational issue is related to the concept of the *Energetic Threshold*. This may sound like a complex physics or chemistry principle, but the concept is quite simple in its application to Leadership and the workplace. Essentially, the principle of an *Energetic Threshold* refers the fact that energy is required to create an interaction, and when we are attempting to create a specific level of interaction and result, then a specific level and type of energy is required.

If we examine this principle in relation to our workplace, there are several key observations that can be made to help us to Lead and serve more effectively. Let's face it, in the typical workplace, on a typical day, the things that are going on are often perceived by our workforce or teams as mostly rote, routine, repetitive and just not all that exciting. There are obviously occasional exceptions to this. But as a whole, most workplace activities do not rise too high on the "excitement scale," once we get beyond our initial experiences in a new position. As a result, the interface between typical workplace tasks and the people performing them does not consistently facilitate an individual's full and passionate attention to many of these common tasks. This can create less than optimal, and at times, even dangerous products, services and results for our organizations.

If we were to look at some example activities that call people to give their very best effort, we need look no further than the sports world or other forms of competitive activity. We could also look to the military, as another example. These types of activities or employment have as an inherent element, a high level of excitement, responsibility, danger or risk. The tasks related to these activities or jobs involve the requirement of giving our best, individually and as a team to be successful, and for us to continue to be able to participate in this role. If we are not giving our best in a highly competitive environment, we will not be allowed to continue on for very long. In more extreme environments, anything less than our best effort can lead to others being injured or worse.

Certain jobs inherently raise our energy, passion and commitment to a level above the threshold needed to support our continuous best effort. Yet most tasks in the majority of our workplaces do not inherently raise our energy, passion, and commitment to support our continuous best effort. Even in those environments that do inherently require and support our continuous best effort, the people within them still need and very much benefit from the support of others (Leaders) who are highly committed to the success of their efforts. In reality, we all benefit from a purposefully supportive environment that helps us to continuously reorient and refocus on giving our best effort on a continuous basis. Great Drill Sergeants do this to help protect their troops. Great Coaches do this to bring out the very best in their players. Great friends or partners do this in support of us. And great Leaders, extra-ordinary Leaders, intimately understand this concept and interact with peers, employees and teams in a way that consistently supports them in rising beyond the *energetic threshold* required for them to give their best for their teammates, customers and for themselves.

When people in the workplace are purposefully supported in more consistently rising and performing at their best, they are able to serve others in better alignment with the best versions of themselves. On an individual level, the result of working and consistently performing in a work environment like this is that it cannot help but more positively impact all other areas of our lives. There is NO separation between our work life and our home life, or any other part of our life! There is only LIFE! And when we step into this life, on a consistent basis, by putting our best self forward, even in some of the more seemingly mundane tasks we face, then our whole experience of life is transformed. This approach can transform the mundane in our workplaces, and our lives, into much more valuable experiences that add significant meaning and depth to our lives. *This is the Leadership Revolution that I am talking about!*

This is one of our primary responsibilities as an extraordinary Leader: to first, thoughtfully and purposefully overcome our own *energetic threshold*, to light our own fire, to consistently give our best. And then, to purposefully and consistently support our coworkers and teams and friends and families in raising their energy, passion and commitment above the *energetic threshold* required for them to give their best. And how we do this is critical to the process. Obviously, yelling at or bullying our workplace teams is not typically a sustainable approach to bringing out their passion and best efforts. That is where the up-leveling processes that we will begin to cover soon come directly into play. They are designed to appropriately and very effectively pull people into the best versions of themselves, and to productively raise their energy and passion around an effort. The AQ Model includes numerous approaches that help us to move more naturally beyond the *energetic threshold* that holds most of us back in the workplace.

As an extraordinary Leader, we must endeavor to understand and apply the foundational elements of real Leadership, and work thoughtfully and purposefully to move ourselves and others beyond the energetic threshold of our workplaces. Anything less does not work in the complex, rapidly changing environments that we all are a part of. Anything less will not generate the level of energy and passion and commitment necessary to move beyond the status quo, to move further on our Leadership journey, our Hero's Journey. We must light our own fire every day to be able to help others do the same. This is a core issue for Leaders across the planet to address, in an effort to raise our collective experience and results beyond the status quo.

CHAPTER 6

The AQ Model
A Functional Model for Leadership development (that means it really works)

There is so much more available to us as Leaders, and so much more available to those we serve.

As I mentioned previously, **AQ** is an abbreviation for Awareness Quotient. The name of this model is indicative of the observation that while much of the currently available Leadership development material has contributed to our understanding and performance, in order to truly achieve the possibility of Leadership, further growth in our Awareness is still required of us. We certainly have grown and benefitted from the past and current Leadership development material, yet key pieces of the Leadership puzzle are still missing. In order to approach our potential and to step further into the possibility of extraordinary Leadership, we must commit ourselves to even *further and deeper and wider explorations in our Awareness.*

Many of us have realized that it is not from a lack of Leadership "content" that we suffer, as there are an enormous number of books, trainings and information sources out there regarding Leadership. What we have come to know, however, is that we lack a comprehensive and integrated Leadership "context" or framework, and that this hinders us from moving more significantly forward in our Leadership growth, to meet the demands of today's complex work environments. What we are missing is the Leadership "context" or the overall "picture" of what extraordinary Leadership looks like and feels like and smells like, so that we can put the pieces of the Leadership puzzle (content) together in a way that creates a more integrated, functional approach to serving our teams and organizations.

Speaking of puzzles, this might serve as an interesting analogy. When we attempt to put together one of those really BIG, complex puzzles, those with the hundreds of small pieces, well, right on the cover of the box is a beautiful picture of what the puzzle will look like when we have completed it. This picture helps to guide and gauge our progress as we work on the puzzle. And as we complete a certain portion of the puzzle, we can clearly see it and appreciate how it fits into and contributes to the overall picture (context), such as when we put together a major part of the scenery of the puzzle. The picture on the box also helps us to clearly see how all of the interrelated puzzle pieces fit together.

Now, let's imagine that someone, a Leadership consultant for example, just dumped out some puzzle pieces (content) on a table in front of us. And let's imagine that this pile of content did not contain all of the pieces of the BIG, complex puzzle of Leadership. And how about if the consultant also did not provide us with the puzzle box that shows the full picture of what we are attempting to put together, perhaps because they did not have it. And then, after some extensive discussion about the puzzle pieces, the consultant said, "Thank you all, that was fun. Now I am going to leave you to finish putting together the pieces of this complex puzzle for your Leadership development. Good luck." So, how would that go?

Well, let's explore that for a moment. We are Leaders with some level of initiative, creativity and commitment, so we would probably do something such as examine the puzzle pieces while trying to remember and understand what each piece represents. And then, based on what we think we heard from the consultant, we would probably use the pieces to start to put together something in hopes that it actually fits or works. And since we are Leaders, we most probably would create something out of the puzzle pieces. And given that we are talking about Leadership here, we might call this puzzle our latest "Leadership Approach." Nice work!

The only problem with this is that if anyone were to really look closely at our new Leadership Approach, and examine our creation in action, they would see that some of the puzzle pieces actually don't fit or work together all that well, and that there are some missing pieces that create glaring holes in our Leadership Approach. The common response to this would usually be, "but that's what the consultant said" or "that is what they gave us." Everyone then goes about their business since, apparently, there's nothing further that can be done with our latest Leadership Approach, with its missing pieces and with the fact that it doesn't seem to work or fit together all that well. Incidentally, some of our peers and those we serve may have a different name for our latest Leadership Approach. They might call it, the latest "flavor of the month."

And there we have it! With just a little exaggeration for fun, that pretty much describes the situation in which many of us have been involved as Leaders over the years. Now, there are most certainly some good Leadership consultants out there and we do have some of the puzzle pieces of Leadership, although as individuals we seem to have a different collection of puzzle pieces as compared to our peers. Many of us have some of the older pieces, while others may also have some of the newer pieces of the puzzle. But we clearly don't have all the puzzle pieces together in the same place to put the whole puzzle together in a way that works and fits the growing needs of our complex organizations.

Worse still, nobody seems able to find the puzzle box, so that we actually can see how everything fits together or what pieces may be missing. It's as if all the puzzle pieces are out there somewhere, amongst the books and articles and blogs and trainings and with individual Leaders, but few Leaders have tried or have been able to pull all the key pieces together, and deeply explore them, and understand how they might fit and work together. Nor have they taken the time to put the pieces into a box that has the picture of the puzzle right on top!

It is this very situation that led to the genesis and continuous growth of the AQ Model of Leadership development. Like many of us, I was also desperately trying to figure out and gain a deeper understanding of Leadership, and to genuinely improve my Leadership performance so that I could serve others at a higher level. Like most of us, I read book after book, and article after article. I went to various Leadership trainings and spoke with many other Leaders. This was fun for me! And I did learn quite a bit about many of the pieces of the puzzle of Leadership. As a result, over time and through much trial and even more error, I most certainly did grow as a Leader. But, even with all the theories and opinions and approaches (puzzle pieces) that I had been exposed to, I continued to struggle with understanding the full picture or the context of Leadership. And therefore, I knew that my expression of Leadership was still limited and failing to provide others with some of the key support pieces needed to help them to thrive in the workplace.

It seemed as if so many people were just surviving in the workplace. I knew that there had to be much more to this thing, this workplace experience. And that Leadership had a key role and responsibility in figuring this out and delivering on a greater possibility for the workplace. So, some years ago, I committed to becoming a serious explorer of Leadership! I became an impassioned and enthusiastic student and deep explorer of extraordinary Leadership. And, the AQ Model emerged from these deeper explorations in Leadership Awareness.

As an explorer of Leadership, I am committed to the ongoing, thorough investigation, experimentation and practice of Leadership, in an effort to significantly improve our ability to serve others. I consider all of us to be fellow explorers. We are all explorers in a sense, discovering and examining pieces of the Leadership puzzle, and sharing them with one another so that we can build a clearer and more complete model of Leadership: One that fits together and works for us and our organizations in a way that supports others in stepping into their best selves, while also contributing to the attainment of our organizational goals.

And let's also add this to the picture: As Leaders, we have a significant opportunity and responsibility to transform our workplaces in a more positive way, and to help others to transform in a way that best supports them and their families, thus contributing to the transformation of our communities, our regions, our nations and our planet. And the purpose of the AQ Model is to provide a clear road map for us to move into this possibility, in the here and now. We have no more time to wait! Evolution takes too long! And the very best version of our Leadership is needed right now! *This is the Leadership Revolution that I am talking about!*

Despite some impressive profits and innovations across many industries, things in many workplaces are clearly coming apart. People in the workplace are coming apart. Many of us in the workplace know this and are experiencing this on some level. So, let's step into this situation with more clarity and commitment to our role as Leaders, in service to others. Let's go on an extra-ordinary Leadership journey, a *Hero's Journey*, and together show ourselves and our coworkers and our organizations, communities and the planet, what is really possible when we step fully into who we are and why we are here as Leaders.

As we explore this functional model for Leadership development, keep in mind that Leadership models are meant to help us organize information and concepts, and present them in a way that helps us to see and understand key relationships, and how things fit together. A useful Leadership model should help us use this information in a way that improves our understanding and performance as Leaders. A functional model should help us begin to immediately understand more of our potential as Leaders and help us to "up-level" our performance, as well as the performance of others, in the here and now.

The AQ Model is not presented in an attempt to convince others of something or as a counter to the research or theories of anyone else. This Functional Leadership Model is simply meant to show us, in a clear, understandable, and integrated way that is provable to ourselves, by ourselves, that performing as an extraordinary Leader is not only possible, but also our responsibility. This model emerged as the result of an ongoing, purposeful, deep exploration of Leadership, and was then thoughtfully refined and applied within the reality of our current, complex work environment. It has been analyzed and assessed, piloted and tested, and further modified within the complexity of the challenges we all face as Leaders. The AQ

Model reflects the reality that we experience as Leaders, as well as the reality of the impact of our Leadership performance on others and our organizations.

The AQ Model actually began as a series of exploratory observations and discussions related to the modern evolution of Leadership development and practice, beginning with the Industrial Age and progressing through the Information Age, the Knowledge Age and so on. The Levels of Leadership in the AQ Model are organized by these Ages of Leadership practice, which creates a degree of continuity and clarity for the explorer of this approach. And as the AQ Model continued to emerge, additional key elements of this functional model also began to come together in a *Revolutionary* way.

Each Age or Level of Leadership is also linked with its associated "Leadership Approach," and includes the "Predominant Leadership Characteristics" for each Level. Each Level also includes an exploration of the major issue that may be preventing us from moving forward in our Leadership development. But the model does not stop there. The AQ Model also includes the corresponding keys to "up-leveling" ourselves, from one level to the next, and also the keys to "up-leveling" others into higher levels of performance, in real time!

This approach has been proven to help Leadership practitioners to more clearly see and understand Leadership development as an interconnected continuum that is progressing in observable and reproducible ways, based on the changing work environment and the changing needs of our organizations and those we serve. And, as explored previously, the AQ Model of Leadership development is NOT a narrowly focused, "trait-based," or "skillset-based" or "tool set-based" Leadership developmental approach. The AQ Model leverages the entire Leadership progression, along with other key Leadership concepts, to support a comprehensive understanding and direct experience with exploring and applying this model to the realities of our current Leadership challenges and opportunities.

And let me be clear at this point, that the information shared within the following Ages or Levels is not meant to disparage any past or present Leader or any Leadership approach based in a certain period of time. The descriptions in each Age or Level are certainly not all-inclusive in their scope, as an incredible amount of advancement or good has occurred or is occurring in any given Age. There is clearly much more information that could have been included within each Age or Level. However, they are meant to reflect some of the more typical Leadership elements of each level, to illuminate certain characteristics and patterns of Leadership practice and performance common of each level, and to provide a road map for moving from one Leadership level to the next.

So, look at the descriptions in each Level as guideposts, and try to get a feel for the flow of the descriptions, for where they are pointing us, for where they are trying to take us. That is the real value of any functional model or map. Remember, the map is never the terrain! Maps point us in a direction, and they help us to find our way a little more efficiently. They can also illuminate what we might find along the way, but it is up to us to actually take the journey and to follow the map, to see and experience for ourselves what is really there!

Now let's begin to look at and explore the first two Levels of Leadership. These first two levels represent the ordinary, status quo of Leadership. We can see versions of the first two levels of Leadership displayed everywhere. We can still move things forward to a degree using these approaches to Leadership. It's just that they are significantly limited in enabling us to express many of the more expanded possibilities of Leadership, along with their associated results. There is so much more available to us as Leaders, and so much more available to those we serve. But we will start here and ground ourselves in the typical, status quo of Leadership, so that we can more deeply understand how this plays out in mostly unconscious ways, in so many of our expressions of Leadership. We will do this so that we can become more *Aware* of ourselves and more *Aware* of the deeper impacts of our Leadership. And to position ourselves to more thoughtfully and purposefully jump into the extra-ordinary journey of Leadership.

CHAPTER 7

Level 1 Leadership
The Industrial Age &
Authoritarian Leadership

Leadership through Command and Control . . .

Leadership Age: *Industrial Age*

The first Level of Leadership illuminated in the AQ Model comes out of the "Industrial Age." We most certainly could go further back in time to explore a number of previous Ages and their associated Leadership Approaches. But, as I stated earlier, this book's purpose is not simply to add historical or research-based information to the already voluminous material available on Leadership. This book's purpose is to provide us with a clear, concise map of what is happening right now, in this complex day and age, so that we can clearly understand and move significantly forward with our Leadership performance. Therefore, the model begins with the Industrial Age, since this Age or its remnants, are still a significant part of the civilization and workplaces that we all live and work in. And the Industrial Age mentality is still very much a part of our inherited or programed Leadership and workplace expectations, cultures and behaviors.

As a brief description, the Industrial Age is characterized by the advent of machines, mechanisms and economic processes that enable the mass production of goods and services. The Industrial Age is responsible for much of the growth of infrastructure and other forms of progress that have been achieved by societies across the planet.

Leadership Approach: *Authoritarian Leadership*

Although the Industrial Age produced significant benefits for the advancement of civilization, and there is no doubt that many incredible Leaders were developed and served others well during this Age, the Leadership Approach most representative of the Industrial Age could be described as Authoritarian Leadership. Many of those who spent their lives working in these environments tell us, "You certainly did not question Leaders back then, if you wanted to keep your job." "Leaders worked behind closed doors. And your job was to show up to work on time, do what you were told and ask as few questions as possible." And in reality, these types of workplace environments are still very common today. The Industrial Age, and it's associated Authoritarian Leadership approach, are still a major influence on the Leadership and workplace performance for many of us.

Now remember, this is only a snapshot of the Leadership Approach from the Industrial Age, but a common one just the same. The Industrial Age certainly produced many incredible Leaders and the workforce of these times built our country, and others around the world. No small feat! Again, please don't fall into the trap of getting too distracted by any negative connotations associated with Industrial Age Leadership, thereby missing the real point being made here at the start of our exploration in Leadership development and Authoritarian Leadership. Those who practice the Authoritarian Leadership approach are not necessarily bad. It's just that this approach can have significant limitations within our complex and evolving workplace environments, as we will see as we continue on with this Leadership journey.

Authoritarian Leadership is typically demonstrated through individual Leadership control over all or most major decisions, with little input from team members. These Leaders make decisions based on their own experience, ideas and judgments and rarely seek input or advice from those who report to them. In problem solving, which is one of a Leader's key functions, the expectation is that a Leader, when confronted with a problem, should have an immediate solution, since, after all, that is what Leaders are paid to do.

Despite its limitations in today's complex environments, the Authoritarian Leadership approach can still be an appropriate approach within certain circumstances. However, in an increasingly complex and evolving workplace, these circumstances are becoming fewer and farther between. And when used inappropriately, this approach can cause significant workplace dissatisfaction and overall organizational dysfunction.

Predominant Leadership Characteristics: *Authoritarian Leadership*

1. **Leadership through Command and Control**, which is typically based on the *Leader's experience*. At this level of Leadership, Command and Control

(Dominance) is the tool that we are most comfortable with and one of the few tools of influence we have access to. This may be due to the way we were taught or programmed as a Leader, which is still quite common today. Our hard-earned experience was and is our primary source of power and influence. Obviously, good experience is still valuable for a Leader, but any form of dominance is typically not a sustainable Leadership approach in an increasingly complex workplace, especially amongst an increasingly well-educated, highly mobile workforce. An Authoritarian Leader's main focus is on maintaining control.

2. **Grounded predominantly in emotion**, with negative emotions, such as anger and frustration, coming up frequently for us at this level of Leadership, especially when challenged in any way by people or circumstances. These negative emotions also create increased fear and anxiety in others, which can become a detriment to the workplace, along with the products and services produced there.

3. **Is "used by" emotion**, with little *Awareness* of, or control over, how our emotions rule us. At this level of Leadership, we very often, consciously or unconsciously, create fear and anxiety in others through a lack of control of our fear-based emotions.

4. **More typically past-oriented** in our view of how things should work. We will often state something like "This is how we did it in the past" or "This is how we did it in my previous organization." Additionally, we often refer to past situations and experiences in

attempt to justify our perspective and get our way. That does not mean that every time someone points out a method they have used in the past that they are coming from Authoritarian Leadership, however. There are clearly methods that have worked in the past, which are still relevant and valuable today. The point is that the past is often the Authoritarian Leader's sole source of perspective.

5. **Focused on hierarchical structures**, while relying on our positional power to gain support from others, as other forms of influence and engagement are mostly unavailable to us. At this level of Leadership, we may frequently feel the need, overtly or just subtly, to remind others of our position over them.

6. **Problem Solving Method** usually involves moving directly from *"Problem"* to *"Solution,"* once again based on our past experience. This approach has a more variable result with increasingly complex problems involving interrelated groups or business units, as it often does not take into consideration the impact on the multiple interrelated systems, processes or people involved. At this level, we typically do not concern ourselves or are not *Aware* of these impacts, since we often do not take the time to explore and understand the full scope of the problem. We can also feel an internal (programmed) pressure, to have instant solutions for any problem, otherwise we may feel that we are not needed.

7. **Common Leadership Statement** may be any version of ***"It's my way or the highway."*** Have we ever heard

any version of this statement from a Leader? There is a good chance that most of us have.

8. **Common Outcome of this Leadership Approach** is often a chronic and ongoing frustration and dissatisfaction by those who report to us, even as the work involved seems to be getting done. And, in a highly educated and/or mobile workforce, high employee turnover and its associated costs are common. Outside the few circumstances where this approach to Leadership is still possibly appropriate, this approach typically works only for the Leader, and for very few others. This approach works mostly to bolster our ego at this level of Leadership, and not much else.

The Authoritarian Leadership approach is typically not adopted by choice, but by default. This approach is often programmed into us and serves mostly as a Leadership survival mechanism for us. The Authoritarian Leadership approach is not inherently bad. And Leaders grounded here are not necessarily bad people. We have all demonstrated some version of this approach and may continue to do so in certain circumstances. The challenge for a Leader is to understand this approach, including its short and longer-term impacts, and apply it only when it is appropriate or necessary, while continuing to learn and grow and perform at increasingly higher levels of Leadership over time. Even with the *Awareness* that we must continue to improve our understanding and performance as a Leader, it can still be extremely difficult to move forward from this level without some support.

Remember, there is a lot of programming around this Leadership approach. So much that it can go on almost invisibly, beneath our *Awareness*. As many of us move into Leadership roles, some version of this approach very often becomes our default mode of Leadership. Over time, this approach gets reinforced and hardwired into our expression of Leadership, despite the obvious examples of where it is not working. This issue is reflective of the power and momentum and the influence that the Industrial Age still has over us. And it is completely understandable, if we take the time to understand it.

In its best expression, Authoritarian Leadership has the capability of effectively organizing people and resources to accomplish incredibly large efforts. This is the hallmark of the Industrial Age. But the secondary impacts of this Leadership approach can include the unnecessary domination, control and marginalization of others. And, when Authoritarian Leadership regresses away from its best expression, these secondary impacts, along with many other unnecessary and troubling outcomes, can become more and more of the primary impacts of this Leadership approach. This is quite common in our workplaces today.

We can do much better than this as Leaders. We should be able to accomplish very large efforts without the need to dominate, control and marginalize others. We can mobilize people and resources without the need to overly command and control them, as we have been programmed to think that we must. But this can be quite a challenge for us at this level of Leadership. As we have explored, there is a lot of overt and subtle programming and modeling reinforcing this Leadership approach to us.

Even though our environment continues to change and our work demands continue to grow, and even though we have attended various Leadership trainings and studied multiple sources of Leadership development material while we are actively trying to improve our Leadership performance, we can still remain stuck in approaches that no longer work or that do not provide for the best performance and outcomes. What might be causing this very common scenario? Well, there must be something preventing us from moving forward on our Leadership journey. And, as we may have guessed, that thing is us! Many Leadership development approaches do not know of, understand or address these parts of us that are holding us back. So, let's identify and begin to address these key elements that limit our Leadership journey. One of the key elements in overcoming obstacles to our development as a Leader is related to the concept of an *Energetic Impediment*. Energetic Impediments are essentially mental/emotional obstacles that require a significant shift or "quantum leap" in our mindset to effectively move beyond. They function as very real obstacles to our growth as Leaders. To ignore this concept is to create unnecessary, additional challenge with our Leadership journey and, quite possibly, ensures a significant limitation with our progression and growth. As explored earlier, simply reading or learning about Leadership is NOT enough to facilitate significant transformation in our consistent Leadership performance. If it was, we would all be extraordinary Leaders by now. Dealing with these Energetic Impediments is another missing link to our real and sustainable Leadership growth.

So, let's explore the primary Level 1 Energetic Impediment that limits our ability to move forward from Level 1, Authoritarian Leadership, and to Lead more productively and effectively. This Energetic Impediment also prevents or impedes us in moving forward with more ease on our Leadership Journey. By the way, this concept is referred to as an Energetic Impediment because there is an energy related to the primary "attachment" at this level. And this energy is holding the attachment in place, making it more difficult or challenging to remove or let go of. Consequently, there is a certain *type* and *amount* of energy required to release this attachment while we simultaneously develop new abilities and hold them in place, to support us in establishing more productive thoughts, beliefs, feelings and habits. Our Energetic Impediments commonly express themselves through our attachments, which reveal themselves as a strong need or strong desire or strong opinion on something.

Our attachments are many times programmed into us through some aspect of our upbringing or daily life but, in the end, we agree to them on some level and it is this agreement that holds them in place. Not all of our attachments are dysfunctional. In fact, many of our attachments serve us well. The challenge is knowing the difference. More on that, later. Specifically, it is our attachments and our related programming around these attachments, that is getting in the way and making it difficult to move forward. The AQ Model, in acknowledgement of this critical issue, also illuminates this matter and provides guidance in moving beyond these obstacles or Energetic Impediments.

If some of us are unfamiliar with the concept of an attachment, think about it in terms of a strong need or a strong desire for a consistent food or substance, or more importantly in this case, a strong, consistent belief pattern related to Leadership and serving others. Attachments are strong agreements that we have made with ourselves or, in many cases, agreements that have been programmed into us related to how something is supposed to be. Any deviations from "the way things are supposed to be" creates dissonance or discomfort within us and can play out in many ways, including our conscious or unconscious resistance to our own growth as a Leader. Our strong attachments to various ideals of Leadership that are clearly no longer working and that continue to create personal and organizational dysfunction and sub-optimal results, are one of the key factors that create limitations in our growth.

Dealing with our attachments is an interesting field of study and practice in itself, and we would be well served to do some additional exploration into this material. The AQ Model will illuminate some of these relevant attachments in an effort to create a degree of *Awareness* with them and as much ease as possible with overcoming them on our Leadership journey, our Hero's Journey.

Our attachments must be acknowledged, explored and purposefully addressed, either by tossing them out, modifying them, replacing them, or by keeping them if they are still working for us and others. We must, at a minimum, become *Aware* of any attachments that are holding us back in life and on our Leadership journey, and apply enough of our *Attention* and *Focus* to overcome the Energetic Threshold required to override them, even temporarily. And then we must rebuild and reprogram more productive thoughts, beliefs, feelings and habits to take their place. This is how we ultimately grow and transform in life and this is how we ultimately grow and transform on our Leadership journey. We must identify what is no longer working within us, and with our full *Awareness*, *Attention* and *Focus*, and as energized further by our clarity of purpose, passion and commitment, create and embrace a more expanded perspective of the purpose and possibility of our Leadership. We must courageously act and move forward in our service to others and our organizations. *This is the Leadership Revolution that I am talking about!*

Now let's move directly into the exploration of the Energetic Impediment (attachment), that often keeps us stuck in Level 1, Authoritarian Leadership.

1st Level Energetic Impediment:

Release the attachment (*the need or strong desire*) *to using "control" to preserve our sense of power.* The illusion of control and the need to control others and situations is one of the major forms of dysfunction on the planet and also in the workplace. It plays itself out in numerous gross and subtle ways. Leaders who are trapped by the need to control can end up pushing away the results we seek, and the people we are responsible for Leading.

As this Leadership approach comes directly out of the Industrial Age, it should be of no surprise that the impacts of this approach are still rampant in our workplaces. Look around. Examples of this approach are everywhere. From small groups and organizations to large groups and major institutions, Leaders spend much of their time and energy vying for control over their competitors, their marketplace, their peers, and even those who support them.

The Authoritarian Leadership approach is so pervasive that even those of us who consider ourselves to be Followers, can also get caught up in this approach either by fighting against it with all of our energy or by jumping onboard with it and playing out versions of this approach from our Followership role. In either case, the outcome of this approach to Leadership is that many of us become even more invested in it. By putting all of this energy into this practice, we end up further strengthening our attachments around this less than optimal approach to Leadership. Our attachment to control, and many of the less productive approaches to fighting against it, help to keep the mechanisms of control solidly in place, along with those who champion them. Please think about this.

Interestingly, using excessive control as a Leader can actually produce results in the workplace, giving a Leader the false sense that using this approach in this day and age is a positive, sustainable practice for Leadership. As stated earlier, this approach (Level 1 Authoritarian Leadership) does have certain applications in limited circumstances, but they are fewer and farther between in the increasing complexity of most workplaces. This approach also comes with numerous negative impacts, such as: limiting the input from others necessary in a complex environment; stifling the creativity and contributions of others; limiting the possible solutions to a given challenge; and pushing others out of an organization while these Leaders become increasingly isolated because of the suboptimal approach to serving others and their organizations. As an extra-ordinary Leader, it is incumbent upon us for the good of all concerned to get very clear about this illusion of control. And to make a very real commitment to move well beyond this approach to Leading and serving others.

It is time for us to be clear about this and make the decision to move beyond this limiting approach to Leadership. And we can do this by making a very real decision to do so (*Being*), and setting our Mindset around this, and then focusing on developing more productive and valuable Leadership habits (*Doing*). As Leaders, we must *Do* things, the right things, to move forward.

In order to break old habits that are no longer working for us and for others, we must establish the appropriate Mindset (*Being*), and then replace this old habit of control with a new, more functional habit (*Doing*). And repeat, repeat, repeat. Simple! We do not have to make this process overly complicated or overly difficult. Just simply do this, over and over again, while sparing ourselves and those around us the typical excuses we use to maintain our comfort zones and the status quo. We are talking about extra-ordinary Leadership here! And the price of extra-ordinary Leadership requires our ongoing, honest, purposeful effort. That is one of the reasons it's called "extra-ordinary" Leadership, because "ordinary" Leaders are often unwilling to apply this much focused, purposeful energy and effort to serve others and their organizations at higher levels. *This is the Leadership Revolution that I am talking about!*

And by the way, if for some reason we are unsure if we have issues or an attachment to control, which is not uncommon in Leadership, we can ask someone for their honest feedback or ask a group of coworkers for some anonymous feedback. This can help us to be clearer about our approach and the impact of any overly-controlling tendencies. Others can be quite helpful with illuminating our blind spots or calling us out in our denial. At this point however, we should stop pretending that we don't know what we most certainly should know about our own behaviors.

So, what could we replace this habit of needing to control other people and things with?

Develop the ability to be open to others' input, to share our power. That's it? Yes, that's it. Develop a consistent habit of seeking input from others, instead of jumping to our own solutions and conclusions whenever an issue arises. We develop this habit simply by doing it, and then repeating it over and over again. That's how it works! As a Leader, we are very much a product of our Leadership habits. So, let's pay close attention to our habitual ways of *Being* and *Doing* (our habits).

The next time an issue arises or if we are currently contemplating a new idea or change in current business practice, just ask some of our peers or coworkers or direct reports for their thoughts and ideas. That's it! The amount of goodwill, collaboration and engagement that can come out of this simple question, asked genuinely and on a consistent basis, is significant. When we share our power in this way, instead of trying to keep it all to ourselves through control and manipulation, we are able to create more meaningful connections with others. These connections encourage an increase in others' engagement and commitment and, in many instances, leads to a more effective decision, and increased effort and collaboration from those involved.

There could be other Energetic Impediments or obstacles preventing a Leader from moving beyond Authoritarian Leadership. However, the need for control is many times at the root of this issue. The concept of control is really an illusion and, in most cases, it is a dysfunctional, or at least sub-optimal, method for engaging others in providing their best effort. It will take some level of *Awareness*, *Attention* and *Focus*, and the acknowledgement of this issue, along with a commitment to change and grow, for a Leader to move beyond it and become grounded in a higher, more expanded expression of Leadership. A Leader can be helped and supported through this growth, and there are many valuable approaches for this type of support, but ultimately the Leader must decide for himself or herself and make the commitment to change and grow.

The AQ Model incorporates an extremely effective process and methodology for supporting ourselves and others with moving beyond these Energetic Impediments, these attachments that hold us back. This process is also key to moving us into the next higher level of Leadership performance. And this process is the "up-leveling" method that has been spoken about earlier. The up-leveling process is another key, overlooked element in many Leadership development models. It is also one of the missing links within genuine Leadership development. Let's explore this important process further.

In an effort to move further on our Leadership journey and begin to ground ourselves in more expansive, productive

Leadership performance, I would like to create some initial understanding of the up-leveling process. Although each of the recommendations for up-leveling is fairly simple to understand, in order for them to actually work and result in the significant growth that we are seeking, then there are most certainly some important prerequisites for us to consider. For example, what is our current level of desire and commitment related to our development as a Leader? Do we possess a *rabid passion* for personal Leadership development and demonstrate an ongoing commitment to growing our *Awareness* and stepping into higher levels of Leadership? If we are at least intrigued and somewhat committed to the possibility of significantly increasing our Leadership performance, then we have the ability to improve our Leadership performance. And, the momentum created by these initial efforts can build into even more productive expressions of Leadership performance.

The up-leveling strategies in the AQ Model are a real-time tactic to address many of the challenges we face each day in the workplace. These approaches are not designed for some kind of theoretical discussion about improving Leadership performance. The up-leveling approaches are meant to be used in the here and now of the very real and challenging situations that we find ourselves in each day as Leaders. In fact, it is in the application of the *Doing* of these up-leveling approaches within the course of the challenges we face, that we learn and grow, and more rapidly move to and become grounded in higher levels of Leadership expression and performance. The up-leveling process is focused on expanding our perspective as a Leader (*Being*), while increasing our access to the possible solutions to the challenges we face (*Doing*).

Let's get even more clear about this foundational and extremely functional aspect of the up-leveling strategies. The up-leveling strategies represent key aspects of the work of a real Leader. By taking responsibility for, and *Doing*, the *nondelegable* work that is ours to do as extra-ordinary Leaders, we become better at our jobs as Leaders. Right? This is how it works in all positions and Leadership is no different. When we do the key elements of our jobs, when we do the right things over and over, and add to this our passion and commitment and purpose and *Awareness*, *Attention* and *Focus*, we can get really good at whatever we are *Being* and *Doing*! That should be no surprise. However, one of the challenges with Leadership has been that very few people actually understand and know what a Leader is supposed to be *Being* and *Doing*, beyond the mechanics of their job descriptions. This may sound crazy, but it is very often true. Once again, that has all changed now.

The up-leveling strategies take place where the proverbial "rubber meets the road." The up-leveling steps are our work as a real leader. This is where real Leadership exists. It does not exist in a text book, or in a weekend workshop on "Super-Leadership," or in the theories of so many others. These are all well and good; however, real Leadership, extra-ordinary Leadership, exists and is expressed in the moment-to-moment interactions between us and those we serve! This is how we, as committed Leaders, change and transform the workplace and beyond. And the up-leveling steps represent a clear pathway for us as Leaders, to *Be* and *Do* just that. *This is the Leadership Revolution that I am talking about!*

The following steps to up-leveling may seem simple, and they are simple, deceptively simple. And many of them are actually quite easy to apply. However, they must be applied with as much *Awareness*, *Attention* and *Focus* (remember those) that we can bring to a given moment. Only then can we as Leaders most effectively apply them and express them and modify them to a given situation to achieve the optimal result. Only then will we be able to perceive the numerous real-time opportunities to grow and apply ourselves, and to help others grow, while in the midst of a chaotic or dynamic and emotionally charged situation. Simply going through the motions with these up-leveling approaches will not achieve the extra-ordinary results that we have committed to.

When confronted with our next workplace challenge, or our next challenging interaction in a meeting, which for most of us can happen multiple times each day, we must commit to the purposeful approach of up-leveling ourselves and others. The up-leveling concept and approach shared in the AQ Model was conceived, tested and refined to address this very issue in Leadership development. This is the grease that helps us to move faster and with more ease on our Leadership journey. We must be genuinely committed to applying the up-leveling strategies in real time. And when we do this, watch what happens!

What follows next are the step-by-step recommendations related to up-leveling ourselves and others from Level 1 Author itarian Leadership to the next level of Leadership performance. In this first step of the up-leveling ourselves exploration, we will need a degree of *Awareness* around the more typical expression and resulting impact of our Leadership approach. We must develop the ability to more deeply observe ourselves in action, as well as the results of our actions as a Leader. We must be able to see the impacts of our Leadership efforts beyond the objective results that have been achieved, and also as reflected in the faces and body language and performance and behaviors of those we serve.

We will need a fair degree of honesty with ourselves about this. It serves no one to pretend or to remain in denial about our more typical and often programmed Leadership approach.

Whether we are grounded in higher levels of Leadership or not, there may be times that we are pulled down by our reactive programming and end up expressing this Leadership approach, even when it is clearly not the most productive method. So, there is no shame in acknowledging here that we might be functioning as a Level 1 Leader presently or that we sometimes go there in times of stress or challenge. We start wherever we are. Acknowledging this is actually the first, courageous step on the journey to extra-ordinary Leadership, where we begin to step out of the ordinary, status quo of Leadership and more purposefully onto the path of the extra-ordinary Leader, on our Hero's journey.

To be clear, this up-leveling maneuver can be quite a challenge for Leaders who predominantly express their Leadership through a Level 1 approach. At this point, our level of *Awareness, Attention* and *Focus* is often scattered or insufficiently "present." This is the foundational challenge for us at all levels of Leadership, but even more so at the lower levels. As our *Awareness, Attention* and *Focus* expands, we position ourselves to more purposefully step into even higher levels of Leadership expression. And conversely, when our *Awareness, Attention* and *Focus* contracts, we tend to fall back into lower, much less effective levels and expressions of Leadership. So, that's the challenge. Bring it on!

As a predominantly Level 1 Authoritarian Leader, it can be quite challenging to gather our *Awareness, Attention* and *Focus* and to commit to making purposeful changes in our historical, heavily programmed way of *Being* and *Doing* related to Leadership. And yet there is no more courageous or compassionate an act as a Leader than to attempt this for the benefit of ourselves and others. The impact of this earnest effort will be felt and appreciated by those we serve. However, as a predominantly

Level 1 Authoritarian Leader, we may need a little help with up-leveling from here. This is where it can become very important to request support from another who is committed to our growth as a Leader. Through their honest and consistent feedback, we are in a better position to see our Leadership-selves, as others are quite possibly seeing us and being impacted by us. At this level of Leadership, outside feedback can be highly valuable, and at times essential, in expediting our growth from this level. Now let's jump into the up-leveling process!

Up-leveling Ourselves from Level 1, Authoritarian Leadership, to Level 2 *(Evidence-Based Leadership)*

Up-Leveling ourselves is essentially the thoughtful and purposeful process of improving our Leadership performance through an ongoing commitment to growing our *Awareness*, *Attention* and *Focus* to better inform the actions (*Being* and *Doing*) that support the real journey of stepping into higher levels of Leadership performance. It's how we systematically transform ourselves into better Leaders.

Up-leveling Ourselves:

Step 1 – Simply recognize and "feel" any negative emotion as it builds up in us. I am referring to acknowledging our desire, or our tendency, or our programming to immediately become defensive or move to a command and control approach when confronted with a challenge. And then, after this acknowledgement, don't allow ourselves to go there! In this moment, just pause and breathe and try to stay relaxed, even if only on the outside. Momentarily suspend the tendency and desire to dominate the situation or to move directly to a solution, our solution. It is OK in this complex and dynamic age, when not in a true emergency situation, to pause and take a moment to collaboratively explore with others, the current challenge. In fact, taking this type of pause in a challenging situation is actually quite valuable and appreciated by others we serve.

So, step 1 involves the simple, but perhaps not easy at first, recognition of mounting negative emotions that then trigger our tendencies or desires or programming, while in the midst of a challenging situation. *Just feel, recognize and pause.*

This can be easier said than done. This is why we must have a rabid passion or burning desire to radically improve our Leadership performance. Without this, we may be unable to overcome the *energetic threshold* or the inertia of our previous habits or programming, required to step fully into a new and more productive way of *Being* and *Doing* as a Leader. Our desire to transform ourselves as a Leader must be stronger than our commitment to our previous habits or programming. Our *Awareness, Attention* and *Focus* around this opportunity to truly serve as a Leader must be keen and unwavering in these moments. Our *Awareness, Attention* and *Focus* will always be the key to effectively accomplishing our up-leveling.

But even if we miss the opportunity or fail with our attempt at up-leveling in our next Leadership challenge, if we continually re-orient our *Awareness, Attention* and *Focus* to our strong desire to improve as a Leader, we can apply this to the very next challenge, which will not be far behind. We just need to keep recommitting ourselves in thought, word and deed and we will succeed, no matter how many times it takes.

Up-leveling Ourselves:

Step 2 – Take some time to clarify the problem. While paused in step 1, and instead of jumping to negative emotion or a domination-type solution, purposefully insert a different response. Take some time to first clarify the problem. This basically means that we take some time to more fully understand all aspects of the challenge. This may involve pausing the current meeting to take some time to reflect. We can do this problem exploration through an informal or formal approach, which can be nothing more than making a list of the possible deeper root causes of the problem. This reflective act can help us to gain further important insights and a more expanded understanding of the problem, along with some potential solutions. And of equal importance is the fact that this act replaces our old tendency of getting anxious or upset and jumping to solution. With repetition and time, and not much time by the way, this act can become our new habit, our new tendency, our new programming. This is the act of an extra-ordinary Leader.

So, Step 2 involves the inserting of a new habit when faced with a challenge or problem. And this new habit is to simply take some time to explore the problem. *Just pause and perform a problem exploration.*

Up-leveling Ourselves:

Step 3 – Perform some further research, seeking supportive data or information regarding potential solutions or approaches to the problem. This involves taking our problem exploration to the next level. Now that we have interrupted our previous, less productive programming, and have taken the time to understand the problem more deeply, we are now in a much better position to develop a more effective solution in our complex environment. Our next step then is to perform some further research, seeking supportive data or information regarding potential solutions or approaches to the problem. This information gathering could be addressed via an internet search or reading additional material or it could be through talking to peers or those involved in the area of challenge.

As a Leader on an extra-ordinary journey, we must take the time to further explore the challenge and potential solutions in order to understand the matter in greater depth. What are the root causes? What are the impacts of the challenge? What other systems or processes are connected to this challenge? Which people are the most knowledgeable and work most directly with this area of challenge? What are the best-practices available for this issue? This approach is valuable for personal Leadership challenges, as well as the challenges that we face as a Leader in the workplace. The act of performing further research can support an expanded, more up-to-date, more present-oriented perspective of the issues, impacts and possible solution(s) related to a problem.

Performing these three up-leveling steps, in and of themselves, automatically up-levels our Leadership performance significantly, moving us beyond the Level 1 energetic impediment (attachment), while simultaneously creating the possibility for us to explore and experiment in earnest with the more expansive and effective characteristics of Level 2, the "Information Age" and its associated "Evidence-Based Leadership" approach. And it does not have to take that much time at all. By performing the pause (Step 1), and the problem exploration (Step 2), and gathering further information (Step 3), we are automatically up-leveled and performing much more effectively as a Leader in today's complex environment. And this can be done in under an hour in many cases, while this time spent up front can save many more hours on the back end of a project. That's how it can work and does work, in real time!

And now for some further clarification with the AQ Model. Occasionally expressing some of the common Leadership characteristics in any given Leadership Level is different from being "grounded" in a given Leadership Level. To be grounded in a particular Age/Level of Leadership is to operate from that level on a consistent basis, *especially* during challenging situations. That is when our Leadership really counts! This then becomes our default level of Leadership. But in order to ground ourselves in higher levels of Leadership, we must first understand and commit to and practice the Predominant Leadership Characteristics of that level. In time, and not that much time, we can establish or ground ourselves in that higher level of Leadership performance. As the Leadership challenges come, we are able to perform more consistently from this next level of Leadership effectiveness. Remember, at Level 1 Leadership, it can be incredibly valuable and sometimes necessary to seek and obtain outside feedback regarding what we are attempting to do and how we are doing it, on our *Being* and *Doing*!

With so many individuals constantly vying for control, the numerous meetings and group projects in the workplace remain common ground for the expression of Level 1-type Leadership approaches. The dysfunction and outright waste created as a result, can be stifling in the workplace. In these frequent meetings and group projects, there is so much unnecessary challenge and drama, yet this is where some of the real opportunities to up-level ourselves and others and to significantly improve Leadership performance can occur. These meetings can become the playground or, more accurately, the proving ground for those committed to extra-ordinary Leadership and growth.

That brings us again to another unique aspect of the utility and value of the AQ Model's approach to up-leveling others. Unlike most other approaches to improving the performance of the Leaders in our group or organization, the AQ Model's up-leveling approach does not require the typical, mass education, multi-day training and buy-in of all Leaders. That may sound kind of crazy, but it is very true, and has been proven many times over. The only requirement to begin to effectively up-level others in the AQ Model is that we, as committed Leaders, first up-level ourselves.

This approach to up-leveling others does not require another Leader's in-depth understanding of this Leadership development approach for them to benefit from it. Now it can certainly help if they have some understanding of the approach, but gaining another Leader's buy-in is not required for them to benefit from this approach. It can be quite valuable to establish some understanding of the AQ Model with a number of additional Leaders in our group or organization, to scale up the effort and begin to spread this Leadership development approach throughout our organization. But to begin to implement the key elements of the AQ Model, all that is required is our genuine, rabid passion and commitment to first up-leveling ourselves for us to then be positioned to apply the up-leveling strategies to others to genuinely support their Leadership performance and development.

This up-leveling approach provides and requires real-time interaction, Leader-to-Leader (or Follower), regarding our performance in the here and now. And it does not accomplish this through the usual methods, such as pointing out a Leader's dysfunctional behavior and requesting that they change it, which rarely works. And it does not accomplish this through persuading some other brave Leader, who is higher up in the organizational hierarchy, to step in and put the problematic Leader in their place, which usually perpetuates even more unnecessary drama. All that is required in this approach is to first up-level ourselves. And then, when things start to escalate into the typical power and control dynamics so common in the workplace, from our more grounded Leadership perspective, we simply make a few basic requests of others based on the up-leveling steps, and then support them in seeing these requests through. And then, just repeat as needed, over and over again. It's that simple!

This reminds me of a common question that can arise at this point! And that is "Well, what if this problematic Leader doesn't get this stuff and won't change? And they continue to show up at meetings with the same Level 1 types of behaviors?" My response is to just up-level them again. And the next question is usually "Well, what if they just don't get it? How many times or how long am I supposed to up-level them?" And my response is, as many times as it takes, and for as long as it takes. Just keep giving them the gift of up-leveling. Give it freely!

I would further explain that the intent in utilizing the AQ Model's up-leveling approach is not to fix or change others. There are a number of Leaders who will, for whatever reason, remain committed to performing at the level of the status quo, driven by their programming. Rather than attempting to convince these Leaders or trying to get their buy-in for this type of effort, our time would be better spent simply and consistently focusing on first up-leveling our own Leadership performance and then working consistently and compassionately to up-level other Leaders' performance in real-time, giving them and everyone else involved this gift, over and over and over again.

And then, watch what happens to those committed to Level 1 Leadership.

If we simply focus on the process of improving the real-time performance of Leaders in the challenging meetings we all attend, then they and everyone else will be much better served. As a result of this approach, we will also naturally see and identify others who really want to grow as Leaders and we can then invite them into a more formal approach to understanding and applying the AQ Model. In this way, we can spend more of our time and effort on the joy of working with the willing and leveraging the commitment of other truly passionate Leaders. We can really do this! *This is the Leadership Revolution that I am talking about!*

IMPORTANT REMINDER – We must FIRST up-level ourselves, before we are even in a position to attempt to up-level others. We must do the work needed to be grounded in at least one level above (Level 1 Leadership), preferably two levels above, to appropriately and effectively up-level another from level 1 to level 2 Leadership performance, for example. Otherwise, this attempt can come off a little messy and ingenuine. There are already enough of those "do as I say and not as I do" examples of Leadership out there. And others know that routine very well. That is not a part of our commitment or vision here. *So, first us, and then them.*

Now let's begin to directly explore the approach to up-leveling others from Level 1 Authoritarian Leadership to higher levels of performance, in real time! And notice that by design, the approach to up-leveling others coincides with and is very similar to the approach to up-leveling ourselves. This same pattern and alignment is utilized at each level of the AQ Model.

Up-leveling Others from Level 1 Authoritarian Leadership to Level 2 *(Evidence-based Leadership)*

Up-Leveling others is essentially the thoughtful and purposeful process of helping others to improve their performance in real time, based on our growing *Awareness* and a commitment to supportive, purposeful coaching. It's how we systematically support the transformation of others into better Leaders.

Up-leveling Others:

Step 1 – Positively and supportively acknowledge the building of high emotion in others. As with Step 1 in up-leveling ourselves, Step 1 here involves first, through our purposeful use of *Attention* and *Focus,* becoming *Aware* of another Leader's desire or tendency or programming to immediately become defensive or move to a command and control approach. And through the purposeful use of our *Awareness, Attention* and *Focus,* this should not be too difficult for us to discern. Next, simply step into the situation and "interrupt" their programming before it takes them all the way there! Many Leadership teachings recommend that, as Leaders, we should "get out of the way" of our groups and teams. I could not disagree more with this Laissez-Faire (lazy way) approach to Leadership. In more complex, challenging environments, I believe that our groups and teams can very much benefit when we instead "get in the way." So, *don't get out of the way, get in the way.* In this moment, just step into the situation and ask for or create a pause in the dialogue, which can produce a temporary cessation in the rising emotions of another. We must stay relaxed and grounded in our more expanded level or perspective of Leadership or we might add further fuel to the situation.

We then, positively and supportively acknowledge the building or elevated emotion of another. We can even reframe this high emotion as a form of passion or excitement, so that we can work more productively with it. We can simply step in and say something like, "Bob, I can see that you are really excited about this topic, and I know that you have the best interests of the organization in mind." This simple statement, or any version of it, spoken from our heart, based in a genuine acknowledgement of what someone is going through in the moment, is a powerful and effective stance to come from. And others, even while in a state of heightened emotion, can sense this and tend to respond somewhat in kind.

This is a BIG Key Point here. As a Leader, purposely committed to extra-ordinary Leadership service to others, we are in a position to positively and supportively acknowledge another's building or high emotion, because we have committed to positively acknowledging our own building or high emotion. Because we have done our own work first. Therefore, based on our similar experiences with this issue, we are in a position to genuinely empathize and connect with and acknowledge another's rising emotion from a real place of understanding. This type of connection and support (remember our exploration of the meaning of Leadership) is extremely important to this approach. We do not come from a place of superiority. We come from a place of equality.

Step 1 here, is very similar to Step 1 of up-leveling ourselves. However, in this case, we simply observe the rising emotion in another, that rising emotion that we have experienced ourselves many times, and we then step in and interrupt this process in them. Just as we stepped in and interrupted this programming in ourselves. We then act by making a statement that positively and genuinely acknowledges the emotional process that others are experiencing. This act creates a productive pause in the action, rather than trying to confront or control a Leader in a heightened emotional state. There is no longer any need to fight with or argue with others in these situations, or to try to out-dominate them, or to try to mediate or accommodate these types of dysfunctional, unnecessary and wasteful activities that are all too common in the workplace. This simple step provides Leadership practitioners everywhere with a simple approach to begin to immediately shift the performance of others, in real time!

Up-leveling Others:

Step 2 – Facilitate a problem exploration. In Step 1, we have created a pause in the action through our acknowledgement of the rising emotion or passion of another. And now, just as in Step 2 of up-leveling ourselves, we next simply facilitate a problem exploration, either formally, on paper, whiteboard or flip chart for more complex issues, or informally, through a discussion for smaller, less complex issues. We do this to bring more insight and expanded understanding of the issue and potential solutions.

We facilitate a problem exploration by facilitating a brainstorming session and capturing everyone's thoughts around the issue, while purposely NOT moving to solution at this point. In fact, during a problem exploration, we will most probably need to remind others to hold their solutions and resist their natural or programmed inclination to launch into an immediate solution in this moment, while we first attempt to more fully understand the issue or problem as a group. It is best to write everyone's thoughts on a whiteboard or flip chart so that everyone can see and connect with and *Attend to* and *Focus on* the same information at the same time.

What we have accomplished through this more reflective approach to addressing a complex, emotionally-filled issue, can help everyone to gain further, potentially important insights and a more expanded understanding of the problem and potential solutions. Of equal importance is the fact that this act replaces the old tendency of Leaders getting anxious or upset and then jumping immediately to solution. And with some repetition and time, and not that much time, this act can become a rather smooth and accepted team or organizational habit that occurs every day in our workplaces. This is a gift we can provide others, as an extra-ordinary Leader.

Up-leveling Others:

Step 3 – Request that the Leader who is experiencing high emotion or passion around the issue perform some further research and collect supportive data or information about potential solutions or approaches to the problem. This involves taking the group problem exploration to the next level. Now that we have interrupted the potentially chronic, negative programming of another Leader and helped this Leader and the group take the time to understand the problem more deeply through a problem exploration, we are in a much better position to develop a solution that actually may work even more effectively in our complex environment.

Our next step is to request that the Leader who is experiencing high emotion or passion around the issue perform some further research, seeking supportive data or information about potential solutions or approaches to the problem, and then present this research back to the group. We simply request that this Leader gathers some evidence-based research or best-practice information on the issue, and report back in a reasonable period of time. This information gathering could be through an internet search or through reading other material or it could be through talking to peers or those involved in the area of challenge. And this part may sound really crazy, but to make this request we do not have to be higher up in the Leadership hierarchy than the Leader in question! It is just a simple request to collect and share information with those involved in an effort to address a challenge. As a courageous Leader on an extra-ordinary journey, we must develop the commitment to and the habit of stepping into these types of situations as they arise. It is in these situations that extra-ordinary Leadership happens! This is where we grow as Leaders, while helping other Leaders to grow also. *This is the Leadership Revolution that I am talking about!*

The act of performing further research supports an expanded, more up-to-date, more present-oriented, perspective of the issues, impacts, and possible solution(s) related to the original challenge, even with Leaders who have a tendency to rely only on the past or past experience for the solutions to complex problems.

Performing these three up-leveling steps, in and of themselves, automatically up-levels another Leader's performance significantly, at least temporarily moving them beyond the Level 1 energetic impediment (Attachment), while creating the possibility for them to explore and experiment in earnest, the more expansive and effective characteristics of Level 2, the Evidence-Based Leadership approach. And this does not require much time at all. By supporting another Leader by creating a pause in their programming (Step 1), and facilitating a problem exploration (Step 2), and having the Leader do some further research and gather some evidence-based information (Step 3), they are automatically up-leveled into the Information Age and its associated Evidence-based Leadership approach.

As a side benefit, when we up-level our own Leadership performance and/or the performance of another Leader, the people who surround us also benefit. They are finally spared the exposure to another unnecessary, overdramatic display of ineffectual Leadership found in too many instances and organizations today. That's just how this can work and does work, in real time!

As an extra-ordinary Leader, we can walk someone else through the up-leveling process, very thoughtfully, productively and compassionately. There is no fighting, arguing, or convincing necessary. Walking someone else through the process of up-leveling accomplishes the outcome of up-leveling automatically, even if it is just temporary for a given Leader. The next time this Leader demonstrates the same sort of negative behaviors, we just repeat the process again, and as often as necessary. We never even have to say the word "up-leveling" or "AQ Model" to them. As stated previously, other's understanding or buy-in is not necessary for this unique approach to be effective. It can surely help, but it is not necessary. All that is necessary is that we, as Leaders committed to extra-ordinary service, understand and relentlessly apply the up-leveling approach first to ourselves, and then give this gift freely to others, anytime they are in need.

I hope this exploration of Level 1, Industrial Age, Authoritarian Leadership and the up-leveling process has helped to gain some deeper insight into the underlying structure of the AQ Model, along with its clarity, relevance and relative simplicity. Since this was the first Leadership Level that we have explored, I wanted to be descriptive enough with some of the finer details for everyone to get a sense of what the model looks like in real life. Please also examine Figure 4, which is a summary chart version of Level 1 Leadership, to help further clarify, at a glance, the key elements of Level 1 Leadership. And as we move further along with the exploration of the additional Leadership Levels and other supportive concepts, I am confident that we will begin to see and appreciate the integration and functionality of this model and start to see the bigger picture or what the whole puzzle of Leadership looks like.

This completes our initial exploration of Level 1, Industrial Age, Authoritarian Leadership. This will probably come as no surprise, but I will point it out anyway. There are many Leaders out there today in our organizations, groups, teams, schools, government, etc., who are very much grounded in Level 1, Authoritarian Leadership. There are also quite a few Leaders that visit Level 1 somewhat frequently as part of their expression of Leadership, especially during times of challenge. There are exceptions but, for the most part, this Leadership approach contributes significant amounts of unnecessary frustration, anxiety, fear and discontent in the workplace. And these things can have a direct and negative impact on service and product quality, employee engagement and turnover, and many other measures of organizational success.

Most people know this, and yet this approach to Leadership is still at least tacitly supported by many organizations and groups. Could it be that they do not yet know how to effectively address this type of suboptimal Leadership performance? And remember, these are not bad Leaders or bad people for the most part. The vast majority of these Leaders were simply trained or programmed in this way. Yet, the majority of these Leaders can demonstrate some level of improvement in their Leadership performance, and some of these Leaders can actually continue forward to create significant improvement in their Leadership performance. However, most often we avoid these Leaders like the plague, because they make most people uncomfortable in dealing with them, and few methods have been developed that actually have a significant impact on them.

Well, that has now changed. We now have an approach that can genuinely shift and improve Leadership performance, in real time. The AQ Model, and it's up-leveling approach, was designed for this very thing! It was actually developed and initially tested with a primary focus on dealing more productively and purposefully with Level 1 (and Level 2) Leaders. This early exploration and experimentation also specifically involved the practice of subordinate employees with up-leveling their senior Leaders. And even in these circumstances, positive changes in Leadership performance were clearly noted. Thoughtfully and purposefully applied, this approach can work across or vertically, up and down an organization.

It's now time to step more fully into our responsibility as Leaders and help the often unknowing, Level 1 Leaders and everyone they impact by supporting their growth through the gift of up-leveling. Remember, with a really committed Level 1 Leader, nothing is 100%. We may need to finesse this approach and tailor it for a specific person or situation, and we may need to repeat it multiple times. But, more often than not, we can improve this suboptimal Leadership performance in the moment, especially when we have done our work first.

And for those really committed Level 1 Leaders who, after being given the gift of up-leveling on multiple occasions, and who still absolutely refuse to improve their Leadership performance based on the needs of the organization, well, that's a different dialogue altogether. But everyone deserves a chance.

Everyone deserves an opportunity to step further into a level of Leadership performance that serves others more completely, as well as themselves. Yet, most Level 1 Leaders have not been truly offered a chance, a real chance to break out of the heavy programming around this Level of Leadership. Let's now give them a real chance. Let's help them and support them, as best we can.

Now that we have explored how a Leadership Level is organized, along with some of the key terms and concepts of the AQ Model, we will be able to move through the subsequent Leadership Levels (2–10) in a more focused manner. Each level of Leadership presented will follow this same pattern of exploration, to reinforce the understanding and integration of the information presented. At each level, we will explore a summary of the Leadership Age and Approach, the Predominant Leadership Characteristics of that approach, the Energetic Impediment that holds us back from grounding ourselves in the next level of Leadership, and then, the Up-Leveling Steps to move us beyond the associated energetic impediment (attachment) and directly into the very next level of Leadership. The pattern and repetition of this structure supports the development of our own mental map of the territory we are exploring. We can also refer back to this chapter as often as needed, to refresh our memory and to deepen our understanding regarding some of the depth and functionality of these key concepts integrated into the AQ Model.

Level 1 Leadership Age & Approach	**Up-Leveling Ourselves** the thoughtful and purposeful process of improving our performance through an ongoing commitment to growing our awareness, attention and focus	**Up-Leveling Others** helping others to improve their performance *"in real time,"* based on your growing awareness and your commitment to supportive, purposeful coaching
Predominant Leadership Characteristics		
Industrial Age: Authoritarian Leadership 1. Leadership through Command and Control – typically based solely on the Leader's experience. 2. Grounded predominantly in emotion. 3. *Is used by Emotion.* 4. Is more typically, Past- Oriented 5. Focused on hierarchical power. 6. Problem Solving Method – Moves directly from "Problem" to "Solution." 7. Common Quote – *"It's my way or the highway."* 8. Common Outcomes – Work can get accomplished, but at the expense of chronically frustrated, dissatisfied and disengaged employees, along with all of the *negative* impacts of this.	Moving from Level 1 to Level 2 1. Recognize the feeling of high emotion/passion building within ourselves 2. Clarify more deeply the problem confronting us (Problem Exploration) 3. Perform further research, seek supportive data, information and perspective	Moving from Level 1 to Level 2 1. Positively acknowledge the high emotion/ passion of others 2. Clarify the problem confronting others or a group (Facilitate a Problem Exploration) 3. Request further research, information or data to expand the group's perspective

1st Level Energetic Impediment (Obstacles requiring a significant shift in mindset [AQ and/or EQ] or "Quantum Leap" to move beyond) – *Release* the attachment (the need or strong desire) to using "Control" to maintain a sense of power. *Develop* the ability to be open to new or novel ways of solving problems.

Figure 4. Level 1 Leadership

CHAPTER 8

Level 2 Leadership
The Information Age &
Evidence-Based Leadership

Leadership through Persuasion . . .

Leadership Age: *Information Age*

The 2nd Level of Leadership illuminated in the AQ Model emerges from the Information Age. As a summary, the Information Age is characterized by the emergence of significant increases in the publication, consumption, and manipulation of information and data, particularly through the use of computer technology and computer networks, which increased at an exponential rate in and around the 1970's. Few of us have been untouched by elements of both the Industrial Age and the more recently emerging Information Age. The growing availability of information and technologies are revolutionizing how we live and accomplish so many of our daily activities.

The key point related to our exploration is that, largely as a result of the emergence of the Information Age, the needs, desires and expectations of people in the workplace have significantly changed, as well as the requirements of Leaders to understand and grow in ways to effectively address these changes. This has created an interesting tension between previous approaches to Leadership and the Leaders who have been developing in response to this progression into the Information Age. Most people are well aware of the many ways that this plays out and impacts issues in the workplace. Our organizations and workplaces are a source of frequent discussion and often some level of verbal bashing of one group by the other. The older generation of Leaders and workers pokes at the younger generations and vice versa. This is common in our workplaces, and there is really no need for this.

Leadership Approach: *Evidence-Based Leadership*

The characteristic **Leadership Approach** in the **Information Age** could be described as **"Evidence-Based Leadership."** In the past, it could take many years of experience for a Leader to amass the information needed to Lead effectively in a given industry. However, as information has become more readily available and accessible as a result of computers and the internet, it has become possible for people to access large amounts of information on any topic of need. Discovering and understanding industry research and evidence-based or best practice approaches has also become a readily available approach to Leadership for those committed to this type of activity. This commitment can help to move our contributions and Leadership performance to this next level.

Evidence-Based Leadership strives to obtain and utilize, as much as possible, empirical (experimental, experiential, observed) evidence related to the most efficient and effective techniques and approaches to address a challenge. This is done to gather and leverage the experiences of many different individuals and organizations, in an effort to apply their discoveries to our current challenges. This has been a growing field of Leadership study and practice, and many Leadership practitioners are committed to this approach. Evidence-Based Leadership includes valuable additions to our Leadership perspective and approach that most certainly have the ability to improve our Leadership performance within our rapidly changing, complex environments.

As we move into our exploration of the Predominant Leadership Characteristics for this next level of Leadership, I would like to highlight a key point. The up-leveling approaches performed in the previous level of Leadership serve to automatically usher us into this next level. However, in order to remain or ground ourselves here, we must begin to practice and to embody and express the Predominant Leadership Characteristics below. We must work to ground ourselves in the *Being* and *Doing* of this level, to gain the Leadership benefits and to achieve the potential results of this level, for everyone we serve.

Therefore, we should continue to utilize the up-leveling approaches we have explored (in the previous chapter), while placing our *Attention* and *Focus* on the Predominant Leadership Characteristics below. By working to understand and practice them, we ground ourselves in the here and now of these characteristics, until they become our default mode of Leadership.

Predominant Leadership Characteristics:
Evidence-Based Leadership

1. **Leadership through Persuasion**, which is typically based on our experience (as in Level 1), with the

addition of *a focus on information and data gathering and/or sharing*. At this level, we recognize the challenges of a rapidly changing, increasingly complex environment and the need to access additional sources of data and information, to Lead, manage and address the issues needed to create effective change. As Level 2 Leadership emerges out of Level 1, with its focus on control, Level 2 Leaders can have a tendency to use information in a coercive way, in an effort to convince others that our way is best. Whereas Level 1 Leaders are focused on exerting control, as our source of power, Level 2 Leaders can be overly focused on needing to be or appearing to be right as our source of power and influence.

2. **Grounded predominantly in the intellect**, which corresponds to the left-brain, analytical part of the mind. At this level, we can more readily see the parts of a process and how they logically fit together. Logic is a very useful tool for us. However, when we rely too much on logic, we can become attached to or trapped by or used by this same logic, which many times results in the need to defend our ideas and thought processes quite vigorously and, of course, to be right.

3. **Is "used by" information** with little *Awareness* of, or control over how data and information rule us. At this level, consciously or unconsciously, we often create anxiety and upset in others through our dominance-based approaches to sharing and discussing information and data. Not only does this approach create dissatisfaction and dysfunction in the workplace, it is another common reason for why employees leave an

organization. However, at this level, we have at least begun to gain a level of insight and control over our emotions through our growing emotional intelligence (EI or EQ), and we are no longer completely ruled by or used by our emotions, as in level 1.

4. **More typically present-oriented** in our view of how things should work. At this level, we will often look to what current evidence says or what the best organizations currently do to address an issue. Additionally, we often refer to case studies or highlight stories of other organizations in attempt to justify our perspective, and to be right or to get our way. That does not mean that we should not utilize case studies and other forms of research as part of our decision-making processes. This approach can bring incredible value to the process. At the same time, we should not discount ideas from the past, simply because they come from the past. There are clearly processes that worked in the past that remain relevant and valuable today. The point is that the Evidence-Based Leader often defaults automatically to whatever is the latest information, as our primary source of perspective.

5. **Focused on current research and discovering evidence of best practices**, while relying almost solely on what the chosen data and information indicates, to make recommendations and decisions and to develop or update key systems and processes. This is most certainly a good place to start but it is important to ensure that the research performed includes a variety of sources and perspectives to minimize our often-biased nature at this level. We may often and overtly

remind others that our recommendations are based on what the best organizations do.

6. **Problem solving method**, usually involves moving from Problem to *Evidence-Based Research* to Solution, based on our specific research. Although this approach to problem solving adds an additional important step of *Evidence-Based Research* to effectively address more complex problems and to achieve the optimal solution, this approach can still have variable results within a particular department or organization, since this approach does not take into consideration the uniqueness or important differences within these areas. At this level, we typically do not concern ourselves or are not aware of these impacts, since we often do not take the time to explore and understand the unique nature of business unit processes and people. We can also feel an internal, programmed pressure to have the right answer for any problem, otherwise we may feel that we don't stand out enough.

7. **Common Leadership statement**, may be any version of *"Why reinvent the wheel."* From this level, our perspective is that someone else has already done the work around this issue. All that we need to do is copy and paste this process into our organization, as if it was that easy. Have we ever heard any version of this statement from a Leader? There is a good chance that most of us have.

8. **Common outcome of this Leadership approach** is, many times, a chronic frustration and upset by those who report to us, even as the work seems to be moving

forward and getting done. And in a highly educated and/or mobile workforce, high employee turnover and its associated costs are common. Although this Leadership approach tends to be more effective than just basing decisions on our previous experience and opinion, this approach many times fails to optimize everyone's effort and results. This Leadership approach also works mostly to bolster our ego.

The Evidence-Based Leadership approach cannot be copied, it must be learned. We can't just casually observe someone utilizing this approach and hope to be in a position to duplicate it ourselves. The skills related to this approach must be purposefully studied and applied over some period of time, and not that much time, to position us to effectively apply this method. The Evidence-Based Leadership approach incorporates the crucial skill of researching and gathering a cross-section of relevant, up-to-date information and data to determine the best way to address complex problems. However, in many cases, there is still more work that needs to be done to more consistently develop the optimal approach to solving complex problems, one that takes into account the uniqueness and important differences in organizations and people. The challenge for an extra-ordinary Leader is to understand this approach more deeply, including its short and longer-term impacts on the specific application of information and data. And of course, to continue to learn and grow and perform at increasingly higher levels of Leadership over time, since that is what is required of us as extra-ordinary Leaders.

I'd like to share a few additional points on the Leadership Levels in the AQ Model as we go along. In book or chart form, the Leadership Levels appear to be separate and to come one after another and to be neatly stacked on top of one another. But I want to make the point early on that the Leadership Levels are not so cleanly separate and distinct. The levels actually flow in and out of each other and their individual characteristics may appear interchangeable between levels. This is to be expected given the complex nature of human development and individual differences in learning and expression.

Remember, *the map is never the terrain*. Individual differences may apply. Nothing in Leadership is set in stone. Nothing takes the place of our own thoughtful experimentation and genuine observations while exploring or following this or any other Leadership model. We should use the AQ Model as a guide for our experiments, observations and experiences, and adjust as appropriate, based on reality. And then this model will have served us very well.

It is now time to take the steps necessary to move to the next Level of Leadership, Level 3, Knowledge Age, "Coaching Leadership." But once again, in order to ground ourselves in this next level of Leadership, as opposed to just visiting there temporarily, we must understand and work through the attachments or programming that keep us grounded back in Level 2 Leadership. Remember, it is not just a matter of looking at a model or reading about it and then moving to another Level, as some Leadership development approaches would suggest. That would be nice, but it is not true in most cases. The AQ Model, in acknowledgement of this critical issue, illuminates this matter and provides guidance around thoughtfully approaching these obstacles or impediments.

As a reminder from the previous chapter, an attachment is represented by a strong need or a strong desire for something, such as a food or attitude or belief pattern or Leadership paradigm. So, attachments are strong agreements that we have made with ourselves or, in many cases, that have been programmed into us, about how something is supposed to be. And any deviations from the way things are supposed to be, creates some level of dissonance or discomfort within us, which can play out in many ways, including our conscious or unconscious resistance to our own growth as a Leader. Our strong attachments to ideals of Leadership that are clearly no longer working and that continue to create personal and organizational dysfunction and sub-optimal results are one of the key factors that creates limitation in our growth.

The AQ Model will illuminate many of these relevant attachments in an effort to create a degree of *Awareness* with them, and as much ease as possible with overcoming them on our Leadership journey, our Hero's Journey. Our attachments must be directly looked at and acknowledged, explored and purposefully addressed by either tossing them out, modifying them or keeping them if they are working for us and others. We must, at a minimum, become *Aware* of the attachments that are holding us back in life and on our Leadership journey, and apply enough of our *Attention* and *Focus* to overcome the energetic threshold required to override them, at least temporarily, while we build and program in more productive thoughts, beliefs, feelings and habits to take their place. This is how we ultimately grow and transform in life, and this is how we ultimately grow and transform on our Leadership journey.

We must identify what is no longer working within us, and with our full *Awareness*, *Attention* and *Focus* as energized further by our clarity of purpose, passion and commitment, create and embrace a more expanded perspective of the purpose and possibility of our Leadership, to courageously act and move forward in our service to others and our organizations. *This is the Leadership Revolution that I am talking about!*

Now, let's explore the primary Level 2 Energetic Impediment that limits our ability to move forward from Level 2, Evidence-based Leadership, to Lead more productively and effectively. And remember, this concept is referred to as an Energetic Impediment because there is an energy related to the primary attachment at this level. Energy that is holding the attachment in place, making it more difficult or challenging to remove or release. Consequently, there is a certain *type* and *amount* of energy required to release this attachment, while we simultaneously develop a new ability and hold it in place to establish more productive thoughts, beliefs, feelings and habits.

Energetic Impediments are essentially mental/emotional obstacles that require a significant shift or quantum leap in our mindset to effectively move beyond. They function as very real obstacles to our growth as Leaders and express themselves through our *attachments*. To ignore this concept is to create unnecessary, additional challenge with our Leadership journey and quite possibly ensures a significant limitation with our progression and growth. As explored earlier, simply reading or learning about Leadership is NOT enough to facilitate real, significant transformation in our consistent Leadership performance. If it was, with all of the Leadership information out there, we would all be extraordinary Leaders by now. Therefore, dealing with these Energetic Impediments is another missing link, another missing piece of the puzzle to our real and sustainable Leadership growth.

2nd Level Energetic Impediment:

Release the attachment to being "right" to maintain a sense of authority. The need or strong desire (attachment) to be right can be just as insidious and damaging to our team and our organization as our attachment was to being in control in Level 1 Leadership. In fact, the need to always be right is very much related to this Level 1 attachment to control. They only differ by degrees but the outcomes or impacts on others is very similar. Often Leaders will attempt to use their rightness in an attempt to ultimately control others or a situation. Can we see how these two behaviors can be closely related? The need to be right is often used as a more sophisticated maneuver to exert control.

Our need to be right can be expressed in different ways, many of which turn out to be rather thinly veiled attempts at bolstering our personal sense of value and our more public persona of appearing indispensable. Continually being in control (Level 1) and being right (Level 2) require a lot of energy by us, energy that could be much better spent by investing in our support of others. Look around. We can see the impacts of this Leadership approach pretty much everywhere. And, Followers are just as likely to get caught up in, or attached to, the need to be right. What we have then is entire groups of people vying with each other to be right. Does this sound familiar? Our collective efforts towards this energetic impediment also serve to hold it in place as a consistent part of our experience in our groups, teams, organizations and institutions. It is happening all around us!

Once again, the first step in moving ourselves beyond this limited perspective is to become *Aware* of it, either on our own, through our fearless self-reflection or through the honest feedback from others. And then to actively commit to replacing this limited habit of needing to be right, with a way of *Being and Doing* that is more expanded and supportive of others and organizations.

And what could we replace this habit of needing to be right with?

Develop the ability to *explore how systems and processes are connected and how they impact each other.* Instead of automatically jumping to the conclusion that based on our present intellectual knowledge around an issue that we know best, we must develop the consistent habit of performing a more structured exploration of other possibilities, while connecting with our deeper purpose around an effort. We should make a habit of involving others as much as possible in this process. What we can learn from opening ourselves to others' perspectives can be quite valuable and the up-leveling processes that follow support us with the above. And once again, as Leaders, we accomplish this by aligning our *Awareness, Attention* and *Focus* around this issue, and then doing it. No excuses necessary.

There could be many other impediments or obstacles preventing a Leader from moving beyond Evidence-based Leadership, however, the desire to be right is many times at the root of this issue. Our singular rightness is another type of illusion. There are often many right answers, and in many cases this issue can get in the way of engaging others in providing their best effort. However, it will take some level of *Awareness* and acknowledgement of this issue, and then a commitment to change and grow, for a Leader to begin to move beyond it. A Leader can be helped and supported through this growth, and there are many approaches for this, but we must ultimately commit ourselves to the change and growth process.

The Evidence-based Leadership (Level 2) approach incorporates the crucial skill of gathering relevant, up-to-date data and information to determine the best way to address complex problems. However, in many cases, there is still more work that needs to be done to more consistently develop the optimal approach to solving complex problems. The following up-leveling steps were developed for this very purpose.

Up-leveling Ourselves from Level 2, Evidence-Based Leadership to Level 3 *(Coaching Leadership)*

Up-Leveling ourselves is essentially the thoughtful and purposeful process of improving our Leadership performance through an ongoing commitment to growing our *Awareness, Attention* and *Focus* to better inform the actions (*Being* and *Doing*) that support the real journey of stepping into higher levels of Leadership. It's how we systematically transform ourselves into better Leaders.

Up-leveling Ourselves:

Step 1 – Simply recognize the feeling and/or strong desire to persuade others by using data, information or research. This can show up as feeling the need to prove that we are right, and/or becoming overly insistent that our information is the right or the best way or the only way. In this step, we acknowledge our desire or tendency or our programming to immediately attempt to convince others, but then we don't allow ourselves to move there! In this moment, just pause and breathe and try to remain relaxed, even if only on the outside. Momentarily suspend the tendency and desire to move directly to a solution that we have discovered through our research. It is OK in this complex and dynamic age, when not in a true emergency situation, to pause and take a moment to explore collaboratively with others the current challenge. In fact, taking this type of pause in a challenging situation is actually quite valuable and will be appreciated by others we serve.

So, step 1 involves the recognition of our feeling of the mounting desire to demonstrate the superiority of our intellect that can then lead to our tendencies or programming to attempt to convince others of our plan, while in the midst of a challenging situation. *Just feel, recognize and pause.*

As in the previous level, this is easier said than done at first. That is why we must have a rabid passion or burning desire to radically improve our Leadership performance. Without this, we will not be able to overcome the energetic threshold or the inertia of our previous habits or programming, required to step fully into a new and more productive way of *Being* and *Doing* as a Leader. Our desire to transform ourselves as Leaders must be stronger than our commitment to our previous habits or programming. Our *Awareness, Attention* and *Focus* around this opportunity to truly serve as an extra-ordinary Leader must be sharp and keen and unwavering in these moments. Our *Awareness* will always be the key to accomplishing this up-leveling.

But even if we miss the opportunity in our next Leadership challenge, if we maintain our *Awareness* and our strong desire to improve as a Leader, we can then apply this to the very next challenge, which will not be far behind. We just need to keep recommitting ourselves in thought, word and deed and we will succeed, no matter how many times it takes.

Up-leveling Ourselves:

Step 2 – Take some time to clarify our purpose. While paused, and rather than jumping to our tendency or our programming to immediately attempt to convince others of our way, purposefully insert a different response. Instead, take some time to clarify our purpose. This basically means that we take some time to more fully understand the depth of our purpose as a Leader. There are many approaches to more deeply clarifying our Leadership purpose and we will review a simple but powerful approach for this in the next chapter of this journey. This self-reflective act can help us to gain further potentially important insights and a more expanded understanding of who we aspire to be as a Leader, and what that looks like and feels like to those we serve. From this place of clarity of purpose, we as Leaders are in a much better position to more consistently perform in alignment with our best version of ourselves.

This is a major issue with many Leaders today. Yet, the reality is that many Leaders have never done this kind of incredibly valuable, self-exploration before. It is not taught in most schools or business programs and it is not yet a requirement in most organizations, even for Leaders. Therefore, a given Leader might move through their entire career with little clarity regarding their vision for their best Leadership-self. And the result of this for a Leader, and everyone that they interact with along the way, is typically a sub-optimal experience and, many times, much worse than that. If we don't have a crystal clear picture of our vision for ourselves as an extra-ordinary Leader, then where do we come from or where are we anchored in the daily, moment-to-moment challenges that we face? If we are not crystal clear about where we stand as a Leader, then we will come from whichever place we happen to be standing at the time, or from wherever our programming dictates. This can lead to many of the inconsistencies and variability of performance with so many Leaders.

It is time to become crystal clear about our vision, our purpose, for ourselves and those we serve. And if we have done this type of activity before, it may be time to review and update our Leadership purpose, in alignment with our growing passion for extra-ordinary Leadership.

Step 2 involves this new habit of bringing a deeper version of ourselves to a challenge, based on our clarity of purpose as a Leader. Simply take the time necessary to develop a clear Leadership Purpose Statement and begin to act more consistently from there. *Just pause and step into our Leadership purpose, instead of allowing our programming to take control.*

The process of developing and implementing our Leadership Purpose Statement on a consistent basis is a necessary step in beginning to reprogram ourselves in a way that produces results that are more consistently in alignment with our best vision for our self and others.

Up-leveling Ourselves:

Step 3 – Align our Leadership purpose to meet the needs of those we serve (customers, team members, employees, etc.) and the organization, and customize our approach for the purpose of the challenge or issue at hand. This involves taking our Leadership Purpose Statement to the next level. So, now that we have interrupted our previous, negative programming and have taken the time to understand our Leadership Purpose more deeply, we are now in a much better position to align our personal Leadership purpose and performance, with the changing needs of others and the organization.

To align our Leadership purpose to meet the needs of those we serve (customers, team members, employees, organization, etc.) and to customize our approach for the purpose of the challenge or issue at hand is to purposefully recognize what our team needs to be successful within the context of the unique environment where the issue exists. This approach can far exceed the results of the Level 2 Leadership approach of taking a best-practice from some other organization and then just, "shoehorning" that best practice into our organization. Yes, we can achieve some results with the Level 2 approach, but there is a huge missed opportunity here to more deeply align our efforts with the more specific needs of our groups, teams and organizations. In Step 3, we move from acting from our Level 2 programming to connecting our deeper Leadership purpose with the real needs of those we serve.

Performing these three up-leveling steps, in and of themselves, automatically up-levels our Leadership performance significantly, moving us beyond the Level 2 Energetic Impediment, while creating the possibility for us to explore and experience in earnest, the more expansive and effective characteristics of Level 3, the "Coaching Leadership" approach. And, it does not have to take that much time at all. By performing this pause (Step 1) and developing our own Leadership Purpose Statement (Step 2) and aligning our Leadership purpose to meet the needs of those we serve and for the purpose of the challenge or issue at hand (Step 3), we are automatically up-leveled and performing more effectively as a Leader in today's complex environment. That's just how it can work and does work, in real time! *This is the Leadership Revolution that I am talking about!*

As a related side note here, many approaches to Leadership development only hint at the specific steps needed to move from one level of Leadership to the next. Many approaches simply present information about certain desirable Leadership traits or a model of their ideal of Leadership approach, and then basically say "just do more of that." And again, this approach is not bad, and it most certainly adds to the overall body of knowledge regarding Leadership, and it can actually lead to some improvements in Leadership performance. It is just that this approach typically does not result in the *Revolutionary Leadership* transformation that is needed in today's complex and rapidly changing environment. Nor does it result in the level of transformational growth that many of us seek on our Leadership journey, our Hero's Journey.

At the same time, there are most certainly some Leadership development approaches out there that do attempt to more specifically outline various steps and methods for the process of growing ourselves and others as Leaders. However, it is not uncommon for these approaches to be missing key pieces of puzzle for them to be more deeply effective. These approaches frequently require the additional knowledge and skills of an outside consultant to facilitate and continue with their process of the Leadership growth. This is not necessarily a bad thing. It is just that this book and the AQ Model are focused on the very real and exciting possibility of significantly improving our Leadership performance and that of others, in the here and now. And with stepping into our full responsibility as a Leader for making this happen.

There are indeed more than a few other Leadership development models out there that are extremely well thought out and presented in a way that can produce some significant results for Leaders, over time. There is certainly more than one path to extraordinary Leadership. *The AQ Model is just one of the more direct paths.*

Up-leveling Others from Level 2, Evidence-Based Leadership to Level 3 *(Coaching Leadership)*

Up-Leveling others is essentially the thoughtful and purposeful process of helping others to improve their performance in real time, based on our growing *Awareness* and a commitment to supportive, purposeful coaching. It's how we systematically support the transformation of others into better Leaders.

Up-leveling Others:

Step 1 – Positively acknowledge the information presented by others, while recognizing the tendency to sometimes use (or *be used by*) data and information, to attempt to vigorously persuade others in a certain direction. This can show up as someone forcefully expressing the need to prove that they are right and/or becoming overly insistent that the information they are advocating for is the right or the best or the only way.

Simply acknowledge another's desire or tendency or programming to immediately attempt to convince others, but don't allow them to move right to their solution. In this moment, we create a pause, and genuinely let others know how much we appreciate their research and their perspective. This can momentarily suspend their tendency and desire to move directly to their recommended solution, the one that they may have discovered through their research. Creating this type of pause in a challenging situation is actually quite valuable and might even be appreciated on some level, even by this passionate Leader, and of course, the others in the group.

Step 1 involves the recognition of someone's mounting desire to attempt to convince others of their plan, while in the midst of a challenging situation. And then, create a pause in the action by thanking them for their research and perspective. *Just recognize, pause and thank.*

As in the previous level, this can be easier said than done. It can be easy to get caught up in someone else's energy and excitement and their momentum with moving forward in a challenging environment. That is why we must have a rabid passion or burning desire to support the Leadership development of others. Without this, we will not be able to overcome the energetic threshold or the inertia of another Leader's habits or programming required to help them to step more fully into a new and more productive way of *Being* and *Doing* as a Leader. Our desire to support the transformation of another Leader must be stronger than their commitment to their typical habits or programming. Our *Awareness, Attention* and *Focus* around this opportunity to truly serve others as an extra-ordinary Leader, must be sharp and keen and unwavering in these moments or they quickly will slip by.

But even if we miss an opportunity, if we maintain our *Awareness* and our strong desire to support others in their Leadership growth, we can then apply this to the very next challenge, which will not be far behind. We must just keep recommitting ourselves in thought, word and deed and we will succeed, no matter how many times it takes.

Up-leveling Others:

Step 2 – Clarify the purpose of the effort by facilitating the exploration and development of a Purpose Statement for the effort. We can do this either informally (verbally) for very small issues or formally (on paper) for more complex issues to bring more insight and expanded understanding for the purpose of an effort. These steps are actually some of the key elements of setting up for any successful project. Too many Leaders and organizations skip these types of details in an effort to jump right into action as they were programmed to do, or they are not even

Aware of these key steps. In either case, skipping these steps almost invariably creates additional, unnecessary waste, frustration, drama and suboptimal results.

The slow way becomes the fast way! Take the time to understand and facilitate this key element of a project. This will help to avoid much of the frustration and waste in a typical project effort, while actually saving time on the back-end of the project. Take the time necessary to clarify the purpose of the effort, through the facilitation of a Purpose Statement for the work, to get everyone on the same page (alignment). Help others to resist the compulsion to jump in and start doing "stuff" before everyone is on the same page and in alignment. This is a significant mistake that plagues projects and organizations everywhere.

A Project Purpose Statement is a simple document that asks and answers, through a facilitated, participative discussion, four key questions related to an upcoming effort. Incidentally, this document and approach is very similar to the document used for our personal Leadership Purpose Statement document, and that is *on purpose*. Anyway, the four questions that must be asked, explored and answered are:

1. **What** are we planning to do?

2. **Why** are we planning to do this?

3. **Where** will this take our department, unit or organization?

4. **How** are we going to accomplish this?

These questions may seem so basic and not nearly worth the time. But I can assure you, if we do not have this conversation and clarify the purpose of the effort at the start, we can pretty much guarantee that those involved will have at least a slightly different perspective on the upcoming effort. This lack of alignment can and does create numerous issues when attempting to move forward in a complex environment. This activity will save everyone much of the unnecessary confusion and frustration related to an effort. As an extra-ordinary Leader, this is a real gift we can support others with.

Up-leveling Others:

Step 3 – Assess the potential impacts of the researched plans to address the specific purpose of the effort, within the uniqueness of our organization (by facilitating a Project Brainstorm/Outline & Work Plan). There are numerous approaches to facilitating a Brainstorm/Project Outline. This activity essentially involves meeting with key stakeholders to share everyone's experience, research and perspective around outlining the key considerations of a project or significant effort, to get as much focused input as possible. This part of the approach creates even further engagement and collaborative ownership around an effort. It also begins the critical step of scoping the effort, which involves determining what is going to be done, and also what is not going to be done.

A simple way to accomplish this Brainstorm or Project Outline is to use a large (2 × 3 ft.) flip chart and some colored sticky-notes. Begin with a row of separate sticky-notes across the top of the flip chart. Write the major issues of consideration for the effort on each sticky-note. Then, beneath each sticky-note in the top row, create a vertical column of sticky-notes going downward that identify all of the key elements of the sticky-note (major consideration) at the top of the column. When complete, the group will have a fairly accurate, but not final, outline for the project or effort. This activity helps everyone to be able to explore and visualize the key elements of the effort, and to have more productive dialogue around the effort, since everyone is able to look at the same document together. Sticky-notes are also very easy to move around and rearrange as needed, as the exploration evolves. The thoughtful, creative use of a flip chart and some sticky-notes, can help us and others to innovate and create alignment around a number of issues. Have fun with it!

The next important element of Step 3 is to create a Work Plan based on the Brainstorm/Project Outline that the group just completed with the flip chart and sticky-notes. Most people are at least familiar with some version of a Work Plan document, and there are many versions to choose from. A Work Plan is basically a simple spreadsheet or chart that we can use to copy all of the relevant elements of the Project Outline, from the sticky-notes, and arrange them in a column on the spreadsheet in a way that most appropriately describes the work that needs to be accomplished for the project. There are usually at least three additional columns on this spreadsheet and these are: "who is responsible" for completing the work on that line of the spreadsheet; "by what date"; and a space for an ongoing "status update" for that individual item. Other columns can be added as needed.

A Work Plan is basically a four-column spreadsheet with a number of rows on it, to plug in the work that needs to be done. But this document is way more than that. This document represents a key accountability structure for this effort. Without it, the project will just go where it goes, like so many of our unsuccessful projects. Organizations everywhere are littered with un-started and unfinished projects. The amount of waste, frustration and dysfunction created by this singular issue is difficult to quantify, but very real. Causing people to waste their time and energy by not supporting them with the tools and skills they need to accomplish the project work of the organization is a common example of Leadership malpractice. And an extra-ordinary Leader would simply not allow this to occur, to have their team and their organization unnecessarily struggle as a result of this issue.

Clearly, Step 3 is a big and critical step, and one that takes some effort on our part. And, as a Leader committed to extra-ordinary service to others, we must fully embrace the utilization of some version of these tools for any project of size or complexity. After we utilize these tools several times, we will quickly become an expert at supporting others with these elements. All of these steps together should take no more than one or two meetings to accomplish. This will be time well spent! We are most probably going to be meeting over the project anyway, so why not make these meetings much more productive? This is a gift that everyone will appreciate.

So yes, extra-ordinary Leadership does require our time and thoughtful effort on an ongoing basis. There is no getting around that one. That is why, by definition, it is "extra-ordinary," because most ordinary Leaders have not yet developed the level of passion and commitment required for this level of Leadership service and performance. But that is what is required to be successful and to continue to bring value to an organization in this complex, rapidly changing environment! Therefore, extra-ordinary Leaders develop a commitment and passion for this type of work.

By the way, as we continue into our complex workplace futures, there won't be much of a place for Leaders who don't embrace this level of commitment and work. Simply standing around or sitting around, and telling others to, "just get it done," or any other version of Level 1 Leadership, won't work for us much longer. And there is a wave of Leaders of all ages coming forward to contribute their commitment, passion and service. This is an exciting time for Leaders committed to extra-ordinary service and performance. As a Leader, we can either step fully into our duty and responsibility as an extra-ordinary Leader, and Lead from the inspiring vision that is within most of us or, in many cases, someone else would be thrilled to step in to assume our position. That is just reality! *This is the Leadership Revolution that I am talking about!*

This is just one of many steps in the up-leveling process and the AQ Model, that requires us to make a very clear decision and to commit to and to deliver real action (*Being* and *Doing*). Think about that one. This is truly a complex, extremely challenging and exciting time to be a Leader.

Performing these three Steps, in and of themselves, automatically up-levels another Leader's performance significantly, moving others beyond the Level 2 energetic impediment (attachment), while creating the possibility for us to explore and experiment in earnest, the more expansive and effective characteristics of Level 3, the "Coaching Leadership" approach. Again, this does not have to take that much time at all. By supporting another Leader or group with creating a pause in their programming and facilitating a Purpose Statement, Brainstorm/Project Outline and Workplan, everyone is automatically up-leveled into the "Knowledge Age," in real time. And as a side benefit, when we up-level our own Leadership performance and/or the performance of another Leader, the people that surround us benefit also. They are finally spared the exposure to another unnecessary, ineffective, overdramatic display of what passes itself off as Leadership in too many instances and organizations today. That's just how this can work and does work, in real time!

In summary, we are basically just walking someone else through the up-leveling process, very thoughtfully, very purposefully and very compassionately. No arguing or convincing necessary. Walking ourselves or someone else through the process of up-leveling accomplishes the outcome of up-leveling automatically, even if it is just temporary for a given Leader, which is common. As stated previously, due to their relative simplicity, after practicing the up-leveling approaches just a couple of times, we should quickly develop a level of expertise with them and also the ability to modify them for specific situations. We are then positioned as an extra-ordinary Leader, who in a thoughtful committed and compassionate way, is continuously working to up-level ourselves and others, to more skillfully and gracefully move things forward in a complex environment.

And remember, we never even have to say the word "up-leveling" or "AQ Model" or use any other jargon with others. As stated before, the full understanding of this model, or buy-in with it, is not necessary for this approach to be effective. It can surely help, but it is not necessary. All that is necessary is that we as Leaders committed to extra-ordinary service, understand, and relentlessly apply the up-leveling approach to ourselves first, and then give this gift freely to others, anytime they are in need or the situation requires it.

Please examine Figure 5, which is a summary chart version of Level 2 Leadership, to help further clarify, at a glance, the key elements of Level 2 Leadership. And as we move further along with the exploration of the additional Leadership Levels and other supportive concepts, I am confident that we will also begin to see and appreciate the integration and functionality of this model and start to more clearly see the BIG, complex puzzle of Leadership.

This completes our initial exploration of Level 2, the Information Age, Evidence-based Leadership. We all probably know this, but I will point it out anyway. There are many Leaders out there today in our organizations, groups, teams, schools, government, etc., who are very much grounded (their typical operating platform or default mode) in Level 2, Evidence-based Leadership. There are also quite a few other Leaders, that visit Level 2 Leadership somewhat frequently as part of their expression of Leadership, especially during times of challenge. There are exceptions but, for the most part, this Leadership approach still contributes significant amounts of unnecessary upset, and under-appreciation of others in the workplace. And these things have a direct and negative impact on others fully engaging and giving their best effort.

And remember, with a really committed Level 2 Leader, nothing is 100%, right out of the box. We may need to finesse this up-leveling approach and tailor it for a specific person or situation, and we may need to repeat it multiple times. But more times than not, we can improve this Leadership performance in the moment, especially when we have done our work first.

Everyone deserves an opportunity to step further into a level of Leadership performance that serves others more completely, as well as themselves. Yet most Level 2 Leaders have not been truly offered a chance, a real chance, to break out of the heavy programming around this Level of Leadership. Let's give them a real chance, now. Let's help them and support them, the best we can.

There is one more important point that I actually need to make before we leave the status quo of Leadership on our journey forward. In discussing the status quo of Leadership, my primary focus has been with illuminating the key characteristics of these two levels of Leadership, along with how we move beyond these more limited approaches to serving others. I briefly discussed the common outcomes of these Leadership approaches but did not go deeply into some of the more troubling impacts of these status quo approaches. Yet I would be negligent with an aspect of my Leadership purpose if I did not directly point out another common aspect of the status quo of Leadership.

At its best, the status quo of Leadership leaves us underperforming and undermotivated as we move things forward in our suboptimal workplaces and organizations. But there is also a very real "dark side" to the status quo of Leadership, and most of us have experienced some version of this. This dark side of the status quo of Leadership is still all too common today in our workplaces and organizations and many of the Followers in these organizations are quite literally suffering on a daily basis as a result of these questionable Leaders. These Followers continue to be exposed to frequent and unnecessary mental and physical torment, that at times borders on abuse. And unfortunately, some of these Leaders actually do cross the line into some form of abuse. This is no exaggeration. This is all too real to ignore.

There are still so many versions of this going on today that it is no wonder that people's commitment to their workplaces and organizations continues to drop precipitously. And it is no wonder that many people feel like they are in survival mode while at work. This is one of the deeper reasons why it is so important for us to move ourselves and others beyond the status quo of Leadership. This is one of the reasons why this Leadership model and approach is so important to our organizations, and even more important to the people within these organizations. The status quo of Leadership is failing us on multiple levels, and unnecessarily. Someone needs to do some-thing about this. And that someone is us! *This is the Leadership Revolution that I am talking about!*

This brings our exploration of Part 1 of this book, and Phase 1 of the Hero's Journey, *The Separation* (from the status quo) to an end. At this point, we should be poised to confidently step beyond the status quo of Leadership. Our exploration of the key elements of the foundation of extra-ordinary Leadership should have helped us to begin to understand the limitations of status quo while and also the possibilities of a more expanded perspective on Leadership. In Part 2 of this book, we will begin our exploration and our journey into *extra-ordinary* Leader-ship, an expression of Leadership that is much needed in our complex environments and that is well deserved by everyone we serve. It is now time to step decisively onto the path of an extra-ordinary Leader!

Level 2 Leadership Age & Approach	Predominant Leadership Characteristics	Up-Leveling Ourselves	Up-Leveling Others
		the thoughtful and purposeful process of improving our performance through an on-going commitment to growing our awareness, attention and focus	helping others to improve their performance *"in real time,"* based on your growing awareness and your commitment to supportive, purposeful coaching
Information Age: Evidenced-based Leadership	1. Leadership through Persuasion – typically based on the above, and on information gathering and/or sharing. 2. Grounded predominantly in the intellect (the "left-brain," analytical part of the mind). 3. Uses Emotion vs. being used by Emotion 4. Is more typically, Present-Oriented 5. Focused on current research and discovering "best practices." 6. Problem Solving Method – Moves from "Problem" to "Best Practice Research" to "Solution." 7. Common Quote – *"Why reinvent the wheel?"* 8. Common Outcomes – Work can get accomplished but at the expense of chronically upset, demoralized and underappreciated employees, along with all of the negative impacts of this. This approach still, many times, fails to optimize everyone's best effort, engagement and the results.	Moving from Level 2 to Level 3: 1. Recognize our desire to persuade others by using data, information or research 2. Clarify our purpose as a Leader (develop a Leadership Purpose Statement) 3. Align our purpose to meet the specific needs of those we serve and the organization, and the purpose of the challenge at hand	Moving from Level 2 to Level 3: 1. Positively acknowledge the information presented by others while recognizing the desire to persuade others by using data, information or research 2. Clarify the purpose of the effort (facilitate the development of a Purpose Statement) 3. Assess the impacts of the researched plans to address the specific purpose of the effort within the uniqueness of your organization (facilitate a Project Outline, Work Plan)

2nd Level Energetic Impediment – Release the attachment to being "right" to maintain a sense of authority. *Develop* the ability to explore how systems and processes are connected and how they impact each other in specific environments.

Figure 5. (Level 2 Leadership)

Part 2

"The Initiation"

Crossing the Threshold and Exploring a New Possibility (the journey into extra-ordinary Leadership)

The preceding chapters were designed to help us explore many of the essential elements of the foundation of our journey into extra-ordinary Leadership. They should serve as a jumping-in point, into the very real journey we have committed to. We explored the *Root Cause* of the challenges that we all face as Leaders, along with the practical model for understanding and working with our *Consciousness, Awareness, Attention* and *Focus*, as well as the deeper *Meaning of Leadership* together with its foundational elements of our *Being* and *Doing*. We explored a practical model for understanding our performance needs, through the *T.S.M.M Model* of our *Tool Sets, Skill Sets, Mindsets* and *Meta-Mindsets*. And we also explored the key concept of the *Energetic Threshold*, which frequently limits our full engagement and best effort in the workplace. And then we explored an overview of the AQ Model to provide some background understanding of where it came from and how it works and what its purpose is.

As part of this foundational exploration, we also explored Level 1, Authoritarian Leadership and Level 2, Evidence-based Leadership. These first two levels of Leadership basically represent the status quo of Leadership across most industries and societies. These first two levels are also a major contributor to much of the unnecessary struggle and drama that we experience as part of groups, teams, and organizations. And as part of this exploration we reviewed the key processes we can utilize to *up-level* ourselves and others beyond the *Energetic Impediments* (attachments) that hold us back from more supportive and productive Leadership performance, while moving us into more expanded levels of Leadership perspective.

This initial exploration was designed to clarify several of the foundational elements of extra-ordinary Leadership and to re-inspire us with their depth and functionality, while illuminating the key elements of moving beyond the status quo of Leadership. Additionally, our exploration established the foundation for us to more deeply understand this BIG, complex puzzle of extra-ordinary Leadership. And now that we have glimpsed what it looks like and feels like and smells like, what do we do next? Well, my hope is that by now we are all feeling the pull and hearing the call for us to step more firmly on the path of extra-ordinary Leadership, our best expression of ourselves in service to others and our organizations.

Part 1 of this book was shared for the primary purpose of inviting us all, in a very real way, onto an extra-ordinary Leadership journey. Yet only we, as individuals, can make the decision to take this journey in earnest. Nobody can make this decision for us. Meanwhile, however, our teams, our organizations, our communities and our countries continue to struggle far more than is necessary. And the need for something far greater from our Leaders continues.

In Part 2 of this book, we transition from Phase 1 of the Hero's Journey, *The Separation* (from the status quo), to Phase 2 of The Hero's Journey, *The Initiation*, where we have made the decisive choice to do the work and access the learning and growth necessary, to achieve the results of our commitment to extra-ordinary Leadership. This dividing line on the Hero's Journey requires a clear, individual choice by us as Leaders, and it is a choice that we must make each and every day. There will be even more challenging days where this choice will need to be made many times throughout. This is what *responding to the call to adventure* is all about! This book is our personal invitation to leave the world of ordinary Leadership, and to go on an extra-ordinary journey, for the benefit of ourselves, our organizations and everyone with whom we interact. Part 1 of this book is the invitation, and now it is up to us as to how we respond.

As we move into Part 2, we will be exploring and mapping out the key elements of extra-ordinary Leadership, so that we can confidently apply what we are exploring to the realities of our individual experiences, while also beginning to develop a level of *self-mastery* with our Leadership performance. Part 2 of this book, this exploration, this journey, is about courageously moving forward in the here and now, with our very real expression of higher levels of Leadership performance. It is time for our own personal *Leadership Revolution*.

CHAPTER 9

The Importance of Our Leadership Purpose

Our Leadership Purpose Statement is our compass, our anchor, and the source of inexhaustible energy that can keep us going through the ups and downs and challenges of our Leadership journey, and life.

Well, this feels good, doesn't it? To make a clear and decisive choice to respond to the call to extra-ordinary Leadership! Incidentally, this is the first major hurdle on The Hero's Journey, *responding to the call.* It is not that the information regarding the need for more effective Leadership performance is unavailable to us. This is the Information Age! Most of us know what many of the issues are and also what is called for at this time as a Leader, along with what our role in these challenges could and should be. And yet, on too many occasions and in too many critical situations, too many Leaders still default away from or outright refuse *to answer the call.* In too many critical situations that have littered our news cycles, too many Leaders have demonstrated an unwillingness or inability to step forward from their default mode of status quo Leadership performance, and the results have many times been just disastrous for so many others. Thanks to the Information Age, we have never before been exposed to so many blatant examples of this.

It can feel very good to draw a line in the sand, and then to step boldly over it, leaving the Leadership status quo far behind, while we move purposefully onto the path towards the best version of ourselves as Leaders. Everyone we serve deserves nothing less, including ourselves. Part 2 of this book will focus on the learning and growth and the work of extra-ordinary Leadership, and with sharing a few more key Leadership concepts, while we explore the more expanded Leadership Levels in the AQ Model. These more expanded levels of Leadership represent the specific concepts, principles and actions needed to begin to ground ourselves as extra-ordinary Leaders. This is where we will put principles into practice. And where we, and those we serve, begin to experience the more positive impacts and results of our commitment to this Leadership stance, in the here and now.

Before we begin our exploration of the more expanded levels of Leadership in Part 2, let's first explore one of the key concepts spoken about earlier in this book, which is the clarification and development of our specific Leadership Purpose. For without significant clarity related to the deeper parts of our Leadership purpose and commitment (Meta-Mindset), it would be difficult, if not impossible, for most Leaders to consistently cultivate and apply the energy necessary to create real, sustainable change for ourselves and others. That is just the reality of this thing. Our Leadership Purpose Statement provides an extra-ordinary Leader with the anchor point and the energy necessary to move from the ordinary to the extra-ordinary, especially during times of significant challenge.

Our Leadership Purpose Statement is an essential tool for us to move from the first phase of The Hero's Journey, *The Separation*, and into the second phase of The Hero's Journey, *The Initiation*. The Initiation involves jumping into an extra-ordinary journey and committing to the work, and trials and tribulations necessary for us to grow significantly as a human being, and to achieve a much higher level of understanding and personal mastery with our Leadership performance. Our Leadership Purpose is also an essential tool for moving from Level 1 and 2 Leadership, the status quo, the ordinary, into Level 3 Leadership which represents the first level of extra-ordinary Leadership. Therefore, let's approach what follows in this chapter as an essential component of our transformation from an ordinary, to an extra-ordinary Leader. As a matter of fact, these next three chapters are meant to equip us with the additional critical concepts and tools necessary for us to more confidently progress on our extra-ordinary Leadership Journey, our Hero's Journey.

To begin our discussion regarding the development and utilization of our Leadership Purpose Statement, I want to be very clear about something. There are quite a few methods out there to develop a meaningful Leadership Purpose Statement, and many of them are quite good. Some of us may have already used one of these approaches to develop a Leadership Purpose or Mission Statement, while others may not yet have been exposed to this type of activity. In either case, the point that I would like to make early on in this chapter is that our Leadership Purpose Statement is more than a piece of paper with some nice sounding words on it that attempt to reflect what we would like to be when we grow up as a Leader.

Part of the outcome of this activity does involve the development of a piece of paper with some nice sounding words on it, but this piece of paper and these words should be crafted to continually anchor us to the depth of our real purpose and the real possibility of our service in Leadership. This is where the needed energy, passion and inspiration can come from, to fuel us on the challenging Leadership journey that lies ahead of us. Without this anchor to our own source of energy and inspiration, it would be incredibly difficult, if not impossible, for us to move into significantly higher levels of Leadership and to sustain ourselves there. The status quo has a significant pull to it, a gravity all its own. Therefore, the journey into extra-ordinary Leadership requires some extra-ordinary effort. Nothing is free! Some form of energy exchange is required of us to do anything in life, and our Leadership journey is no different.

Another essential element of the journey into extra-ordinary Leadership includes living and acting on purpose as a Leader, each and every day. What does it mean to live on purpose? What is this purpose we are living on? Well, in this case, it is our Leadership Purpose. That is why we must be crystal clear about, and anchored in, our Leadership Purpose. We must be continually immersed in and present to our Leadership Purpose for it to become a consistent, moment-to-moment expression of our thoughts, words and actions as a Leader.

Without this type of genuine inner exploration along with the development of a clear reflection of this effort, which is the piece of paper with the nice words on it, we will have no purpose to live on. A very typical result of Leading without clarity and commitment to our purpose is a potentially well-meaning Leader who moves from one Leadership theory to another, or a Leader who is a mere reflection of someone else's approach to Leadership. The focus of the development of our Leadership Purpose Statement is to explore and clarify, and develop and connect with, the very core of why we are here as a Leader, in service to others. Our Leadership Purpose Statement is our compass, our anchor, and the source of *inexhaustible energy* that can keep us going through the ups and downs and challenges of our Leadership journey, and life. *This is the Leadership Revolution that I am talking about!*

As I stated earlier, there are many methods to create a Leadership Purpose statement. Some focus much more time in the exploration of our strengths and desires in life. Others focus more on the concept of beginning with the end in mind, which involves projecting ourselves to the end of our careers or the end of our lives to explore how we would like to be remembered. These are valuable approaches and I recommend them highly. But what I would like to share is that no matter which approach to developing our Leadership Purpose Statement we choose, we must make sure that it includes the following essential elements. These essential elements are designed to ensure that this effort produces a clear and actionable exploration of our purpose and commitment as an extra-ordinary Leader. And, that the resulting document can be used to ground us in a very real, daily expressions of our Leadership commitment.

We should choose any approach or method that we are drawn to for this effort, but also make sure that it either includes what follows, or that we incorporate what follows into our chosen approach. We can do this today! Just search this on the internet and go from there. And if we have already done this type of activity in the past, this might be a good time for an update, as our Leadership Purpose Statement definitely changes over time.

The essential elements of an actionable Leadership Purpose Statement involve the exploration and clarification of four key questions, the "What, Why, Where and How" of our Leadership Purpose. And then, as an extra-ordinary Leader, we must pay *Attention* to and *Focus* on our *Being* and *Doing* of these things, on a daily basis.

The first basic but essential question that we must answer is **"What am I committed to, as an extra-ordinary Leader?"** This question can be explored in any way we choose. However, the outcome should include two to five bulleted, clear and relevant statements that could be easily understood by anyone we read this to, which we should definitely do after we develop this. We can be as expansive or descriptive as we choose to be with these answers, as long as they are also clearly actionable. This is one of the keys to this effort.

One additional element of our response(s) to this first question, and with each following question, is that our answer must include at least one response related to our Being (our extra-ordinary Leadership Mindset, *Attention*, attitude, or paradigm that we will stand in), and at least one response related to our *Doing* (our physical expression of extra-ordinary Leadership that creates movement forward).

By the way, this first question is where many Leadership Purpose Statement activities end. This is sort of like creating a New Year's Resolution, where many of us may have stated "what" we intend to do in this upcoming year, and then mostly not followed through with it for very long. That is one of the problems with these New Year's Resolution-type approaches to developing a Leadership Purpose Statement. They don't take us deep enough into the issue for it to create the necessary clarity of purpose and the necessary energy for us to overcome the energetic threshold or gravitational pull of the status quo.

That is why this next foundational question is so essential to this effort. This next question takes us deeper into this exploration. Now that we have brought some level of clarity to "What" we are committed to as an extra-ordinary Leader, the next question supports our deeper exploration into the all-important, "Why" of our Leadership Purpose.

The second essential question is then, ***"Why am I committed to this?"*** In other words, describe the deeper reasoning for our bulleted answers in question one, the "What" question. And again, our exploration of this question should result in two to five bulleted, clear and relevant statements that could be easily understood by anyone we read this to. This "Why" (Meta-Mindset) question requires us to more deeply explore what's in our field of *Awareness* related to the depth of reason for being here as a Leader. It can also further inform the "What" (Mindset) question of our Leadership Purpose, since our Mindset flows out of our Meta-Mindset. The "Why" question also can help us to clarify and connect with the deeper drivers of our commitment to extra-ordinary Leadership. The "Why" of our Leadership Purpose, is critical to the sustainability of our journey in extra-ordinary Leadership. It is directly connected to the source of inexhaustible energy (in our Meta-Mindset) that we will need for this journey.

And, as with the first essential question, the "Why" of our Leadership Purpose Statement should include at least one response related to our *Being* (our extra-ordinary Leadership Meta-Mindset, AQ, EQ and Intent, the foundation of who we really are), and at least one response related to our *Doing* (our physical expression of extra-ordinary Leadership that emerges out of being present to who we really are). The exploration and response to this question can also Lead us into one of those BIG questions of life, which is "Why am I here?" So, this question is BIG and deep and an extra-ordinary Leader will not hesitate to go here and then, of course, to share this with others.

The third essential question for us to answer is the "Where" question. Once we have some degree of clarity around "What" we are committed to and "Why" we are committed to this as an extra-ordinary Leader, the next logical but often overlooked question we need to explore and be clear about is basically the "So what" question. In other words, what will be the outcome of this effort. *Where* will this effort take us? So, the third essential question is, **"Where will my commitment to extra-ordinary Leadership take me and those who I interact with?"** What will this future state look like and feel like. It is critical for us as extra-ordinary Leaders to be clear about where our efforts are pointing us towards, and what the intended outcome of our actions will be.

Once again, our exploration of this question should result in two to five bulleted, clear and relevant statements that could be easily understood by anyone we read this to, and should include at least one response related to our *Being* (our extra-ordinary Leadership Mindset, *Attention*, and goal for our future destination), and at least one response related to our *Doing* (our physical expression of extra-ordinary Leadership that illuminates the results of our efforts). This third essential question helps us to explore and clarify our vision of what our extra-ordinary Leadership destination will look like and feel like, for ourselves and others we interact with. Having some clarity around where we are going is one of the keys to getting there! This can also serve to fuel us on our journey, since we are now clear and can see where this effort is taking us and others.

The fourth essential question is critical to actually manifesting and grounding our journey in extra-ordinary Leadership, in the here and now. Even if we were to get clear about and answer the first three questions, all we really have at that point are a few thoughts and ideas or at best, a blueprint for what our Leadership Purpose looks like and feels like and where it could potentially take us, which is a really good start, by the way! But without clarity and commitment to the answers of the fourth question, our beautiful vision of our extra-ordinary Leadership journey may never really get off the ground. It would remain stuck in the planning phase or trapped in R&D (research and development), never quite making it to production. It would be like the blueprint for a beautiful house, that never gets built.

Therefore, the fourth essential question is *"How will I ensure that I am implementing or expressing my extra-ordinary Leadership Purpose, on a daily basis?"* In other words, describe in detail how we will actually express our Leadership *Being* and *Doing*, on a daily basis. The responses to this essential question make up our daily, weekly, monthly work plan for our extra-ordinary Leadership effort. This fourth exploration should result in two to five bulleted, clear and relevant statements that could be easily understood by anyone we read this to, and should include at least one response related to our *Being* (our extra-ordinary Leadership *Mindset* and daily *Attention* related to our attitude in action) and at least one response related to our *Doing* (our extra-ordinary Leadership Skill Sets and Tool Sets, and daily *Focus* related to the specific things we will do as an expression of our extra-ordinary Leadership).

The responses to this question are analogous to the construction plan/schedule for building and completing the beautiful house that we created a blueprint for, in our previous example. Without a clear plan for bringing our vision to reality, how will it come into *Being?* Just haphazardly doing stuff or using some other random, trial-and-error approach to this type of extra-ordinary journey will not get us there in the here and now, or even in the near future. This haphazard method is the slow evolutionary approach to things, which works just great over longer time frames. But, as we explored earlier, we don't have that kind of time anymore. We, they, our workforce, our customers, our communities have had enough of the mediocre or just plain poor Leadership that plays out in too many places. It is time to get really clear about our Leadership Purpose and ground ourselves in this, in today's reality. We all deserve nothing less. *This is the Leadership Revolution that I am talking about!*

These essential questions must be explored and clarified if we are to move significantly and confidently forward on our Leadership journey (see Figure 6.). It would be a good idea, or better yet, an extra-ordinary idea, if we were to create or update our Leadership Purpose Statement today. Use any model that we are drawn to, while including these four essential questions, or we can most certainly just simply use these four essential questions as our Leadership Purpose Statement. The key here is that we get present with this activity and take the time to put ourselves into this activity. And that we endeavor to create a document that is reflective of our highest and deepest version of our Leadership, at this time. And also, that we put some level of *Attention* on it, and *Focus* and connection to it, as we move through the moment-to-moment activities of our day. It has to come alive for us to be of any real value to us or those we serve as a Leader! It has to be real, and only we have the power and responsibility to make it real. No one else can do this for us.

And very importantly, we must begin the implementation, the "How" of our Leadership Purpose Statement, immediately, in the here and now. Our extra-ordinary Leadership journey should have a bias towards purposeful action. There are these dual but related elements of our Leadership *Being* and *Doing* that are inherent in nearly all parts of our journey, and these elements are analogous to the process improvement elements of planning and implementation. They should go hand and hand or, otherwise, like too many Leaders out there, who remain committed to the status quo, we are just talking. There is lots of talking out there but not enough *Doing*. Extra-ordinary Leaders talk and then we do; we plan and then we implement the plan; we *Be* and we *Do*.

One additional step that we alluded to earlier is that, although there is significant value in developing a comprehensive Leadership Purpose Statement, we can create even more accountability for ourselves when we share our Leadership Purpose Statement with others. I am talking about actually reading it to our peers, direct reports and those we report to. We can even email it to others that we don't have the opportunity to interact with as frequently. This may sound a little crazy, and it is definitely out of the ordinary, but as we have discussed multiple times already, extra-ordinary Leadership requires extra-ordinary efforts on our part. This is a valuable opportunity for us as Leaders to stand in our purpose and commitment in front of those we serve. This extra-ordinary Leadership act can create many significant, positive impacts.

By standing in front of those we work with and serve as a Leader, and by sharing our Leadership Purpose with this level of honesty, vulnerability and accountability, we may just inspire others into their deeper purpose. And we can actually support others in doing this same thing, developing their own Leadership Purpose Statement and sharing it with others, to multiply the impact of this type of effort. The other significant impact of sharing our Leadership Purpose Statement with others is that it creates an accountability loop for us. When we tell others what to expect from us . . . wait, what? I know, that is not how it typically works with Leadership! Leaders are usually telling others what the Leader expects from them. However, we are talking about extra-ordinary Leadership here. So, when we tell others what *they* can expect from *us*, we establish a clear and transparent bar for ourselves, that everyone now knows about. There is no place to hide as an extra-ordinary Leader, nor do we want or need to hide.

This type of accountability loop is a real gift to ourselves as Leaders, and to those we serve. This is actually one of the reasons why many Leaders avoid this type of Leadership Purpose activity. When no one knows our responsibilities or commitments, we as Leaders get a wide leeway as to what we do with our Leadership performance. Leaders basically get to do whatever we want (within some degree of reason), while those we serve have a much more defined and transparent set of expectations and performance requirements. And many Leaders who are committed to the status quo would like to keep things this way. So this activity serves to create even more motivation for us to be more consistently accountable to what we said we would *Be* and *Do*. What a gift! *This is the Leadership Revolution that I am talking about.*

Leadership Purpose Statement

1. "What am I committed to as an extra-ord nary Leader?"

   a. Being Elements:

   b. Doing Elements:

2. "Why am I committed to this (describe the deeper reasoning behind our answers to question 1)?"

   a. Being Elements:

   b. Doing Elements:

3. "Where will my commitment to extra-ordinary Leadership take me and those that I interact with (describe the future state)?"

   a. Being Elements:

   b. Doing Elements:

4. "How will I ensure that I am implementing or expressing my extra-ordinary Leadership Purpose, on a daily basis (describe in detail)?"

   a. Being Elements:

   b. Doing Elements:

Figure 6. (Leadership Purpose Statement)

CHAPTER 10

The Drama Triangle

*Look around! The dysfunction of the
Drama Triangle is everywhere!*

This next critically important Leadership exploration may be familiar to some of us. The "Drama Triangle," as a concept and a working model, has been around since the late 1960's and was developed by Dr. Stephen Karpman, MD. Karpman performed extensive work and writing around this concept, and many others have added their commentary over the years. As an extra-ordinary Leader, this would be a valuable topic for some additional research and exploration. My intent with this chapter is to briefly share some perspective, based on some of the fundamentals and implications of this model, and also, how we might apply it from a Leadership perspective to create a more productive and inspiring workplace. I have adapted some aspects of this model to more directly relate to our present workplace challenges (a Level 3 Leadership approach), without altering the original intent of the model. I am confident that even with just this brief exploration, there will be much that we will be able to immediately take away and apply to our extra-ordinary Leadership Journey.

I cannot emphasize enough, the importance of this next exploration. Understanding and working with The Drama Triangle, is one of the MAJOR KEYS to genuinely moving forward in extra-ordinary Leadership. Taking responsibility for this component of our Leadership and our lives, is essential for us to step out of the realm of the status quo, the ordinary, and into the realm of the extra-ordinary! The Drama Triangle has been unconsciously impacting us and nearly everyone else we interact with, and quite negatively, for most of our lives. Yet few people are aware of this simple model for understanding and extricating ourselves from this trap. This is some of the most important work that we can commit to in phase two of our Hero's Journey, to position ourselves to move forward in our Leadership commitment. So, let's address this nagging issue for ourselves and everyone we serve.

As a basic summary, this model is set up to reflect the three key elements of the Drama Triangle. In the model, there are essentially three unconscious (outside of our *Awareness*) behavioral elements that are behind much of the dysfunction that we all experience in our families and social interactions, and these are clearly rampant in our workplaces. These unconscious dysfunctional behavioral elements are reflected in role of the "Victim," the "Persecutor" and the "Rescuer."

The "Victim" is a role we play when we consistently believe and express that life and many of our life situations are unfair or against us. Our position is further supported by our consistent, self-fulfilling stories about the injustices we have experienced, along with our own consistent negative self-talk. The Victim is at the effect of most people and most situations, and our locus of control is outside of ourselves. Something is frequently wrong in the Victim's world, and it is very often the result of someone doing something purposely to us. We all probably know a few people who are unconsciously trapped in this way of *Being*. And, quite honestly, there is a very good chance that we have expressed ourselves from this perspective before, and probably many times. I know that I most certainly have.

Typical behaviors of a Victim in the workplace include, but are certainly not limited to, frequently expressing a feeling of hopelessness, powerlessness or being incapable of making decisions or making positive changes, or a feeling that others perceive us in this way. Other behaviors can include subtly manipulating others or using some form of guilt to get help or to get what we want or need. Frequently blaming others or our circumstances for our own personal challenges, is also common, along with many other behaviors. This should begin to clarify the Victim personality trait a bit.

Another interesting aspect of the Victim is that the Victim cannot exist in a vacuum. The Victim actually needs the other two roles (Persecutor and Rescuer) to play out our Victim role and to get the "payoff" that we seek. Although these three roles are largely unconscious, there is definitely a payoff that each role seeks to reinforce. For the Victim, one of the payoffs is gaining attention from others in a way that helps us to feel cared for. Therefore, the Victim must identify a Persecutor who is attacking us, and then seek out a Rescuer to save us. Victims are very adept at this dynamic. We many times know exactly who we can enlist in our Victim-based dramas. When in this role, we know very well from experience, who will listen to us and support our victimhood.

As a Victim, we must enlist others into our perspective and dynamic to justify our continued behavior. Our dysfunctional interaction here consists of several effective elements. They are the "con" (our poor me story), and then a "hook" (garnering sympathy and support from others), followed by a series of complementary interactions that provide each role player with their own benefit or payoff. The Drama Triangle is magnetic in nature and it too, has a gravitational or habitual pull on us and others. However, once the "roles" and the "cons" and the "hooks" and the "payoffs" of the Drama Triangle are known, and no longer unconscious to us as an extra-ordinary Leader, we are then well-positioned to potentially get ourselves off of the Drama Triangle and then to support others in doing the same. We can then leave behind so much of the unnecessary drama in our workplaces, the unnecessary drama that negatively impacts our systems, processes, products and services, and just about everything else. Karpman's Drama Triangle illuminates this pervasive type of dysfunctional social interaction in a way that we can plainly see it, and then more productively address it.

As Victims, we actively seek out Persecutors, which could be people, events or even things, to use them in our attempt to get others (Rescuers) to listen to us and to agree with our story and to sympathize with our plight. We then attempt to control these Rescuers to a degree, by enlisting their support in somehow dealing with our issue. And most importantly, as a result of this interplay, the Victim receives the payoff that we seek, which is to feel listened to and taken seriously and cared for and loved.

Let me also be clear at this point, NOT to confuse the Victim role with someone who comes to us, as a Leader, with a legitimate issue or problem. Not everyone who comes to us with an issue is seeking payoff as a Victim. Our job as an extra-ordinary Leader is to discern the difference and to understand the reality of a situation, and then to address that reality, directly.

The next dysfunctional role frequently played out in the workplace is that of the Persecutor. The Persecutor is a role we play when we consistently criticize the Victim or others or situations or try to control others or a situation through our perceived, superior power, expertise or knowledge. As an important aside, and to create a connection to the Leadership Levels we have explored so far, Level 1 and 2 Leaders can, and many times do, develop and express and justify our role as a Persecutor to a very high level. Persecutors, through our condemnations of others and events, also seek to be in control and to be right, just like Level 1 and Level 2 Leaders. To clarify this issue even further, the Drama Triangle actually overlays Level 1 and 2 Leadership. All three roles of the Drama Triangle play out fairly consistently with ourselves and others when we are part of the status quo of Leadership.

As a Persecutor we must also enlist others into our perspective and dynamic to justify our behavior, and for our own payoff (benefit). We will often share our condemnations of others with three groups of people in the workplace: those that report to us, to demonstrate to them our superior power, expertise or control; to our peers, so that we can attempt to convince others of our superior knowledge base and the importance of our opinion; and to Leaders above us, so that we can attempt to manipulate and control this group, through planting fear or doubt in their minds. As we can see here, the Persecutor role is also made up of a complex and well-orchestrated set of behaviors designed to create a benefit for the "actor," albeit a dysfunctional, nonproductive benefit.

Typical behaviors of the Persecutor in the workplace include being *very invested* in making sure others know what should be done to solve the problems or the issues at hand. Persecutors see others, especially Victims, as incapable of making appropriate decisions for themselves, and, needing to be "fixed." They are overtly and consistently critical of others, while many times insisting that Victims have some negative intent in mind. Persecutors also often speak and act in a more rigid, insistent, dominating, or bossy manner. Persecutors are very often the bullies of the workplace.

As Persecutors, we need Victims as fodder or material to obtain our own needs, which are similar to the Victim's needs. As a Persecutor, we also want to be heard and to have others understand and agree with our perspective, and to control the actions of others to a degree through this interplay. Persecutors also have a strong desire to be respected and, of course, loved. We all know the classic Persecutors in our workplace and we may have even performed in this role ourselves. And, to tell you the truth, I have performed in this role many times in the past, and at an award-winning level.

The last key role on the Drama Triangle is that of the Rescuer. The Rescuer's role is sort of like that of Superman or Superwomen, or how about Super Leader! The Rescuer needs both Victims to save and impress, and Persecutors to thwart or sometimes to gain the favor of. The Rescuer seeks to make the Victim feel safe and the Persecutor feel important. And when this is accomplished, all three roles are in balance and "the play" has been another success.

As the Rescuer, we feel the strong desire to insert ourselves into or be pulled into challenging situations because we feel that we alone can fix the situation. The Rescuer feels compelled to save the Victim and feels somewhat responsible for the outcome of the Victim's problem or the issue at hand. At the same time, we also feel compelled to thwart the Perpetrator or, at times, actually to gain their favor. The Rescuer attempts to gain favor from the Persecutor in hopes that when the Persecutor inevitably speaks to others about the Rescuer, it will be a positive representation of the Rescuer, although this is rarely the case. Often, the underlying motivation to Rescue others is so that the Rescuer can feel invaluable and needed and recognized for their role.

As a Rescuer, we must also enlist others into our perspective and dynamic to justify our behavior. The Rescuer does this, many times, by making sure that we explain in intricate detail the many things we are doing to address the problems of a Victim and the condemnations of a Perpetrator. We want everyone to know how challenging a situation is, and how fortunate everyone is that we are there to save the day. The payoff for the Rescuer in the workplace is, that like the Victim and the Persecutor, we also desire to be acknowledged and heard and appreciated and, of course, loved. And we believe that the best or only way to obtain this from others, is to show up, just in the nick of time, and Rescue others in distress. This helps us to feel good and to look good, in our own minds.

The Rescuer perceives others as incapable of handling challenges without our direct involvement, and perceives our role or mission as saving others and the organization. We are convinced that without our intervention, others and the organization would fail. Many Leaders actually gravitate towards and feel at home in this role. I personally have made much of my Leadership career about starring in this role. I actually thought for quite some time that my role as a Leader was to run around and save everyone and the organization. I am not even sure where I picked up that programming, but I certainly ran around a lot, jumping from challenge to challenge. And while in this role, I missed so many opportunities to more productively serve others and the organization.

We should also note here that some individuals gravitate towards a particular role, while others can move around the Drama Triangle quite cleverly, switching roles to best suit our needs, and keeping others guessing on how to best respond to us. For example, a Victim may, after sharing how we have been wronged, turn into a Persecutor, where we then begin to point our finger at others as the cause of all of our problems. And after that, we might take on the Rescuer role to project that only we can vanquish the challenge. Each time we show up, we might randomly be in a different role.

It is also important to point out that those playing out a role on the Drama Triangle are not bad or dumb. After all, so many of us have performed quite expertly in these roles in the past and may still get pulled into them from time to time. It is important for us as Leaders to understand that the main reason that these roles show up so frequently, in the workplace and in our lives, is as a result of the consistent programming we have received from so many sources, ever since we were children. This creates our mostly unconscious (outside of our *Awareness*) experience and consistent involvement in these roles.

We should be able to clearly see at this point that these three roles are rampant in the workplace (and society), and that they depend on each other, and that we ourselves as Leaders have probably played each of these roles, unwittingly, many times in the past. And as a reminder once again, not everyone who shares with us that they have been mistreated is a Victim. And not everyone that points out to us a problem with a person or situation is a Persecutor. And not everyone that steps in to help in a challenge is a Rescuer. The differences can be subtle but can significantly impact others and an organization, either positively or negatively.

As we look at many of our past experiences, and even at our present situation, we should be able to clearly discern when we have acted out one of these dysfunctional roles and also be able to determine when someone else is doing the same thing. And we should be able to discern this, not because we are smarter than others but because we have also performed in some version of these roles many times in the past. We are able to discern when someone is playing out one of these roles, not because we are better, but because we can identify with them through our own experiences with these roles.

More specifically, how do we know if we or others are operating on or playing one of the roles on the Drama Triangle? For example, when we *consistently* feel like it is our job to single-handedly solve everyone's problems and it becomes a consistent focus of our internal and external dialogue, then there is a good chance that we are on the Drama Triangle. When we experience *consistent* feelings and emotions that include out of proportion frustration, anger, guilt, resentment, entitlement, hopelessness, feelings of oppression, then there is a good chance that we are on the Drama Triangle. When our sense of power is experienced as either feeling powerless or feeling power over others, then there is a good chance that we are operating from the Drama Triangle. When we consistently blame ourselves or others or the situation, rather than taking appropriate responsibility for our actions, then there is a chance that we are on the Drama Triangle. When, as a Leader, our actions are *consistently* reactive to people, circumstances and problems, then we just may be on the Drama Triangle.

We could explore many other examples at this point regarding what Leading while on the Drama Triangle looks like and feels like, but the main point we must acknowledge is that when we as Leaders operate from any one of the roles on the Drama Triangle, even the Rescuer, we add to the already plentiful dysfunction of many of our workplace interactions. We also contribute to the unnecessary drama of the workplace, while we sub-optimize everyone's performance and results. Additionally, performing in one of these roles as a Leader, models or sets the standard for the types of behaviors and performance the workplace culture supports. This is one of the most dysfunctional elements of the status quo of our organizations and society. And as an extra-ordinary Leader, it is our responsibility to get off of the Drama Triangle, to model and to create a new possibility in our workplaces and in society. *This is the Leadership Revolution that I am talking about!*

There is a lot of great information out there on the Drama Triangle, and an extra-ordinary Leader will do some extra-research on this important topic. So, how do we as extra-ordinary Leaders go about getting off of the Drama Triangle, so that we can finally serve others in a way that models and calls out the best in others? Our *Being* and *Doing* while off of the Drama Triangle is the opposite of our *Being* and *Doing* while on the Drama Triangle, and so is the impact on others. While on the Drama Triangle as a Victim, we see ourselves as powerless and at the effect of others and circumstances. The opposite of this way of *Being* and *Doing* is that of an empowered "Creator" or Co-Creator. As an empowered Creator, we see ourselves as responsible for our own actions, and with an internal locus of control we tend to respond to challenges as opposed to reacting. A Creator sees challenges as an opportunity to exercise our creativity and ingenuity and to collaborate with others to create a new possibility.

The feeling and impact of working through a challenge with someone with a Creator mindset is quite the opposite of that of a Victim. The Creator is typically fun and easy to work with during a challenge, without the unnecessary drama of the Victim that can drag down a team's efforts. And the payoff that the Creator receives as a result of this way of *Being* and *Doing* is that we are actively involved in living out our Leadership Purpose, which includes taking responsibility for a more positive stance in life, while exercising our creativity and contributions in the face of a challenge.

As a Persecutor, we spend our time pointing our finger at others. The opposite of this is the "Catalyst," who sees challenging people simply as those in need of some support or direction. So, instead of wasting our time and energy with tearing down people as a Persecutor, a Catalyst shows up to support and encourage other's growth and more productive performance. The Catalyst sees the challenges others are experiencing as simply an opportunity to provide some key additional input, to help to move things forward more efficiently and productively. The Catalyst may offer a word of encouragement or some potential supportive course of action, or even challenge us to bring out our best. The Catalyst helps to create a much more positive experience and outcome for others and the organization, while the Persecutor wastes the precious time and energy of others. The payoff that we receive for our efforts as a Catalyst is that our *Being* and *Doing* is in alignment with our Leadership Purpose, which includes the positive and productive support of others in the face of a challenge.

Where the Rescuer's ego is more focused on how good we will look to others, the "Coach" is focused on the role of a guide, who sees others as capable individuals, who at times, benefit and thrive on thoughtful, supportive and targeted input and motivation. Coaches see challenges as opportunities to facilitate and support individual and team excellence. Coaches work to bring out the best in others to overcome challenges and achieve objectives. The payoff that a Coach receives for this way of *Being* and *Doing* is that we get the opportunity to live our Leadership Purpose, which includes the deep work of understanding others and the ever-changing environment, while creatively facilitating the best efforts of others in their contributions to the team. The Rescuer's efforts are mostly focused on building up our ego, while the Coach's efforts are mostly focused on building up other's self-esteem, confidence and performance.

As extra-ordinary Leaders, we must work to transform ourselves first, and then support the transformation of others, from a *Victim* to a *Creator*, from a *Persecutor* to a *Catalyst*, and from a *Rescuer* to a *Coach*. This is stepping off of the Drama Triangle and supporting others in doing the same. And when we find ourselves back on the Drama Triangle, for whatever reason, our first responsibility is to recognize this and then to work to step back off of the Drama Triangle, so that we once again position ourselves as an extra-ordinary Leader, to serve others exceptionally.

Stepping off of the Drama Triangle can be a fairly straightforward process, but our years of negative programming and our ego's habitual behaviors can complicate this process. Essentially, as an extra-ordinary Leader, all we need do is to first understand the Drama Triangle and its negative impacts on individuals, a team and an organization, and then commit to changing and transforming this at a very deep level. What I mean is to deeply and genuinely commit and take consistent and real steps with this, especially during challenging situations, to create a much more productive and positive experience for others. This commitment must be grounded in our very real *Being* and *Doing*, expressed through our moment-to-moment thoughts, words and deeds.

And once we understand the very real impact of our Leadership *Being* and *Doing* while on the Drama Triangle, we must also become clear about what it looks like and feels like and what the impacts are of operating as a Leader while off the Drama Triangle. We must simply understand, and then drop any of our efforts or energy that supports ourselves or others with continuing to perform in the role of a Victim, Persecutor or Rescuer. We must thoughtfully and purposefully replace these efforts and energies with a Mindset and associated behaviors that are reflective of the Creator, Catalyst and/or Coach. And then we must just repeat this process over and over and over, forever, as there are numerous subtle variations of performing while on the Drama Triangle, just as there are numerous subtle variations of its opposite, performing while off the Drama Triangle.

So, once again, there are no special tips or tricks or external devices necessary for this effort as an extra-ordinary Leader. We just do it! We can start by just looking back at our Leadership Purpose Statement, the one that we just developed or updated. I would be willing to bet that our Leadership Purpose Statement does NOT say anything about us acting like any version of a Victim, Persecutor or Rescuer. So then, what could possibly be a justification for us to adopt these roles in any circumstance, even challenging ones? Some Leaders claim to be committed to some version of higher level Leadership, yet when we find ourselves in the middle of a challenge, these superficial commitments often fly right out of the window and we immediately default back to our dysfunctional programming and operating from the Drama Triangle. Everyone around us sees this and knows this, by the way. Did we get that? We are not invisible when we are on the Drama Triangle and operating outside of our deeper Leadership commitment. In these moments, our active Leadership commitments are exposed to the light of day, for everyone to see. But this is not the journey of an extra-ordinary Leader! Extra-ordinary Leaders draw a very real line in the sand with this all-too-common approach to Leadership.

Extra-ordinary Leaders stare very intently at the Drama Triangle and how it plays out in very real ways in our lives, and we contemplate the very real impacts of the associated behaviors. Look around! The dysfunction of the Drama Triangle is everywhere! It exists in almost every industry, from education to politics . . . especially politics! Extra-ordinary Leaders also stare very intently at and contemplate the roles and behavioral transformations that remove us from the Drama Triangle. And then we make the only choice possible for an extra-ordinary Leader, which is to thoughtfully and purposefully step off the Drama Triangle by adopting a way of *Being* and *Doing* that is in alignment with our Leadership Purpose Statement and that truly serves the needs of others and our organizations, right here and right now. And by paying special *Attention* to this when we are involved in a challenging situation.

Look at the Drama Triangle Model. Pull it up online. Print out or draw a picture of it. We should contemplate it until it comes alive for us, and then we need to act as an extra-ordinary Leader. Like all of the concepts discussed here, we must literally reach out to this concept, and wrap our mind around it and incorporate it into our *Awareness*. And we must place our *Attention* on it and *Focus* on it, in a way that informs and supports the further transformation of our *Being* and *Doing* as an extra-ordinary Leader. That is our responsibility with this type of material, and all Leadership material for that matter.

We typically cannot make significant changes in our Leadership *Being* and *Doing* by just reading about something. We must *immerse* ourselves in it, and engage with it, and experiment with it. Otherwise, what we read or hear will, in time, just fade into the background of our default programing. We must actively connect with this information to be able to express our version of it in any meaningful way. That's how it works with everything we choose to take on! From playing sports to acting in a play to performing a hobby. It's all the same. If we want to do something well, then we must genuinely apply ourselves to it! We must get into it! So, let's get into it!

It all starts first with us. As an extra-ordinary Leader, we must take the first step and we must take this step over and over again, if we are to expect to more positively impact and influence others. *First us, and then them.* We must firmly establish our way of *Being* and *Doing*, as an extra-ordinary Leader, not perfectly but consistently, before we are in a position to Coach others along the way. And this should not take years or even months to accomplish. As extra-ordinary Leaders, this process can begin right here and right now.

We must establish our Mindset (*Being*), grounded in our Leadership Purpose, and then act from there (*Doing*). We must be positive and supportive and remain committed to understanding and addressing the reality at hand, and not be pulled into unnecessary drama, innuendo, assumption or other forms of illusion. We must establish and model our way of Leadership *Being* and *Doing* and then extend it out to others, by thoughtfully and purposefully coaching them towards an expression of their best selves, their best performance. This Coaching approach is clearly part art and part science. As an extra-ordinary Leader, we begin with others wherever they are, and engage with them on a journey to what is possible for us, individually and collectively. That is one of the reasons why we, as extra-ordinary Leaders, must first step into our best version of ourselves. We cannot call others into their best selves unless we are solidly on this journey ourselves. *This is the Leadership Revolution that I am talking about!*

Since this issue, the Drama Triangle, is so important to our extra-ordinary Leadership journey, let's briefly touch on some of the keys for Coaching others off the Drama Triangle before moving on. As stated previously, first, we must ensure that we are off the Drama Triangle, by understanding the Drama Triangle and many of its more common expressions, and also its dysfunctional impacts on people and situations. And then, though the energy of our personal commitment, grounded in our Leadership Purpose, we must actively and purposefully step off the Drama Triangle by dropping any of the programmed roles here, and instead, acting by choice as a Creator, Catalyst and/or Coach. Only when we have accomplished this, are we in a position to effectively Coach others.

Now, positioned as an extra-ordinary Leader and off the Drama Triangle, we can now focus our Coaching on others. When someone approaches us and begins to act out one of the roles of the Drama Triangle, while we remember the difference between a legitimate concern versus the need to express one's programmed perspective, we must listen and watch, and from a perspective of understanding, compassion and non-judgement, we can begin to Coach the person in front of us. We do this by temporarily ignoring wherever their accusatory finger is pointing, and we focus on and Coach the person in front of us by engaging with them in an exploration or fact-finding dialogue.

We do this primarily through a series of thoughtful, purposeful *questions*, directed at uncovering the facts, and separating them out from any additional opinions or assumptions or judgements around these facts. There is no standard approach to this type of questioning. As an extra-ordinary Leader, we must stay present to the person in front of us, and just begin to ask whatever questions seem appropriate to understand the facts, based on the specifics of the situation being presented. Just let our *Awareness*, *Attention* and *Focus* guide us along this process.

Coaching the person in front of us involves helping others to focus their energies inwardly and to take the time to understand and acknowledge the issues (internal & external) to be able to develop more creative, productive solutions. Coaching the person in front of us helps to redirect a person's energy towards how they can more positively and productively influence or address a situation. It involves an exploration regarding what their thoughts and beliefs are about the situation, and how these may be influencing their feelings and emotions and subsequent behaviors related to the issue. It may also involve supporting others in questioning some of their own long-held thoughts and assumptions about their coworkers and the workplace.

Some example questions that could get the process of Coaching the person in front of us started, could include any version of:

▶ *What is it about this situation that is creating frustration or upset within you?*

▶ *What are your thoughts and beliefs related to this situation that might also be contributing to your frustration and upset?*

▶ *Is it possible for you to temporarily suspend your current thoughts and beliefs about this issue, to try to look at this issue from a different perspective?*

▶ *How might you be contributing to this situation?*

▶ *What have you done so far to help to improve the situation?*

▶ *What else could you do to improve this situation and move it forward?*

▶ *What could you do right after this meeting, to begin to move this issue forward in a more positive, productive manner?*

▶ *After you have done that (answer from the question above), please follow up with me and let me know how things went and what your next steps might be!*

As we can see, these questions are all focused on the person in front of us, not what they are trying to point us towards.

These example questions are just a starting point, and the answers we receive should guide our follow-up questions and approach. These questions can create the initial foundational dialogue around empowering others towards more productive behaviors, while setting a more positive and productive tone and expectations around future dialogues with us. And this can be accomplished without the need to give someone a lecture about the Drama Triangle. We, as extra-ordinary Leaders, through the clarity and purposefulness of our interactions and dialogue, can model and Coach others towards significantly higher levels of performance, while also genuinely supporting others with stepping further into the best versions of themselves.

We should coach *Victims* towards a *Creator* mindset, by helping them to experience their own abilities, creativity, power and responsibility. We should Coach *Persecutors* towards a *Catalyst* mindset, by helping them to understand the *Victim* mindset and their opportunity and responsibility in collaborating with this person in a way that helps the *Victim* more productively through their current challenge. And we should coach *Rescuers* towards the *Coaching* mindset, by helping them to understand how to create an experience for the *Victim* or the *Persecutor* to grow in their ability to take responsibility for their circumstances and create more positive interactions and results. And at the appropriate time, we can Coach all of the *Players* in *the game* itself (the Drama Triangle), to help them to see it and to understand its dysfunctional impact, and ultimately to help them to stop playing it. *This is the Leadership Revolution that I am talking about!*

To reiterate and to connect this discussion more directly to the AQ Model, the Drama Triangle overlays atop Level 1 and Level 2, the status quo of Leadership. Think about it. The pay-offs within the Drama Triangle are things like being in control, being right, looking important to others, etc. Just as in Leadership Levels 1 and 2. When we operate at Leadership Levels 1 and 2, we very often add to the already high levels of unnecessary drama in the workplace. Unnecessary drama is stifling our workplaces and creating so much dysfunction, and an extraordinary Leader does their best to decrease drama, not add to it! Coincidently, one of the main roles we take on as a Leader when we step off the Drama Triangle is that of a Coach. In the AQ Model, Level 3 is represented by the *Coaching Leadership* approach, the first level of extra-ordinary Leadership. As we can see, the AQ Model itself also supports us in stepping off the Drama Triangle as we journey along, when we earnestly engage with it. And we will be exploring Level 3 Leadership soon!

CHAPTER 11

The Value of Others
on our Journey

We are here for others, and others are here for us.

We are almost ready to jump in and explore Level 3, Coaching Leadership, but before we do, let's briefly cover one additional topic that is both key to our journey in extra-ordinary Leadership and our Hero's Journey. That topic is centered around people. At this stage of our extra-ordinary Leadership journey, there can be incredible benefit gained from a close association with a mentor, advisor or co-creator; one who has made the same type of commitment that we have, and who has possibly walked this path and experienced many of the challenges that await us.

The only problem is that there are not yet enough of these types of individuals out there in Leadership circles. Now don't get me wrong, there are most certainly many good Leaders out there, and also quite a few great ones. And there is much to be learned from them and their work. But, quite frankly, there are not enough *extraordinary* Leaders out there to meet all of the mentorship needs for the journey that we are exploring here. Once again, not yet. But as the Hopi Prophecy states, *"We are the ones we have been waiting for."* There will be many more good, and great, Leadership mentors and coaches available in the very near future, as a result of *our* commitments to extra-ordinary Leadership. So, what do we all do in the meantime?

Well, as valuable as a competent mentor can be, our real learning and growth actually occurs in our moment-to-moment interactions with others within our specific challenges. And through these challenges and interactions with others, we can give and receive all of the feedback we really need to effectively learn and grow and proceed along our journey, and to course correct when needed. There is so much valuable feedback available to us, each and every day, from all of the mentors and teachers that we are surrounded by. Those around us are incredibly valuable in and of themselves, and we are truly all in this thing together when it comes to improving our Leadership performance. And when we actually see others, I mean all others, in this way, every interaction can inform and transform our journey. Everyone and every situation, *especially* the challenging ones, then becomes our own personal mentor and coach.

As a committed, extra-ordinary Leader, we can make significant improvements in our Leadership, and its impact, when we truly see and connect with the purpose and value of everyone around us. People are important! And we are all on our own incredible journey, no matter how it may appear on the surface. When we see others as adversaries or obstacles or inconveniences to our agenda, well, our performance as a Leader will reflect this. This is part of the status quo of Leadership that we need to move far beyond. We are here for others, and others are here for us. So, when we see and engage with others in alignment with our Leadership Purpose, our performance, their performance, and our collective experience will reflect this instead.

So, let's stop for a moment, and look around. And let's reorient ourselves and place our *Awareness, Attention* and *Focus* on all of the incredible teachers and mentors and co-creators that surround us right now, and with whom we will be interacting with in the future. This path, this journey in extra-ordinary Leadership, is paved with and enlivened through our interactions and associations with others. This journey is not some super-secret, solo, lone wolf, individualistic, look-at-me approach to Leadership excellence. This path to extra-ordinary Leadership actually requires and depends on our committed, purposeful interaction with others. We literally cannot do this on our own, since Leadership and our growth cannot occur in a vacuum.

We are not retreating to a cave to receive some secret Leadership knowledge, so that we can eventually come back into society and look really cool as a Leader. We are instead stepping fully into the middle of the stream of life, into the middle of our workplaces, into the middle of our challenges, to more thoughtfully and more purposefully interact with and serve others. And when we make this type of commitment and then actually step into it on a consistent basis, then others are also uplifted in some way. And as a result, other people may also step forward to directly support our commitment and our journey, as we support theirs. Many others will begin to join with us in a way where we begin to support each other in remarkable ways. These types of relationships can be amongst the most rewarding in our lives. This is a KEY PART of our work in Phase 2 of our Hero's Journey, and the most rewarding part of it!

The world is waiting for us to take real action here. Others have been waiting for us for a long time. They need our commitment and our courage to give them permission to start to step further into the best version of themselves. These people are everywhere, and in every organization, waiting for us step into and invite them into an extra-ordinary journey through life. As extra-ordinary Leaders, the workplace and everyone in it are part of this adventure, this Hero's Journey. We must really look at our teams, and look at our peers, and look at everyone as a reflection of ourself, at different points on their own journey. And from this perspective, understand them, appreciate them, honor them, love them, support them, reach out to them, connect with them, learn from them, and as a result, everyone's journey becomes a little more extra-ordinary. *This is the Leadership Revolution that I am talking about!*

Now let's jump deeply into the exploration of the "extra-ordinary levels of Leadership!"

CHAPTER 12

Level 3 Leadership
The Knowledge Age &
Coaching Leadership

Leadership through Guidance . . .

Leadership Age: *Knowledge Age*

The third Level of Leadership illuminated in the AQ Model represents the functional progression of a more thoughtful application of individual experience (*Industrial Age*), information and data gathering (*Information Age*), expanded into the "*Knowledge Age*." As a brief summary, the Knowledge Age is characterized by the more thoughtful exploration and application of experience, and information and data, through a deeper understanding of the impacts of distinct interventions within a unique part of a system as it relates to the entire system as a whole. The Knowledge Age appreciates and respects individual experience and the gathering of relevant information and data but sees these as simply starting points to more thoughtfully and creatively determining next steps. Although as a consistent Leadership approach within and across an organization this

Level is not all that common, there are many examples of this level of Leadership that can be directly observed. The sports world is one of these examples.

High-level sports teams very frequently make large and small adjustments to their "game plan" based on the uniqueness of the next team they will face. And these changes can occur week after week and be based on numerous variables such as each individual's growing Skill Sets versus the changing Skill Sets of the other team, or the shifting strengths and weaknesses of both organizations. Each change must be meticulously explored related to its impact across the team and to the goal at hand. Leadership or Coaching in sports is quite a dynamic, agile endeavor.

The key point here related to our exploration is that, in our rapidly changing and increasingly complex workplace environments, more and more we are required as Leaders to make both large and small adjustments to our key plans, systems, processes, and with our team or personnel mix. And simply cutting and pasting someone else's best practice into our organizations often results in some form of negative, unintended consequences. The easy way rarely works for us in our present, complex environment. If we are to serve as extra-ordinary Leaders, we must embrace this fact and apply ourselves to the real work of Leadership by bringing all of our *Awareness, Attention* and *Focus* to moving our organizations forward. And we do this by continuously looking deeply into our environments and systems and people and plans, and by asking the deeper questions that bring about a more thoughtful approach to the challenges we all face.

Leadership Approach: *Coaching Leadership*

The characteristic **Leadership Approach** in the **Knowledge Age** could be described as **"Coaching Leadership."** Coaching Leadership seeks to guide and motivate others to achieve their individual and group potential, through focused work and ongoing learning and growth based around shared goals. Coaching Leaders leverage our experience and the experience of the team, along with a relentless exploration of relevant information and data with an eye for the modification of the subtle details that can make or break the implementation of a game plan, or strategic plan. Coaching Leaders are constantly observing reality and learning and growing from it to better position our teams for success.

A Coaching Leader's primary focus is always on our people, our team. Coaches know for a fact that we can go nowhere without a motivated, high-performing team. Therefore, with as much time as we spend with our research and discussion and planning, and on our own personal learning and growth, and on the business of our business, as a Coaching Leader we focus even more so on the individuals and groups within our team. People are paramount to a Coaching Leader.

As we move into our exploration of the Predominant Leadership Characteristics for this next level of Leadership, I would like to again highlight a key point. The up-leveling approaches that we performed in the previous level of Leadership serve to automatically usher us into this next level. However, in order to remain or ground ourselves here, we must begin to practice and to embody and express the Predominant Leadership Characteristics below. We must work to ground ourselves in the *Being* and *Doing* of this level to gain the Leadership benefits and to achieve

the potential results of the level, for everyone we serve. Therefore, we should continue to utilize the up-leveling approaches
we just explored (in the previous chapter) while placing our
Attention and *Focus* on the Predominant Leadership Characteristics below and working to understand and practice them until
we ground ourselves in the here and now of these characteristics, until they become our default mode of Leadership.

Predominant Leadership Characteristics: *Coaching Leadership*

1. **Leadership through Guidance** is typically based
    on experience (Level 1) and information and data
    gathering (Level 2), *and on assessing and reorganiz-
    ing information to customize it, based on the specific
    requirements of the team, business unit or organiza-
    tion.* At this level, we recognize the need to use various
    sources of data and information to then develop a
    more customized game plan, to meet the specific needs
    of the individual and/or team. At this level, we also
    realize that employees respond better to a more shared,
    team-oriented, guided process of learning and growth,
    and planning and implementation. Where Level 1
    Leaders are focused on exerting control as their source
    of power, and Level 2 Leaders can be overly focused on
    being or appearing to be right as their source of power
    and influence, Level 3, Coaching Leaders focus on
    supporting and empowering others, as their means of
    guiding a team towards objectives. *A Coaching Leader's
    power comes from empowering others.*

2. **Grounded predominantly in the "mind"** (the left and right-brain, holistic function of the mind that can simultaneously see the whole and its parts), we can see the whole process (the BIG Picture) in relation to the most desirable outcome, and also how the parts fit together and can be re-arranged or interchanged to produce the desired results.

3. **Uses Information vs. being used by Information,** due to our whole-brain approach to addressing challenges. At this level, we can understand that information is merely a Tool that can be utilized and applied in a variety of ways, depending on the needs of a situation, which is a Skill.

4. **Typically, both Present and Near-Future Orientated,** with the ability to understand the past and the present while looking a little further down the road to evaluate the impact of our present actions on the near-term outcomes.

5. **Focused on "systems-thinking"** (understanding that everything is connected), while looking at how individual processes impact other related processes, and also how all of these processes relate to the overall objective of a System (group of related processes). Utilizing this approach tends to produce even more effective results, that come closer to optimizing our efforts.

6. **Problem Solving Method,** usually involves moving from *Opportunity* to Research to **Customization** to Solution. At this level of Leadership, and because of our more expanded perspective, we now see "Problems" as "Opportunities." This language distinction is

not just a matter of arbitrary terminology. It is more of an indicator of our own personal level of growing perspective and resultant Leadership. A problem can have a more negative connotation for many people, while an opportunity tends to be perceived as more positive, somewhat exciting prospect, especially to an extra-ordinary Leader. Additionally, the added element of the *Customization* of best-practices further increases the potential of an effective outcome for our specific group, team or organization.

7. **Common Leadership statement** may be any version of *"Let's put a plan together in a way that works for us."* This type of statement has a much different feel and impact on others than the common statements of a Level 1 or 2 Leader. This statement is much more inclusive of others' expertise and abilities and is focused on our entire team's needs, not just the needs of the individual Leader. Have we ever heard any version of this statement from a Leader? This is much rarer than the common statements of the status quo of Leadership (Level 1 and 2).

8. **Common outcome of this Leadership approach** is frequently a more inclusive, engaged, team-oriented approach to the daily work or activities of a team, and a more collaborative approach to change management and solving the challenges an organization faces. Those in a work group or team begin to feel that their contributions are actually valued and appreciated as the work moves forward and gets done. This Leadership approach tends to establish a work environment where people want to stay and be part of a team and

are motivated to contribute even more of their effort
(body and mind) towards each other and the goals of
the group, creating more optimal results. This Leadership approach works to bolster the confidence, courage
and self/group-esteem of the entire team. This brings
a sense of excitement to a Coaching Leader.

*The Coaching Leadership approach cannot be bought, it must
be earned!* We can't just attend a few presentations on Coaching
Leadership, even if given by a really famous Coach, and expect
our team to then rally around us. We must put some time in
with this approach, and not that much time, by the way. We
must spend some time "on the field" with the other members of
the team, to earn their support around an effort. This level of
Leadership incorporates the Leader's *Awareness, Attention* and
Focus on the value of others, in the process of moving forward
to achieve the objectives of a group, team or organization. This
Leader, as a part of our Mindset, has the desire to motivate
others to give their best effort towards a cause. We also commit
to developing a strong Skill Set with the numerous coaching
Tools available to us. A group or team, in collaboration with
a Coaching Leader, can achieve much and learn and grow
together, creating valuable bonds through our interactions. The
Coaching Leadership approach represents our initial expression
of extra-ordinary Leadership, and everyone we interact with
benefits from this, including ourselves.

Because of our Coaching Leader Mindsets, we develop high-
level Skill Sets with thoughtfully and purposefully modifying
and adjusting both large and small, gross and subtle, elements of
an effort. Our deepening levels of *Awareness, Attention* and *Focus*
support us with seeing, understanding and discerning the most
appropriate elements of an effort to address or adjust. Coaching

Leadership does this through and in collaboration with others, our team! There is nothing more exciting for a Coaching Leader than to be on the field, with our team. This is where it all happens! This is where the dirt and the sweat and the spit and the creative friction of a team comes together in action, in an effort to achieve something of value together. This is a big part of the motivating force behind a Coaching Leader.

Coaching Leadership represents the baseline level of Leadership that we should aspire to and operate from as an extra-ordinary Leader. It marks the beginning of our real journey and adventure on the path. If we were to establish all or most of the Leaders in a given organization at this Level, we would experience a much greater level of consistency and ease with our collective performance and results. Most organizations, however, function from an overall Leadership performance level that averages or bounces back and forth between Level 1 to Level 2. An initial goal we could set as an extra-ordinary Leader could be to first up-level our own Leadership performance to at least Level 3, to enable us to effectively support the up-leveling and performance of other Leaders in our organizations. And then, to work to shift the overall Leadership performance level from the more typical Level 1 and 2, and up to where most Leaders are consistently performing between Leadership Levels 2 and 3. This small but significant shift in the overall Leadership performance of our teams or organization would have a marked and quantifiably positive impact with our organizational experience and results.

And yet, there is still more available within the possibility of Leadership. There is more to share with and give to others, our organizations and ourselves. There remain still untapped reserves within ourselves and others, that when understood and unleashed, can bring even further levels of results and even further degrees of growth and satisfaction, experienced by those we serve, including ourselves. The challenge of an extra-ordi-nary Leader at this point is to not yet be satisfied with all of the positive change and results that are now a more consistent experience for our teams and ourselves.

Although a commitment to Leading through guiding and motivating others, while being grounded in the right/left brain, holistic function of the mind, and as a systems thinker who can see how everything is connected while collaborating with others to create customized solutions, brings more significant results and experiences to those involved, without an active focus on "the heart" of the matter and "the heart" of others and ourselves, we can still be left wanting and fall short of the results and extra-ordinary experiences that still await us.

The Coaching Leadership approach serves as an excellent baseline and springboard into even higher levels of Leadership performance. Coaching Leadership brings much more value to the Leadership equation and moves us and those we serve well beyond the status quo. From this level we can use, as opposed to being used by, Level 1 and 2 Leadership elements, while doing this from a more expanded perspective. This also positively changes the look and feel of any needed Level 1 or 2 approaches to Leadership that we may be required to utilize. A Level 1 Lead-ership act looks and feels completely different when utilized from a Level 3 Leadership perspective, as it replaces the uncon-trolled, negative emotion and need for control, typical of a Level 1 Leader, with a motivating quality and desire to support the best effort of individuals and groups (Level 3). Think about that.

I'd like to share an additional important point on the Lead-ership Levels in the AQ Model. Remember, these levels are not as separate as they appear to be in a chart or book form. Ele-ments of any of the levels may randomly appear in any of the other levels as expressed through our individual Leadership.

However, at higher levels of Leadership, we have purposeful access to all of the Leadership approaches in the preceding levels and can use them much more productively. As a general rule, when grounded in lower levels of Leadership, we do not necessarily have access to the higher-level, more productive approaches to Leadership, especially in a challenging situation.

At lower levels of Leadership, we still have the ability to occasionally perform aspects of higher levels of Leadership but these expressions are too few and too far between for what is needed from us in our complex work environments. At lower levels of Leadership, we can still achieve some significant results, but many times these results are at the expense of others. At lower levels of Leadership, we typically can't even see what we are missing related to the possibilities of our Leadership. We simply don't know what we don't know. And this lack of knowing can limit our ability to best support others, our organizations and ourselves.

And one more thing before we begin to move on from Level 3 to Level 4 Leadership. Most of us have performed to some degree at each of the Leadership levels in this book. At times, we have all done aspects of these things! Through our exploration with the AQ Model, we should be able to see how these elements of Leadership fit together in this puzzle, and how these elements support a more purposeful progression with our efforts. So that we can move with more *Awareness, Attention* and *Focus* and ease, and ground ourselves into higher levels of Leadership performance in the here and now of our teams and organizations. And perform from these higher levels of Leadership more thoughtfully and purposefully and more consistently. Our performance in higher levels of Leadership should not be an accident or only an occasional experience for our teams. As extra-ordinary Leaders, our performance in higher levels of

Leadership should be the norm for all situations and for everyone we interact with. What reason could there be for this to be any other way? What excuse could be acceptable at this point on our Leadership journey?

It's now time to move to the next Level of Leadership, Level 4, the Understanding Age and "Transformational Leadership." But once again, in order to ground ourselves in this next level of Leadership as opposed to just visiting there temporarily, we must understand and work through the attachments or programming that keep us grounded back in Level 3 Leadership. As valuable as Level 3, Coaching Leadership is, it still has limitations that hold ourselves and others back from a fuller expression of our passion and purpose, and the results that are possible. Remember, it is just not a matter of looking at a model or reading about it and moving to another Level of performance. As extra-ordinary Leaders, we must apply what we are discovering to ground ourselves in higher levels of performance and to create the further benefits that are possible for our teams and organizations.

Now, to enable ourselves to move effectively past Level 3 Coaching Leadership, let's explore the primary Level 3 Energetic Impediment that limits our ability to move forward from Level 3. And remember, this concept is referred to as an Energetic Impediment, because there is an energy related to the primary attachment, or strong need, desire or habit at this level. Energy that is holding the attachment in place, making it more difficult or challenging to remove or let go of. So, there is a certain type and amount of energy required to address this attachment, while simultaneously establishing a new ability, and to hold in place these more productive thoughts, beliefs, feelings and habits.

Once again, Energetic Impediments are essentially mental/emotional obstacles that require a significant shift or quantum leap in our Mindset to effectively move beyond. They function as very real obstacles to our growth as Leaders. To ignore this concept is to create unnecessary, additional challenge with our Leadership journey, and quite possibly ensures a significant limitation with our progression and growth. As explored earlier, simply reading or learning about Leadership is NOT enough to facilitate real, significant transformation in our consistent Leadership performance. If it was, with all of the Leadership information out there, we would all be extraordinary Leaders by now. Therefore, dealing with these Energetic Impediments is another missing link or missing piece of the puzzle to our real and sustainable Leadership growth.

3rd Level Energetic Impediment:

Release the attachment to *"the mind" as our singular tool for facilitating change or transformation.* Our programming around the use of this amazing tool, our mind, runs deep, especially in Leadership circles. Traditional logic-based and analytical skills are prized among Board Members and Leaders in many organizations. And yes, the mind is a fantastic tool. But it has been proven time and time again that, as brilliant a tool as the mind is, when it is used as our *singular* tool for moving through the challenges of our daily Leadership activities it can have significant limitations.

The mind is a great tool for so many elements of our Leadership performance but by definition, it lacks "heart." It is great for analyzing and performing mathematical computations and presenting information and data, and other such activities. Yet, the mind is also great at justifying why we should remain in the status quo of our Leadership approach. The mind is very good at telling us that everything is fine just the way it is, and justifying this perspective through very selective data gathering, and with maintaining its programmed-in biases, stereotypes and prejudices. "After all, I got a bonus last quarter, and my paycheck keeps coming every week, and my boss just gave me another glowing performance review last month, so I must be doing just fine. Why should I risk all of this by changing anything?" The mind, very often, works to keep us "safe," by maintaining the status quo. And only when there is a true burning platform will the typical mind even begin to consider the possibility of change.

This tendency of the mind is one of the primary limitations to our true potential as a Leader. Therefore, we must address this here and now. As an extra-ordinary Leader, through our passion and clarity of purpose, we can create our own burning platform. As an extra-ordinary Leader, we light our own fire each and every day. An extra-ordinary Leader fearlessly examines the deeper reality of a situation, to discern the most appropriate course of action, and then acts. And we can further deepen this experience by connecting with our heart.

Before we go any further here, let's explore some of the biases, stereotypes or prejudices that we may have around the concept of connecting with our heart. Many of us have probably been programmed similarly around this issue, especially as a Leader. We have been taught that this "heart stuff" is just a bunch of fluff and nonsense, and that to be a good Leader we have to be tough or cut-throat and that the end justifies the means. And, anyone that offers a different perspective, by bringing up the "ways of the heart," is usually, very quickly marginalized, made fun of and dismissed by the well-programmed minds of others. That's the mind at work, maintaining dysfunctional perspectives in order to preserve the status quo. It works constantly to maintain our own perspective and status at all costs, and very often does this by putting others down in some way. Our mind, or more accurately our mind's programming and attachments, can be our major source of limitation on our journey as an extra-ordinary Leader.

The mind is a great tool, but an unqualified master, as has been pointed out by numerous thought Leaders over the centuries. It can't be a good master, since in reality, it is more like a tool or a Tool Set, albeit a pretty sophisticated one. Our mind as a tool, must be skillfully utilized (Skill Set) by the deeper parts of ourselves that come from our Mindset, as informed by our deeper *Awareness*, purpose, passion and heart, through the exploration of our Meta-Mindset. It's all connected!

As an extra-ordinary Leader, it is time to work through our programming around these issues of the heart, and to brave the ridicule that will most likely come as a result of questioning this programming and the status quo. For on the other side of our questioning of the status quo, lies our freedom as a Leader to express what is really most important to us and to others, even the ones making fun of us. *This is the Leadership Revolution that I am talking about!*

In order to create a smooth transition through this Level 3 Energetic Impediment, here is a little food for thought. The heart does have an amazing capacity to provide us with additional key information and perspective related to a given issue. Investigations over the past two decades suggest that the heart may even have a type of "information processing center" that actually connects with and sends signals to key brain areas such as the amygdala, thalamus, and hypothalamus. These areas of the brain can significantly influence our perceptions and emotions. This research seems to imply that "connecting with our heart" can help us to access perspectives that are not directly accessible through the use of the mind alone.

And remember, my goal here is not to try to convince anybody of anything. We should do our own additional research and experimentation for ourselves. We should also consider suspending our judgements, at least temporarily, related to what we have been taught about the heart. And with a more open mind, and heart, simply experiment with it, and adjust from there. We should prove these things for ourselves. Just know that there are many other extra-ordinary Leaders out there who have already developed the courage to face the "guardians of the status quo," and who are working to serve others and our organizations exceptionally. We are not alone with these explorations. The *Leadership Revolution* has already started!

Once again, the first step in moving ourselves beyond this limited perspective is to become aware of it, either on our own, through fearless self-reflection or through the honest feedback from others, or by placing some level of provisional trust in another, who is also committed to the journey of extra-ordinary Leadership. We should seek each other out and share our perspectives and experiences to help to bolster our journeys, as we actively commit to replacing this limited habit of utilizing the mind as our singular tool for facilitating change or transformation and adopting a way of *Being* and *Doing* that is more expanded and supportive of others, our organizations and ourselves. And what could we replace this habit with?

Develop the ability *to see and understand from our heart, to genuinely connect with and support our own and other's passion and purpose.* Instead of continuing to move forward while centered and focused in the mind only, and limiting our experience and results, we can begin to connect to and ground our *Awareness, Attention* and *Focus* into our *heart-center*, and work from there. From our heart, we can guide our mind and use this amazing tool much more appropriately. So, through the exercising of our *Awareness, Attention* and *Focus* in our heart-center, and connecting to the heart-center of others, we are able to move beyond our previous, programmed, self-limiting attachment and replace this with a more expanded way of *Being* and *Doing* as an extra-ordinary Leader.

We should definitely NOT think too much about this one. That would be the mind doing what it habitually does, analyzing things in an attempt to control them and maintain the status quo. It's the tail wagging the dog, so to speak. We must just try this one to experience it for ourselves. It most certainly takes a growing *Awareness* (Meta-Mindset), and a real commitment (Mindset) to up-level ourselves (Skill Set and Tool Set) at any level. However, it is even more essential when moving from the Level 3, Coaching Leadership, to the Level 4, Transformational Leadership. The Energetic Impediments to up-leveling ourselves associated with the first two levels of Leadership are more related to the mind, and we can typically move beyond these through the discipline of using a more standard set of tools like the project management approach to create higher levels of performance. Whereas, the Energetic Impediment to moving from level 3 to 4, involves the somewhat elusive and sometimes controversial (in the workplace anyway) connection to our heart, and the hearts of others.

At this stage on our Leadership journey, and through this process, we are positioned to move from a 2-Dimensional (2D) approach to a 3D approach to Leadership. It's like the difference between a picture of something (2D), and the thing itself (3D)! 2D Leadership is flat with only an x and y axis and deals with a more limited number of variables. While a 3D approach to Leadership adds in the z axis or "depth," along with the ability to perceive and integrate significantly larger amounts of information or feedback from our environment while performing and expressing our Leadership purpose. This 3D Leadership approach, adds significant depth to our experience, the experience of others, and the results of our organizations. The depth of our Leadership *Being* and *Doing* at this stage of our Leadership journey adds significant and extra-ordinary value to those we serve, our organizations and ourselves. That's 3D value!

There could be many other impediments or obstacles preventing a Leader from moving beyond Level 3, Coaching Leadership; however, the habit of using only the mind in our approach to improve things is at the root of this issue. Although the right use of Knowledge can take us and our team a long way on the improvement journey, Leading with the mind only can get in the way of connecting others with their passion and purpose to provide their best effort. It will take some level of *Awareness* and acknowledgement of this issue and then a commitment to continued growth, for us to recognize our further potential and the further potential of our team. A Leader can be helped and supported through this growth and there are many approaches for this, but, ultimately, we must decide for ourselves to grow further.

The Level 3, Coaching Leadership approach definitely moves us well beyond the more limited expressions of Leadership of Levels 1 and 2 (Authoritarian and Evidence-based Leadership). At Level 3, we are finally beginning to stand and perform more consistently as an extra-ordinary Leader, and others and our organizations will be experiencing this difference also. The Coaching Leadership approach incorporates the additional skill of customizing data and information to best meet the changing needs of an organization. The Coaching Leadership approach is also quite valuable with promoting change. Change however, is not the same thing as "Transformation." Many industries, and the people that work in them, are requiring even more from the workplace. Many people want to be a part of something bigger than themselves, something more meaningful. They want and deserve more out of their workplace experience.

Coaching Leadership, for all of its benefits, is still limited in its ability to facilitate even higher levels of experience and results. So, the journey of an extra-ordinary Leader continues. We may choose to remain at a given level of Leadership for a time, to acclimate there and to more thoroughly explore its benefits and limitations but eventually we may be pulled forward again, inspired to explore and express even higher levels of performance as a Leader, in service to others. *This is the Leadership Revolution that I am talking about!*

Now let's move into the process of up-leveling ourselves and others from Level 3 (Coaching Leadership) to Level 4 (Transformational Leadership), since, as we discussed a few paragraphs ago, without an active focus on "the heart" of the matter and "the heart" of others and ourselves, we can still be left wanting and not fully achieve the results and extra-ordinary experiences that still await us. And as a reminder, these explorations of up-leveling ourselves and others is where the rubber meets the road in the AQ Model. This is where our work occurs, our emotional labor, our exercising of our *Awareness, Attention* and *Focus.* Each set of up-leveling approaches contains both *Being* elements and *Doing* elements but the focus of the up-leveling approaches is on the real-time application of the recommendations. The journey of the extra-ordinary Leader and Phase 2 of the Hero's Journey (The Initiation) involves *Doing,* and lots of it. We can memorize every concept in this book or any other book, but if we don't immediately begin to *DO* something, very purposefully, then what have we accomplished?

The up-leveling processes help us and others, to overcome the *Energetic Impediments* (our attachments) to our current level of Leadership performance, while the *Predominant Leadership*

Characteristics of the next level of Leadership serve as an anchor point for us to focus on and ground ourselves in. So, we should repeat the up-leveling approaches for ourselves and others as much as needed, while grounding ourselves or adopting the consistent practice and expression of the Predominant Leadership Characteristics of the next higher level of Leadership. And once we are comfortable and confident in our Leadership understanding and expression at a given level of Leadership, then it is time for us to move to the next higher level.

With a real commitment to extra-ordinary Leadership, the time spent grounding ourselves at each level does not have to be overly long or arduous. We may find that we progress though some of the levels very easily and quickly, while others may take a little more time, *Attention* and *Focus*, based on our individual attachments and other factors. What I am talking about here in the AQ Model is not a long drawn out *Evolutionary* process to improving our Leadership performance, as is with many other Leadership development approaches. What I am talking about is a *Revolutionary* approach to Leadership development that through our commitment to more expanded ways of *Being* and *Doing*, begins to achieve results for us and others almost immediately, in the here and now of our lives.

Up-leveling from Level 3, Coaching Leadership, to Level 4, Transformational Leadership

Up-leveling Ourselves:

Step 1 – Simply recognize the impulse to want to move immediately to implementation. This can show up as a feeling of perceived pressure or emergency when, in reality, there is still time before the need to act. Once again, the slow way becomes the fast way. Have we ever become aware of this feeling of an emergency when, in actuality, none really existed? I most certainly have. And many times in the past I have proceeded as if things were a real emergency, when clearly they were not.

We must acknowledge our desire or our tendency or our programming to immediately attempt to jump into action, but then, not allow ourselves to move there! In the moment, just pause and breathe and try to stay relaxed, even if only on the outside. Momentarily suspend our tendency and desire to jump right into action, just for a bit. It is OK in this complex and dynamic age, when not in a true emergency situation, to pause and take a moment to make sure that we have understood all of the impacts of our pending effort, while aligning ourselves once again with our purpose or connecting with our heart. In fact, taking this type of pause in a challenging situation is actually quite valuable and appreciated by others we serve.

Step 1 involves the recognition of our feeling of the mounting desire to demonstrate that we are an action-orientated Leader, which can then lead to our tendencies or programming to jump into fixing or changing something before we understand the full potential impact of our pending actions. *Just feel, recognize and pause.*

As in the previous level, this is easier said than done, at first. That is why we must have a rabid passion or burning desire to radically improve our Leadership performance. Without this, we will not be able to overcome the energetic threshold or the inertia of our previous habits or programming required to step fully into a new and more productive way of *Being* and *Doing* as a Leader. Our desire to transform ourselves as a Leader must be stronger than our commitment to our previous habits or programming. Our *Awareness, Attention* and *Focus* around this opportunity to truly serve as an extra-ordinary Leader must be sharp and keen and unwavering in these moments.

Our *Awareness* will always be the key to accomplishing this up-leveling. But even if we fail in our next Leadership challenge, if we maintain our *Awareness* and our strong desire to improve as a Leader, we can then apply this to the very next challenge, which will not be far behind. Just keep recommitting ourselves in thought, word and deed and we will succeed, no matter how many times it takes.

Up-leveling Ourselves:

Step 2 – Consider the intended and unintended impacts of processes on people (ourselves and our team, customers and organization). This can be done as an introspective process or on a written list of some kind. This type of exploration takes a thoughtful, open mind, and just a little time. While paused, take some time to consider even the subtler impacts that a change might have on others and on the existing systems and processes. And consult with others when needed for this effort.

There are many approaches to more deeply clarifying the intended and unintended impacts of a change. This can be done in our head or on a scrap piece of paper for a small change but many times it is best to document this process in some way (on paper, sticky-notes or with a program or app) so that it can be looked at and built upon and reflected upon. This type of approach tends to add the most value to this process. And although we were able to put together a very good, custom-ized plan as a Level 3 Leader, this additional process step will position us to make the further, sometimes subtle, adjustments necessary to more thoughtfully and purposefully move forward, and in a way that deepens our appreciation for and ability to optimize our results.

Just pause before jumping directly into action (Step 1), and then reflect on the possible or potential intended and unintended impacts of our pending actions or efforts (Step 2).

Up-leveling Ourselves:

Step 3 – Align our actions with "the heart" of our Leadership purpose. This is accomplished by re-orienting and re-grounding ourselves in our Leadership Purpose Statement and the purpose at hand. This process reconnects us with our deeper purpose, "the heart" of our Leadership. We cannot re-ground ourselves in our Leadership purpose often enough, as each day's events will attempt to pull us away and back into the status quo. This process may include rereading our Leadership Statement daily and/or at other key times, but once our Leadership purpose has been internalized, we should be much more aware in the moments when we begin to stray from it, enabling us to re-orient back to it in a matter of seconds. Once internalized, our Leadership purpose can become a strong and constant driver of all of our actions, even in the most challenging of circumstances.

Once grounded in our purpose and in our heart as a Leader, and with a clear understanding of the subtle impacts of a pending effort (from Step 2), we are then in a much better position to begin to move things forward more thoughtfully and purposefully. From this position our thoughts, words, actions and results are inspired from a much deeper perspective of Leadership.

Performing these three up-leveling steps automatically deepens our *Awareness, Attention* and *Focus* and understanding of our potential pending action, and in a way that can signifi-cantly inform our next steps. This process can help us to avoid many of the mistakes and unnecessary drama that we have created through our programmed, immediate action-oriented approach to Leadership.

These up-leveling steps automatically move us into higher levels of Leadership performance. By pausing and paying *Attention* to, and adjusting our *Being* in Step 1, and by *Doing* the exploration of intended and unintended impacts process in Step 2, and then by re-grounding ourselves in the heart of our Leadership purpose and acting from this inspired position (*Being and Doing*), we are automatically up-leveled in our Leadership performance. That's just how it works! Just *Be* and *Do* and repeat and repeat. The entire Leadership puzzle can appear quite complex, yet there is a thread of simplicity that runs through the whole thing. Just *Be* and *Do*. Just be nice (compassionate, professional and service-oriented) and move things forward.

Up-leveling Others:

Step 1 – Positively acknowledge the team's effort to customize the plan, while recognizing the impulse of others to move directly to implementation. This step involves acknowledging that this effort now represents a potential best-practice for the specific business unit, team or organization, and that there may be even more of an opportunity to further improve or refine the plan. It is not unusual for team members to want to jump right in and get to work at this point, just like us, especially after taking the time to go through the previous planning (up-leveling) steps. Step 1 of up-leveling others is similar to the Step 1 that we went through as an individual, except that in this circumstance we are facilitating a pause with a potentially diverse group of others. It is important to watch and be aware of the reactions of others to this pause that we are introducing as a Leader, and to support others through this potentially uncomfortable but purposeful pause.

Other's uncomfortableness with this pause may show up much as it has within us in the past. They may perceive a sense of emergency and react to this, when no real emergency actually exists. Remember, others often come from the same programming that has impacted us. None of these potential reactions by others should be taken personally by an extra-ordinary Leader.

Step 1 involves the simple recognition of other's feeling of the mounting desire to demonstrate that they are an action-orientated team member, and that this can then lead to our tendencies or programming to jump into fixing or changing something before everyone understands the full potential impact of the pending actions, and with missing the opportunity to reconnect with the deeper purpose of the effort. Just watch, recognize and facilitate a pause in the action.

This can be easier said than done with a group of others. That is why we must have a rabid passion or burning desire to radically improve our Leadership performance and to improve the performance of others. Without this, we will not be able to overcome the energetic threshold or the inertia of other's previous habits or programming required for them to more fully express their best efforts. Our desire as an extra-ordinary Leader to support the transformation of others must be stronger than our previous habits or programming related to allowing for mediocrity of the status quo. Our *Awareness*, *Attention* and *Focus* around this opportunity to truly serve as an extra-ordinary Leader must be sharp and keen and unwavering in these moments.

But even if we miss this opportunity to support others in our next leadership challenge, if we maintain our *Awareness* and our strong desire to improve as a Leader, we can then apply this to the very next challenge, which will not be far behind. Just keep recommitting ourselves in thought, word and deed and we will succeed, no matter how many times it takes.

Up-leveling Others:

Step 2 – Explore and list the intended and unintended impacts on people (the team, customers, and the organization) of the processes being addressed. This type of exploration takes a thoughtful, somewhat open-minded group, and just a little time. During this activity, take the time to consider the subtler impacts that a change might have on others and on the existing systems and processes. As a committed Leader, facilitate a thorough process by offering some of the deeper questions to be considered to support the group's exploration.

When endeavoring to up-level others, this process should be accomplished typically through some sort of visible, documented process. If everyone can't directly see the process as it unfolds, they will not be in the best position to contribute to the process in a productive way. This process could be accomplished on a white board or with sticky-notes or with the use of any version of this such as a Failure Mode and Effects Analysis. Endeavor to include or draw out everyone's perspective and input, whenever possible.

Remind everyone that although we were able to put together a very good, customized plan as a group (based on our Level 3 work), that this additional process step will position us to make the further, sometimes subtle, adjustments necessary to more thoughtfully and purposefully move forward, and in a way that deepens our appreciation for and ability to optimize our results.

Just facilitate a pause before the group starts jumping directly into action (Step 1) and then, facilitate a reflective process and exploration of the possible or potential intended and unintended impacts of the team's pending actions or efforts (Step 2).

Up-leveling Others:

Step 3 – Connect and align proposed processes and people's actions with their purpose (*heart – head – heart* approach). Although this step resembles the corresponding Step 3 we explored with Up-leveling Ourselves, the fact that as a Leader we are endeavoring to now connect our own passion, purpose and heart with others, to inspire them to do similarly, adds some interesting complexity to this process. This maneuver is definitely more art than science and it may very well look a little different each time we attempt it, depending on the people we are interacting with and the circumstances. But at its core, as an extra-ordinary Leader, what we are actually attempting to do in real time, is to use our own clarity of purpose to explore and connect others a little bit more to their purpose.

Now, if we have had the luxury of working with a group that has already processed through some of the preliminary work that we have been exploring so far here, then connecting with other's passion, purpose and their heart can be somewhat more straightforward. But many times, as a Leader, we will find ourselves working with individuals and groups that have never been exposed to any version of this type of material. And the good news is that, as stated previously, the AQ Model does not require other's knowledge, understanding or buy-in with the model to improve their performance. If applied thoughtfully and purposefully by an extra-ordinary Leader, this model and approach will consistently produce the intended results. And through consistent repetition, these results will continue to be compounded.

What it really comes down to is that, in order to develop our performance as an extra-ordinary Leader, we must simply do a few key things over and over and over. And none of this is very hard to do. We simply must continually exercise our *Awareness*, *Attention* and *Focus* on the things that are in alignment with our purpose (*Being* and *Doing*). After all, if we are going to be paying *Attention* to something throughout our days anyway, then why not pay *Attention* on purpose, instead of allowing our *Awareness*, *Attention* and *Focus* to just go where it goes, based on our potentially dysfunctional programming?

We must then also do the things that are in alignment with our purpose (*Doing*), especially during challenging situations. And again, we are going to be *Doing* things throughout our day anyway. Why not then disrupt our habitual dysfunctional programming and purposely choose to do things that are in alignment with our purpose? And when we do these things over and over again, our lives and our Leadership will begin to look and feel very different, and so will our results. So, once again, I wanted to ground us in the fact that this or any approach of value requires consistent effort. But in this case, it does not require hard effort or excessive effort, just consistent, purposeful effort. This type of effort becomes a joy for an extra-ordinary Leader.

Now getting back more specifically to Step 3 of up-leveling others. The approach to connecting our passion and purpose with other's passion and purpose uses a fairly simple formula that many of us may have seen before, and that is the "heart-head-heart" approach. This formula is actually a very real and powerful way to more deeply and genuinely connect with others. And if we can remember from Chapter 2, our discussion of *The Meaning of Leadership*, we might remember that the deeper meaning of Leadership is grounded in *Love in Action*. With *Love* being defined as *connection*, and *Action* being defined as *movement* forward.

So, real Leadership involves *connection* and *movement*. That is why this approach (heart-head-heart) starts with the heart as our point of connection. The reality is that our hearts often serve us much better as a point of connection than our minds. Our individual minds are often very different in the things we believe and focus on. This can make it more than a little challenging and time consuming to use what's in our mind to reach out and genuinely connect with the mind of another. Our minds have a tendency towards debate and argument, and to be in control and to be right. But our hearts are very often a different matter. Our hearts represent, in a very real way, our deeper shared beliefs and needs and are actually, at their core, quite similar between people and across cultures.

Based on this understanding, using our hearts as a connection point just makes much more sense and is a much more efficient approach than solely using the mind. This approach also brings us and others much more value, satisfaction and ease with our interactions. We are going to be interacting anyway, so why not more purposefully craft our interactions to be more satisfying? Applied genuinely and thoughtfully, the heart-head-heart approach can even disrupt the programming of the most committed *Victims*, *Persecutors* and *Rescuers* in our organizations.

So, we connect first with our heart. We center our *Awareness*, *Attention* and *Focus* into our anatomical and energetic heart area, while connecting with and then using the deeper faculties of our mind to reach out to the hearts of others with our more thoughtful word choice and body language and gestures, to more purposefully interact with them, based around the issue at hand. We take the time to establish our interactions from this place. The slow way becomes the fast way. And we don't have to first provide some kind of in-service about "the heart" to the other people we are interacting with. As an extra-ordinary Leader, we just *Be* it and *Do* it. There is an unlimited number of ways to establish this initial heart connection to another. But each of these ways essentially revolves around genuinely *recognizing* and *acknowledging* the connection we all share as human beings, along with a deep appreciation of and respect for our or another person's humanness and their unique experience, challenges and gifts, and including the deep desire to serve and support each other. This is a foundational element of our *Being*, right out of Chapter 2's *meaning of Love*.

From this level of *Being*, we simply start our interactions by demonstrating our deeper perspective, through communicating to others how much we appreciate the opportunity to connect with them and work with them through this present challenge. Any version of this will begin to create a deeper connection with others, if done genuinely and repeated over time. That is why we must first up-level ourselves! Just do it, and the words will come, and we can refine them as we go along. Don't think about it too much. That is the mind's work. We can simply experiment with connecting with our own heart and begin to use our mind from there. We should *use our mind*. It should not *use us*! And, don't over-think this process. We actually already know how to do this. We used to do it as children all the time. Most of us have just programmed ourselves out of this much more effective and satisfying way of interacting. This is just like riding a bike again! Just do it and adjust from there!

And then, after we have established this deeper heart connection on some level, we move more specifically to the issue at hand, the "head" part of the formula. From this more connected perspective we are in a much better position to discuss the particulars of an issue or move through whatever process is necessary to conclude the specific elements of the dialogue. And when finished discussing the specific issues at hand, we close out the interaction by moving back to the heart, to remind us of our deeper connection as human beings, working together through a challenge. This is where we can re-center our *Awareness*, *Attention* and *Focus* in our heart-center, if we have moved away from here during our dialogue, which can be common at first. We close out our interaction with a genuine statement and gesture of our appreciation for this opportunity to collaborate together, even if the interaction became a little challenging during the discussion. As an extra-ordinary Leader, we should make this our new habit, our new programming around all of our interactions, including our emails, and then watch what happens.

There we have it. A summary discussion of the powerful, efficient and very satisfying, heart-head-heart approach. As an extra-ordinary Leader, we might just be feeling the pull right now to apply this approach to our very next interaction. That's understandable, so please do it. And one more point about the heart-head-heart approach. I want to be very clear that it is NOT the same thing as the "compliment sandwich," which is that transparent attempt to make someone feel good on both sides of a challenging dialogue. Some version of this approach is taught in many Leadership development approaches and if we have ever been on either end of that type of interaction we might clearly remember how sort of fake and "cheesy" it felt. The compliment sandwich lacks the depth of genuine connection of the heart-head-heart approach for it to be of any real value.

In Step 3 of up-leveling others we genuinely connect with others through a heart-head-heart approach while aligning next efforts with the things that others are passionate about. If, for example, through our ongoing exploration of what others are passionate about, we discover that they have an interest working with spreadsheets or data, we are then in a position to connect them with this aspect of a project to leverage their passion and skills. This simple act has the ability to move an individual from being motivated (a Level 3 experience) to *Being* inspired (a Level 4, transformative experience). Think of all of the possible examples that could come up here. Again, this is not hard. All it takes is our consistent *Awareness*, *Attention* and *Focus* towards this approach. All it takes is a way of *Being* and *Doing* that is in alignment with our Leadership purpose. That, along with continuous repetition and ongoing refinement. This is easy from that perspective, and fun and rewarding to an extra-ordinary Leader.

The up-leveling of others from a Level 3 to Level 4 experience includes Step 1, creating a pause in a group's natural tendency to jump right into action, and then facilitating a process to explore and identify as many of the intended and unintended impacts of a change effort on both processes and people (Step 2), and then connecting processes and people's actions with their purpose, through an ongoing genuine curiosity as to what they are passionate about and through the consistent application of a heart-head-heart approach (Step 3). Performing these three up-leveling steps automatically deepens our *Awareness* and understanding of everyone's potential pending action and in a way that can significantly inform the group's next steps. This process can help everyone to avoid many of the mistakes and unnecessary drama that we have created in the past through our programmed, immediate action-oriented approach to achieving objectives.

These up-leveling steps automatically move us beyond the Level 3 Energetic Impediment, and into higher levels of Leadership performance, while creating higher level experiences and higher levels of performance for those we interact with. By pausing and paying *Attention* to and adjusting our *Being* in Step 1, and by *Doing* the exploration of intended and unintended impacts process in Step 2, and then by re-grounding ourselves in the heart of our Leadership purpose and acting and connecting with others from this inspired position (*Being* and *Doing*), we and others are automatically up-leveled into higher levels of performance, in real time. With no drama or buy-in necessary. That's just how it works! Just *Be* and *Do* and repeat and repeat. This is a thread of simplicity that runs through the whole model. Just *Be* and *Do*.

So now it's time to step more fully into our responsibility as extra-ordinary Leaders and help others by supporting their growth through the gift of up-leveling. And once we have moved ourselves and then others beyond the more fixed mindsets of Level 1 and 2 Leaders, there can be much more ease and growth and results achieved, through working within the challenges we all face. As a reminder however, even under the best of circumstances, nothing is 100% as expected. We may need to finesse these approaches and tailor them for a specific person or situation, and we may need to repeat it multiple times to achieve the desired or needed impact. But more times than not, we can improve Leadership performance and everyone's overall experience in the workplace, consistently and in real time, especially when we have done our work first.

Everyone deserves an opportunity to step further into a level of Leadership performance that serves others more completely. Everyone working with a Leader deserves the opportunity to work and contribute within an environment that inspires them towards their best effort and expression of their purpose. Let's do our part as an extra-ordinary Leader to give everyone a real chance for this, here and now. Let's help them and support them the best we can. It's time to transform the whole experience of Leadership! *This is the Leadership Revolution that I am talking about!*

Level 3 — Leadership Age & Approach	Predominant Leadership Characteristics	Up-Leveling Ourselves	Up-Leveling Others
Knowledge Age: Coaching Leadership	1. **Leadership through Guidance** – typically based on all the above, and on assessing & reorganizing information to tailor a course of action based on a set of particular considerations. 2. Grounded predominantly in the "holistic" function of the "mind" (left & right-brain) that can see the "whole" and its parts. 3. *Uses Information vs. being used by Information* 4. Is more typically, Present and Near-Future Oriented 5. Focused on "systems-thinking" (everything is connected). 6. Problem Solving Method – Moves from "Opportunity" to "Research" to "Customization" to "Solution" (PDCA Approach). 7. Common Quote – *"Let's put a plan together in a way that works for us."* 8. Common Outcomes – Work gets accomplished but now with more of a sense of a team approach where employees can begin to feel valued, appreciated and *motivated* to engage more fully with their best effort, along with all of the positive impacts of this.	the thoughtful and purposeful process of improving our performance through an ongoing commitment to growing our awareness, attention and focus Moving from Level 3 to Level 4: 1. Recognize our impulse to move directly to implementation 2. Consider the intended and unintended impacts of processes on people (ourselves & our team, customers and the organization) 3. Align our actions with "the heart" of our Leadership Purpose	helping others to improve their performance "in real time," based on your growing awareness and your commitment to supportive, purposeful coaching Moving from Level 3 to Level 4: 1. Positively acknowledge the effort to customize the plan while recognizing the impulse of others to move directly to implementation 2. Explore and list the intended and unintended impacts of the processes being addressed on people (the team, customers and the organization) 3. Connect and align proposed processes and people's actions with their purpose (heart-head-heart approach)

3rd Level Energetic Impediment *– **Release** the attachment to "the mind" as our "singular tool" for facilitating change or transformation. **Develop** the ability to see and understand from our heart, to genuinely connect with and support our own and other people's passion & purpose.*

Figure 7. (Level 3 Leadership)

CHAPTER 13

Level 4 Leadership
The Understanding Age &
Transformational Leadership

Leadership through Connection . . .

Leadership Age: *Understanding Age*

The fourth Level of Leadership illuminated in the AQ Model represents the functional progression of a more thoughtful application of individual experience (Industrial Age), information and data gathering (Information Age), and customization (Knowledge Age), further expanded into the ***"Understanding Age."*** Experience, if shared, leads to Information and Data, which if more closely examined, leads to Knowledge, which when connected to our purpose, leads to Understanding (Transformation). That's the progression here, so far.

As a brief summary, the Understanding Age is characterized by an even more thoughtful exploration and application of experience, information and data gathering, and customization through a deeper understanding of the more positive impacts that can be gained through connecting our efforts to our purpose, passion and heart. The Understanding Age appreciates all of the efforts of the previous Ages and is obviously an outgrowth of them, and sees them as a strong foundation with which to introduce our more impactful influences as an extra-ordinary Leader. There have most certainly been many examples throughout history of this level "understanding," applied to numerous challenges that have brought forth the "transformation" of entire industries, cultures and civilizations.

At this point, it would valuable to note that although the concept of "Ages" has historically been used to refer to the dominant characteristics of a distinct time period, in the AQ Model, all of the Ages discussed have actually been expressed and represented in many areas of the planet and during many different time periods. And at this time, all of these Ages are actually overlapping each other and expressing themselves simultaneously! Yes, there are very clear examples of all ten Leadership Ages or Levels in the AQ Model happening right here and now, all over the planet. They are all around us, often hiding in plain sight.

Quite a few Leaders are performing at very high levels, without even necessarily being completely *Aware* of the details of their approach. Some Leaders are just more naturally drawn to express their Leadership from a certain level of performance, based on their life experience and their perspective. One of the objectives of the AQ Model then, is to gather these important pieces of the Leadership puzzle, and to further clarify these Leadership Levels, and to illuminate the progression into each, and to map out the path into and through each level, so that more of us, as extra-ordinary Leaders, are positioned to more purposefully and more consistently perform and serve from higher levels of Leadership.

Leadership Approach: *Transformational Leadership*

While Coaching Leaders seek to *motivate*, Transformational Leaders seek to *inspire*. Much has been written about Transformational Leadership over the past few decades and it is a well-documented Leadership approach to achieving a number of additional benefits for our organizations and those we serve. Transformational Leaders seek to inspire others to learn and grow and to achieve new heights through their creativity and innovation, and by creating mutually supportive relationships aligned with an inspiring, shared vision.

Transformational Leaders endeavor to connect with us in a way that brings out our best effort and our best performance and our best version of ourselves. In this type of Leadership environment, we have the potential to more fully express the best parts of ourselves, individually and as a team. And as a Transformational Leader, we are positioned to very purposely and consistently express the depth of our purpose, passion and heart, through our moment-to-moment interactions, especially during times of significant challenge.

Whereas Leadership Levels 1 and 2 are more transactional in nature, and often based on a Leader's expression of their dominance over others, Leadership Levels 3 and 4 are focused on the motivation and inspiration of others to create personal, group and organizational transformation. Our focus here as an extra-ordinary Leader is to express the best version of ourselves first, and to create a more supportive environment through our consistent way of *Being* and *Doing*, that seeks to bring out the best versions of others.

Predominant Leadership Characteristics:
Transformational Leadership

1. **Leadership through Connection** is typically based on experience (Level 1), and information and data gathering (Level 2), on assessing and reorganizing information to customize it based on specific requirements of the team, business unit or organization (Level 3), *and on our purposeful Awareness, Attention, Focus and "Intent" regarding individual, departmental and organizational transformation.* Transformational Leadership is not the same as "Change Management." Transformation involves a purposeful approach to creating a profound and fundamental shift in individual and organizational perspective, culture, or in key systems and results, and includes a significantly expanded experience for those involved.

2. **Grounded Predominantly in both the Mind and the Heart** (the integration of thought, experience, feeling, empathy, intuition, etc.). At this level, we can see the BIG picture as well as how all the parts fit together, and then we add to this a strong heart connection, which can open us up to genuinely connect with the passion and purpose of others.

3. **Uses Knowledge vs. being used by Knowledge,** which is due to our heart connection. At this level, we are not solely bound by information, ideas or mental processes and therefore, we can use knowledge as a stepping stone to create more significant innovations and experiences, to improve both systems and people's experience within those systems.

4. **Typically, Near to Longer-Term Oriented**, with the ability to understand the past, present, the near-term impacts and the impact of our actions or that of a team or group in the longer-term. At this level, we are positioned to move a group, team or organization confidently into the future.

5. **Focused on the relationship between systems and people**, we are able to understand the gross and more subtle interdependence between systems and people, or the degree to which systems and people mutually depend on each other for success.

6. **Problem Solving Method**, usually involves moving from Opportunity to Research to Customization to *Process and People Integration* to facilitate *Transformation*. By adding the elements of a heart connection and the understanding of the *interdependence of Processes and People*, we are positioned at this level to create real *Transformational* experiences for teams and individuals, through connecting with others around a shared, inspiring vision, and through understanding and eliciting their passion and purpose.

7. **Common Leadership statement** may be any version of *"Now, how could we further improve our approach, so that it also engages people's passion and connects them with their purpose?"* Has anyone heard any version of that one lately? I wonder.

8. **Common outcome of this Leadership approach** is frequently a more inspired, team-oriented approach to the daily work or activities of a team and a more innovative approach to addressing, in a transformative

way, the challenges an organization faces. Those in a work group or team begin to feel that their efforts are actually contributing to something larger than themselves, as the work moves forward and gets done. This Leadership approach tends to establish a work environment where people want to stay and are inspired to contribute even more of their discretionary effort (body, mind and heart) towards each other and the goals of the group, creating even more optimal results. This Leadership approach works to inspire the confidence, courage, self/group-esteem, and heart of the entire team. This brings a sense of deep appreciation to a Transformational Leader.

The Transformational Leadership approach can't be taught, it must be caught! This is not a matter of simply reading about Transformational Leadership theory and then magically performing at this level. We must first have or develop a strong desire to make a significant difference in our life and the lives of others. And then, we must passionately and relentlessly follow our purpose. The Transformational Leadership approach incorporates the Leader's *Awareness, Attention, Focus* and *Intent* on the necessity of the contribution of others in the process of moving forward to achieve the objectives of a group, team or organization. This Leader, has as a part of our Mindset, the deep desire to inspire others to unleash extra-ordinary effort towards a cause. Our Transformational perspective emerges out of this way of *Being* and *Doing.* A group or team in collaboration with a Transformational Leader can achieve amazing things together, while they learn and grow and create meaningful relationships through their interactions. The Transformational Leadership approach represents a clear expression of extra-ordinary Leadership and everyone we interact with benefits from this, including ourselves.

Transformation is a very real and impactful experience that we can access as an extra-ordinary Leader and share with others in our workplaces. *Change makes things different, while Transformation makes us different.* Transformation speaks to a deeper impact and experience that is available to anyone who seeks it. Transformational experiences involve all levels of our body, mind, heart, and our relationship to the environment. This is what so many of us crave on some level, and the Transformational Leadership approach supports us with serving as a catalyst for these types of experiences. This approach serves our groups and teams and organizations much more deeply and effectively.

It should be clear to us by now that so many others in our workplaces, community groups and governmental agencies are asking and, in many cases, begging to be part of something bigger than themselves, something real and something gratifying. People are so tired of having their time and their energy and their thoughts and passion wasted within a group or organization led by others who have neither the *Awareness* nor the desire to serve others exceptionally.

If we were to establish a growing group of Leaders in a given organization at this Level, we would experience a much greater level of consistency and ease and gratification with our collective effort, performance and results. As stated previously, most organizations function from an overall Leadership performance level that averages or bounces back and forth between Level 1 and Level 2. An initial goal we could set as an extra-ordinary Leader could be to up-level as many Leaders as possible to Level 3, Coaching Leadership. And to most effectively accomplish this, we must first up-level ourselves to at least Level 4,

Transformational Leadership. This is our initial challenge and responsibility as an extra-ordinary Leader.

And then, when we are able to establish an overall level of Leadership performance within our group or organization in the Level 3 (Coaching) to Level 4 (Transformational) range, the compounded impact of all of our efforts becomes even more valuable and meaningful to those involved as well as our customers. Establishing this level of Leadership across multiple organizations and industries would impact our groups and teams and organizations, and communities and nations in extra-ordinary ways. This is how Transformational Leadership can contribute to the transformation of the planet! As a Transformational Leader, we are positioned to finally begin to fulfill not only the strategic objectives of a group or organization, but also the more foundational desires of those involved. *This is the Leadership Revolution that I am talking about!*

And yet, there is still more available within the possibility of Leadership. More to share with and give to others, our organizations and ourselves. There remain still untapped reserves within ourselves and others, that when understood and unleashed, can bring even further levels of results and even further degrees of growth and satisfaction experienced by those we serve, and ourselves. The challenge of an extra-ordinary Leader at this point is to remain committed to the very real practice of Transformation, while continuing to learn and grow and expand our Leadership perspective even further, for those we serve. Although a commitment to Leading through inspiring others and facilitating the experience of others with being part of something larger than themselves is a valuable experience, we can still be left with the clear knowing that there is still more available to all of us on our journey as an extra-ordinary Leader.

The Transformational Leadership approach serves as an excellent vantage point to more clearly see and explore even higher levels of Leadership performance. Transformational Leadership brings even more value to the Leadership equation and moves us and those we serve well beyond the status quo. From this level, we can more freely access any of the more positive elements within the first three levels of Leadership, while adding to them even more *Awareness* and understanding of all of the possibilities involved. The Transformational Leadership approach further enhances the look and feel and experience and results of those involved. The freedom we experience at this level of Leadership, and our ability to help others to access greater levels of freedom for themselves, brings everyone involved into much greater alignment with our purpose and passion, as expressed through our work or task at hand. And yet, there is more that awaits us as an extraordinary Leader.

Before we move on to the energetic impediment of this level and the process of up-leveling ourselves and others into the next level of Leadership, I would like to share another consideration related to the AQ Model. There are obviously numerous, valuable Leadership *Tool Sets* and *Skill Sets* that we need to use and develop along the way on our Leadership journey. Things such as the ability to engage in *crucial conversations*, the ability to hire committed personnel, and the ability to *separate out* people who ultimately choose not to perform as agreed upon, along with hundreds of other Leadership *competencies*. These types of Leadership activities are often covered in Leadership development materials and they can be quite necessary for us as growing Leaders.

The AQ Model obviously does not cover all of the *competencies* necessary for a given Leader but instead focuses on the framework needed to most appropriately apply these *competencies*. My point here, is that there are many *tools* and *skills* that could be of value to us in our specific Leadership area, and that these should be incorporated into our Leadership approach as needed. And that, as we continue to up-level ourselves, these Leadership *tools* and *skills* will be even further enhanced through our growing *Awareness, Attention, Focus* and *Intent* and our ability to subtly and effectively tailor and apply these *tools* and *skills* to the uniqueness of a given situation. Remember, the AQ Model is primarily focused on the *context* of Leadership, the supportive framework of understanding needed to more effectively apply whatever *content*, the tools or skills or competencies that are most appropriate. And it is the *context* that more directly influences and supports the use of *content*, not the other way around. This key point is missed by many Leadership development approaches.

And now it is time to move to the next Level of Leadership, Level 5, the Wisdom Age, and "Servant Leadership." But once again, in order to ground ourselves in this next level of Leadership as opposed to just visiting there temporarily, we must understand and work through the attachments or programming that keep us grounded back in Level 4 Leadership. As valuable as Level 4, Transformational Leadership is, it still has limitations that hold us and others back from a fuller expression of our passion and purpose and the results that are possible. Remember, it is just not a matter of looking at a model or reading about it to move to another Level of performance. As extra-ordinary Leaders, we must apply what we are discovering to ground ourselves in higher levels of performance and to create the further benefits that are possible for our teams and organizations.

To enable ourselves to move more effectively beyond Level 4, Transformational Leadership, let's explore the primary Level

4 Energetic Impediment that inhibits our ability to move forward on our Leadership journey.

4th Level Energetic Impediment:

Release the attachment *to more immediate gratification or short-term activity and results.* Our programming around seeking more immediate gratification through shorter-term activity and results runs deep, especially in these complex and rapidly changing times. Pressures seem to come to us from everyone and from every direction, to make quick decisions to address challenges. Therefore, we must remain strong and resolute in our commitment to serve others and our organizations at the highest levels, or the gravity of other's perceptions of an emergency will pull us back into suboptimal levels of Leadership performance, back towards the status quo, and away from our purpose as an extraordinary Leader.

As extra-ordinary Leaders, we must cast off the blinders that limit our ability to see farther in every direction, to actually view the past in a way that helps us to genuinely learn from it, and to not continue to repeat the same mistakes over and over again. And, to be able to perceive the key patterns, trends and cycles of action and reaction, effort and results, that position us to envision the most likely impacts of our efforts as they unfold over a selected timeframe.

We must become more intimately familiar with the past, present and potential future and in a more unified, connected manner, as these domains of time are NOT separate. They flow out of and back into each other in a steady stream of connected events. The present flows out of and is influenced by the past, just as the future flows out of and is influenced by the present.

And once these future events occur, and by the way, they can only occur in the present, they then quickly flow back into the past. This cycle is going on all of the time, right in front of us. It is happening right now. It happens so imperceptibly that most people miss the significance of this flow. And, therefore, we are not in a position to engage with this flow of time in a way that creates a more participative, informed experience.

For many, time just happens to them. What I am pointing at here is that it is most certainly possible to transform our relationship with the flow of time. We can really look at it and explore it and dance with it in much more creative ways when we become *Aware* of this possibility, and then place and hold our *Attention* there, while *Focusing* on all of the possibilities available to us within this flow of time.

And let me be very clear here. I am not talking about some kind of "magical," "woo-woo," "time lord" kind of thing here. What I am trying to remind us of is the fact that we already do versions of this in many other areas of our lives and we do this quite effectively. Do we not very often contemplate and then somewhat accurately predict the potential results of our actions within very complex, social situations? We also very often and very accurately predict and adjust to issues related to our education and career goals, our health, and so many other areas of our lives. Think about it! There are just endless examples of how we so frequently do this kind of thing within varying degrees of complexity. But for some reason, most probably our programming (beliefs and habits), we pretend that this skill does not apply or is not welcomed in our workplaces, groups or teams. Yet nothing could be further from the truth!

This tendency or attachment to more immediate gratification (in all of its many forms) and shorter-term results can create significant limitations to our true potential as a Leader.

Therefore, we must address this here and now. An extra-ordinary Leader, through our passion and clarity of purpose, understands the pressures and programming around immediate gratification and shorter-term results, yet continually looks in all directions, and at the past, present and potential future to thoughtfully contribute to the most impactful outcome for everyone involved. This is role of a true Servant Leader.

So, as an extra-ordinary Leader, it is time to work through our programming around these issues with time, and to brave any resistance or ridicule that may come as a result of actively moving beyond the status quo. For on the other side of our questioning of the status quo, lies our freedom as a Leader to express what is really most important to us and to others. That is why we are here.

The first step in moving ourselves beyond this limited perspective is to become *Aware* of it, either on our own, through fearless self-reflection or through the honest feedback from others or by placing some level of provisional trust in another, who is also committed to the journey of extra-ordinary Leadership. There are others like us out there. We should continually seek each other out and share our perspectives and experiences to help to bolster our journeys, as we actively commit to replacing our more limited perspectives and habits and adopting a way of *Being* and *Doing* that is more expanded and supportive of others, our organizations and ourselves. And what could we replace this time-related habit with?

Develop the ability *to "see," discern and appreciate the broader perspective, along a connected and continuously unfolding timeline within a wider time-frame.* As extra-ordinary Leaders, we must develop the ability to look very deeply at and observe the impacts of our actions and how this cause and effect relationship may very likely play out over time. We must very thoughtfully and purposefully look at and study the relevant past and present of the issue we are dealing with, and connect these insights with the impending variables involved, to more effectively determine the most likely future impacts related to our efforts. We must ground ourselves more actively in the flow of time, to serve others and our organizations even more effectively.

Once again, there is no overly complex, sanctioned process for accomplishing this. We simply add to our expanding expression of our Leadership performance, the consistent practice of engaging with or stepping into the flow of events along a specific timeline to explore where these efforts may lead. And we don't need to create this as a separate step in addition to all that we are already doing as a Leader. At this point in our growth, we may be able to just "layer" activities like this over the things we are already doing. We can do these things at this point, simultaneously, and very efficiently. By the way, I am not referring here to what some might call multi-tasking, which has some well-known limitations to it. What I am continuing to refer to is the expansion of our *Awareness*, and the refinement of our *Attention* and the concentration of our *Focus*. Through this process, we, as extra-ordinary Leaders, on a Hero's Journey, in service to others, can develop astounding abilities related to our Leadership understanding, perspective and performance, on multiple levels simultaneously.

At this stage on our Leadership journey, and through this process, we are positioned to move from a 3D (spatial) Leadership approach to 4D (space/time) Leadership. This 4D Leadership experience adds the element and *Awareness* of time as a component and key consideration with our efforts. The 360-degree perspective of our Leadership *Being* and *Doing* at this stage of our Leadership journey adds significant and extra-ordinary value to those we serve, our organizations and ourselves. That's 4D value!

So, by consistently performing the up-leveling processes at this level of Leadership, and with the added *Awareness* of the value and necessity of moving beyond the Energetic Impediment or primary attachment associated with this level, we can more easily and naturally continue to grow on our Leadership journey. There could be quite a few other impediments or obstacles preventing a Leader from moving beyond Level 4, Transformational Leadership, however, and the habit or attachment to more immediate gratification or short-term activity and results can be at the root of this issue.

Although the right use of "Understanding" can take us and our team through a transformative journey, the lack of our ability to be able to see the connection between our efforts and the longer-term impacts of our efforts can get in the way of creating and maintaining an environment where others can more consistently connect with their passion and purpose to provide their best effort. It will take some level of *Awareness* and acknowledgement of this issue and then a commitment to continued growth for us to recognize our further potential and the further potential of our team. A Leader can be helped and supported through this growth, and there are many approaches for this but, ultimately, we must decide for ourselves to grow further.

And with a real commitment to extra-ordinary Leadership, the time spent grounding ourselves at each level does not have to be overly long or arduous. Again, we may find that we progress though some of the levels very easily and quickly, while others may take a little more time, *Attention* and *Focus*, based on our individual attachments and other factors. What I am talking about here in the AQ Model is not a long drawn out *Evolutionary* process to improving our Leadership performance, as is with many other Leadership development approaches. What I am talking about is a *Revolutionary* approach to Leadership development that, through our commitment to more expanded ways of *Being* and *Doing*, begins to achieve results for us and others almost immediately, in the here and now of our lives.

Now let's move into the process of up-leveling ourselves and others from Level 4 (Understanding Age, Transformational Leadership) to Level 5 (Wisdom Age, Servant Leadership), as we step even further into our ability to serve others and our organizations exceptionally.

Up-leveling from Level 4, Transformational Leadership, to Level 5, Servant Leadership

Up-leveling Ourselves:

Step 1 – Seek to perceive and explore a more expanded and connected time frame. We are often programmed or trained as Leaders to look at either more shorter-term (six months – one year) impacts and results or more long-term (three to five years or more) impacts and results, as if these scenarios are completely separate entities. We tend to focus on discrete segments of time to isolate the variables impacting the internal and external elements of the environment we are concerned with. Have any of us experienced this approach to either short or long-term planning? I most certainly have, and many times in the past I have become constrained or limited in my thinking by this siloed perspective.

This up-leveling step begins with widening our perspective and our appreciation for the connectedness between the people and the processes we are involved in, along with tapping into the wisdom to perceive the potential patterns, trends, cycles of activity, and outcomes that may result from our pending actions. In other words, in this step, as extra-ordinary Leaders, we are purposefully and thoughtfully acknowledging and looking at the connectedness of an entire set of actions and reactions related to processes and people, to project these along a continuous, connected, series of potential events over time. We can certainly do this if we put our *Awareness, Attention, Focus* and *Intent* into this area.

We all have heard the Einstein quote about the definition of insanity, " . . . doing the same thing over and over again but expecting a different result." And yet, we continue to see too many versions of this played out by Leaders in all industries. Leaders spend lots of time gathering and reviewing data and options and scenarios, in order to make decisions around future efforts. However, when done in isolation, without a clear understanding of the genuine connectedness and cause and effect nature of all of our actions and interactions over time, we as Leaders continue to expose our teams and organizations to too much unnecessary struggle. And this continues over and over again. As Leaders, we sometimes refer to these struggles as the "unintended consequences" of an effort, and although these types of things actually do exist, many times these unintended consequences could have been avoided with just a little more *Awareness, Attention* and *Focus* on the reality of the connectedness of our actions.

Step 1 involves the recognition of the reality that the interactions between people and processes are connected to the complex micro and macro results that will continuously manifest over time. Therefore, after we have supported the process of creating a customized plan that works for our organization (Level 3), and after we have taken the time to look for opportunities to connect people's passion and purpose with the work ahead (Level 4), it is time for us, as extra-ordinary Leaders, to apply our *Awareness, Attention, Focus* and *Intent* to the task of perceiving the potential downstream impacts and results of the ensuing actions. And honestly, this exercise in *Awareness* is as valuable as it is intriguing and fun for an extra-ordinary Leader. Also, to be clear, although this is not an exact science, many of the scenarios we are involved in as Leaders, do play out in a somewhat predictable series of events, creating probable trends in data and/or likely patterns of behavior and/or prospective cycles of overall experience. *We know much more than we pretend not to know.* We have access to much more than we choose to access.

As an extra-ordinary Leader, it is our responsibility to connect the dots, and to then extrapolate the impacts and results of our efforts and behaviors over a continuously unfolding timeline. Therefore, Step 1 involves understanding and accepting this, and then taking the time to center our *Awareness, Attention, Focus* and *Intent* around this very real and valuable component of extra-ordinary Leadership.

And by the way, this step does not necessarily need to occur in a step-wise progression, waiting until after we have performed all of the up-leveling steps of the previous Leadership levels. At this point in our more expanded perspective of Leadership, the various aspects of our expanded *Being* and *Doing* tend to occur simultaneously and overlap the other activities we are involved in. It is quite possible, and also quite advantageous in many cases, to be considering the impacts of our potential efforts over an expanded and connected timeframe while we are actively involved in exploring the planning process.

As in the previous level, this can be easier said than done, initially. That is why we must have a rabid passion or burning desire to radically improve our Leadership performance. Then, this step can be easy and fun. Without this, we will not be able to overcome the energetic threshold or the inertia of our previous habits or programming required to step fully into a new and more productive way of *Being* and *Doing* as a Leader. Our desire to transform ourselves as a Leader must be stronger than our commitment to our previous habits or programming and the results we created. Our *Awareness, Attention* and *Focus* around this opportunity to truly serve as an extra-ordinary Leader must be sharp and keen and unwavering in these moments. This will always be the key to accomplishing this up-leveling process. And no matter how challenging we may find certain aspects of this process, we simply need to keep recommitting ourselves in thought, word and deed and we will succeed, no matter how many times it takes.

Up-leveling Ourselves:

Step 2 – Consider the intended and unintended impacts on everyone and everything over an expanded and connected time-frame. Step 1 involves centering ourselves in this possibility and responsibility of ours as an extra-ordinary Leader (*Being*), while Step 2 involves the active, thoughtful, predictive modeling of the full range of the probable impacts and effects of a proposed course of action over time (*Doing*).

This can be done as an introspective process or on a written list of some kind. This type of exploration takes a thoughtful, open, purpose-driven *Mindset*, and just a little time. While involved in this process, consider even the subtler impacts that a change might have on others and on the existing systems and processes, in the more immediate and over an unfolding timeline (series of events over time) within the appropriate timeframe (designated duration of time). And don't hesitate to consult with others when needed for this effort.

There are many approaches to more deeply clarifying the intended and unintended impacts of a change. This can be done in our head, through a thoughtful, structured process or on a scrap piece of paper for a small change, but many times it is best to document this process in some way (on paper, sticky-notes or with a program or app), so that it can be looked at and built upon and reflected on. This type of approach tends to add the most value to this process. And although we were able to put together a very good, customized plan that connects people's passion and purpose as a Level 4, Transformational Leader, this additional process step will position us to make the further, sometimes subtle adjustments necessary to more thoughtfully and purposefully move forward over time, and in a way that deepens our ability to optimize and sustain our results.

So, with this up-leveling process, we center ourselves into this possibility and responsibility of ours, related to considering the intended and unintended impacts on everyone and everything over an expanded and connected time-frame (Step 1), and then reflect upon, explore and model in some form, the possible or potential intended and unintended impacts of our pending actions or efforts over the continuously unfolding timeline (Step 2). And the "how" of these two steps is quite flexible and adaptable and up to our individual and growing experience and perspective. We just need to do it for ourselves and everyone we interact with through our Leadership. And at this level of Leadership, and at this point on our extra-ordinary journey, it is not as much a matter of forcing ourselves to perform the details of Leadership, as it is that we are more consistently drawn to perform these types of activities because we very clearly and more deeply know and understand the value and responsibility of our actions as a Leader.

Performing these two up-leveling steps automatically deepens our *Awareness* and understanding of our potential pending actions, and in a way that can significantly inform our next steps. This process can help us avoid many of the missteps and unnecessary drama that we have created through our more programmed approach to considering more limited and disconnected timeframes. These up-leveling steps automatically move us into higher levels of Leadership performance. By pausing and paying *Attention* to and adjusting our *Being* in Step 1, and by *Doing* the exploration of intended and unintended impacts of processes along an unfolding timeline in Step 2, we are automatically up-leveled in our Leadership performance. When we actually *Do* what we should be doing as a Leader, we perform at a higher level for everyone. That's how it actually works! Just *Be* and *Do* and repeat and repeat. The entire Leadership puzzle can appear quite complex, yet there is a thread of simplicity that runs through the whole thing. Just *Be* and *Do*.

Before moving to the process of up-leveling others at these higher levels of Leadership, let's clarify another key point. Since the up-leveling process is essentially a "pull-strategy," versus a "push-strategy," we must first firmly position or ground ourselves in higher levels of Leadership to be able to thoughtfully and purposefully invite or *call* others into their next best level of performance. So, in general, to most effectively "pull" or support another into their next level of Leadership performance, we must first be solidly grounded in a level of Leadership that is at least one level beyond the level of Leadership that we are supporting another into. It is most certainly possible to collaboratively pull someone into the same level of Leadership that we ourselves are grounded in, but without a thorough understanding of the challenges and limitations of this level, we can be hampered in our ability to effectively support and help to sustain others in these higher levels of Leadership performance. Therefore, in order to continue to support others' ongoing growth, we ourselves must remain committed to our own ongoing growth and with grounding ourselves in successively higher or more expanded levels of Leadership. This is our duty and responsibility as an extra-ordinary Leader.

Up-leveling Others:

Step 1 – Facilitate the exploration of a more expanded and connected timeframe. As explored previously, actions, reactions, interactions, and events unfold along a timeline that is often observable and also somewhat predictable, if we consistently place our *Awareness*, *Attention*, *Focus* and *Intent* there.

Therefore, one of our responsibilities as an extra-ordinary Leader is to first develop this faculty within ourselves, to gain a level of familiarity and proficiency with this. And second, to extend this valuable approach out to include others' perspectives. As an extra-ordinary Leader, we clearly understand the significant value of more and more people on our team or in our organization, who can express higher, more expanded levels of performance. This is how, over time, we are able to up-level the overall Leadership performance baseline within our teams and organizations.

Step 1 of up-leveling others involves the genuine acknowledgement of all of the great work and contribution that has gone on so far throughout the process that included all of the previous elements discussed. And this is followed by the facilitation of an exploration into a more expanded, connected, continuously unfolding timeline, and within the appropriate timeframe. And we can do this by introducing a dialogue with others regarding this most obvious but often overlooked fact, that our actions or a significant change in a system or process will inevitably create reactions, and those reactions will create further reactions, and on and on. This cause and effect relationship is an inevitable fact, and yet it is often left unexplored, to the detriment of our teams and organizations.

So, before moving into full implementation of an effort, we facilitate a thoughtful, purposeful dialogue to orient the group's *Awareness*, *Attention* and *Focus* towards this very real concept, by simply reminding others of the connection of events over time, while engaging their thinking and perspective around the potential impacts of the proposed efforts. Once again, we don't need to do a presentation around this topic to try to convince others of its validity, we just need to remind each other of this obvious fact by placing it on the table for discussion. And we do this over and over and over again.

We model this approach just as we are modeling all of the previous approaches, and we do this pretty much forever. This is what establishes this approach as a valued, expected behavior within others and our organizations. This is what establishes this level of performance as part of an organization's culture. Talking about it does not ingrain it in the culture, only *Doing* it does. That's what extra-ordinary Leaders *Do*. We take full responsibility for our Leadership and the effects of our Leadership, in every moment of every day. And that is as fun as it gets for an extra-ordinary Leader. There is never, or very seldom, a time when we are not expressing who we really are and why we are here as a Leader.

Step 1 of up-leveling others is similar to the Step 1 that we went through as an individual, except that in this circumstance we are facilitating a dialogue with a potentially diverse group of others. It is important to watch and be aware of the reactions of others to this dialogue, and to inspire others through our actions to stretch their thinking and perspective through this potentially novel discussion. But, once this dialogue begins, most team members are able to quickly perceive and appreciate the value in this interesting exploration, even the ones who just want to jump more immediately into action.

At this point in our Leadership journey, facilitating this type of dialogue is not hard to do, yet it still requires our extra-ordinary commitment to thoughtfully and patiently and consistently engage with others in this way. That is why we must have and continue to cultivate a rabid passion or burning desire to further improve our Leadership performance and to support the improvement of the performance with others. Without this, we will not be able to consistently overcome the energetic threshold or the inertia of others' previous habits or programming required for them to more fully express their best efforts. Our desire as an extra-ordinary Leader to support the transformation of others must be stronger than our previous habits or programming related to supporting mediocrity or the status quo. Our *Awareness, Attention, Focus* and *Intent* around this opportunity to truly serve as an extra-ordinary Leader must be sharp and keen and unwavering in these moments.

But even if we miss this opportunity to support others in our next Leadership challenge, if we maintain our *Awareness* and our strong desire to improve as a Leader, we can then apply this to the very next challenge, which will not be far behind. We just need to keep recommitting ourselves in thought, word and deed and we will succeed, no matter how many times it takes.

Up-leveling Others:

Step 2 – Identify the intended and unintended impacts on everyone and everything, over an expanded and connected timeframe. We may have already accomplished part of this step when we explored and listed the intended and unintended impacts of the processes being addressed on people (the team, customers and the organization), when we were working on a challenge with others and endeavoring to up-level the team's performance from Level 3 to Level 4. During that step, we once again initiated the process of expanding the team's *Awareness* and guided their *Attention* to a specific area of exploration and requested their *Focus* on a specific set of variables. And now in Step 2 of this up-leveling approach, we take this process just a little bit further, by introducing the very real concept of cause and effect and how it might play out over an interconnected timeline within an established timeframe.

During this activity, we consider through a group brainstorm even the subtler impacts that a change might have on others and on the existing systems and processes over time. Things sometimes appear to work just fine in the short-term, but how many times have we implemented a change that appeared to work very well in the short-term, only to discover later that our fix has created problems down the line? This exploration, therefore, is focused on the thoughtful investigation of the impact of our efforts over time to minimize the potential negative impacts of our efforts.

As an extra-ordinary Leader, our responsibility is to facilitate a thoughtful, thorough, interesting and potentially fun exploratory process. And we can kick this off, if needed, by offering some of the deeper questions to be considered to support the group's exploration. The more we perform this step, and all the other steps for that matter, our teams will more comfortably and confidently transition into these types of explorations, and our role in facilitating these dialogues will become less and less. These more expansive and inclusive dialogues and explorations, more consistently then, replace the previous status quo of quick, unnecessarily siloed, and unexamined solutions and changes. *This is the Leadership Revolution that I am talking about!*

Additionally, this process should almost always be accomplished through some sort of visible, documented process. If everyone cannot directly see the process as it unfolds, they will not be in the best position to contribute to the process in the most productive way. This process could be accomplished on a white board or with sticky-notes or with the use of any version of a process related to this, such as a "Failure Mode and Effects Analysis." We should also attempt to include or draw out everyone's perspective and input whenever possible.

It is also helpful to remind everyone that although we were able to put together a very good, customized plan as a group (based on our Level 3 work), and that our work to connect others' passion and purpose to the effort should create even further benefits for the project (based on our Level 4 work), that this additional process step will position us to make even further, sometimes very subtle adjustments, necessary to more thoughtfully and purposefully move forward, and in a way that deepens our appreciation for and ability to optimize our results, over time.

So, before moving into full implementation of an effort, we facilitate a thoughtful, purposeful dialogue to orient others' *Awareness, Attention* and *Focus* towards this very real concept, by simply reminding others of the connection or cause and effect relationship of events, while engaging their thinking and perspective around the potential impacts of the proposed efforts, over time (Step 1). And then, we facilitate a reflective, documented and visible process and exploration of the possible or potential intended and unintended impacts of the team's pending actions or efforts as they play out over time (Step 2).

Performing these two up-leveling steps automatically deepens everyone's *Awareness* and understanding of the pending action and in a way that can significantly inform the group's next steps. This process can help everyone to avoid many of the mistakes and unnecessary drama that we have created in the past through our programmed, immediate action-oriented, unexamined approach to achieving objectives. These up-leveling steps automatically move us beyond the Level 4 Energetic Impediment (attachment), and into higher levels of Leadership performance, while creating higher-level experiences and higher levels of performance for those we interact with. By pausing and paying *Attention* to and adjusting our *Being* in Step 1, and by *Doing* the exploration of intended and unintended impacts process over time in Step 2, we and others are automatically up-leveled in higher levels of performance in real time. That's just how it works! Just *Be* and *Do* and repeat and repeat. This is a thread of simplicity that runs throughout the AQ Model. Just *Be* and *Do*. And these additional dialogues do not have to add significant amounts of time to the overall process once we get the hang of it. The slow way becomes the fast way.

Now it's time to step more fully into our responsibility as extra-ordinary Leaders and serve others by supporting their growth through the gift of up-leveling. And once we have moved ourselves and then others beyond the more limited mindsets of Levels 1, 2, 3 and even Level 4, there can be much more ease and growth and impactful results achieved through working with greater levels of *Awareness* within the challenges we all face. As a reminder, however, even under the best of circumstances, nothing is 100% as expected. We may need to finesse these approaches and tailor them for a specific person or situation, and we may need to repeat it multiple times to achieve the desired or needed impact. But more times than not, we can improve Leadership performance, the performance of others and everyone's overall experience in the workplace, consistently and in real time, especially when we have done our work first.

Everyone deserves an opportunity to step further into a level of Leadership performance that serves others more completely, as well as ourselves. Everyone working with a Leader deserves the opportunity to work and contribute within an environment that inspires them towards their best effort and expression of their purpose. Let's do our part as an extra-ordinary Leader to give everyone a real chance for this, here and now. Let's help them and support them the very best that we can, as our very best continues to expand. Leadership is about service. It's time to serve exceptionally! We are just getting warmed up here!

Level 4 Leadership Age & Approach	Predominant Leadership Characteristics	Up-Leveling Ourselves	Up-Leveling Others
Under-standing Age: Transformational Leadership	1. **Leadership through Connection** – typically based on all the above, and on purposeful awareness and intent regarding individual, departmental and organizational transformation. 2. Grounded predominantly in both the mind and heart (the integration of thought, feeling, empathy, intuition, etc.). 3. *Uses Knowledge vs. being used by Knowledge* 4. Is typically, Present and Near to slightly Longer-Term Oriented. 5. Focused on the *relationship* between systems and people. 6. Problem Solving Method – Moves from "Opportunity" to "Research" to "Customization" to "Process & People Integration" to "*Transformation*" (Lean Approach, *Respect for People*). 7. Common Quote – "*How could we further improve our approach so that it also connects people's passion with their performance?*" 8. Common Outcomes – Work gets accomplished with more of a sense of an engaged team approach where employees can begin to feel respected, partnered with and *inspired to dig even deeper into their best effort, along with all of the* positive impacts of this.	the thoughtful and purposeful process of improving our performance through an ongoing commitment to growing our awareness, attention and focus Moving from Level 4 to Level 5: 1. Look at and explore a more expanded and connected timeframe. 2. Now consider the intended and unintended impacts on everyone and everything, over an expanded, connected timeframe.	helping others to improve their performance *"in real time,"* based on your growing awareness and your commitment to supportive, purposeful coaching Moving from Level 4 to Level 5: 1. Facilitate the exploration of a more expanded and connected timeframe. 2. Now, identify the intended and unintended impacts on everyone and everything, over this expanded/ connected timeframe.

*4th Level Energetic Impediment – **Release** the attachment to more immediate gratification or short-term activity and results. **Develop** the ability to "see," discern and appreciate the "broader perspective," along a connected and continuously unfolding timeline within a wider time-frame.*

Figure 8. (Level 4 Leadership)

CHAPTER 14

Level 5 Leadership
The Wisdom Age & Servant Leadership

Leadership through Clarity of Vision . . .

Leadership Age: *Wisdom Age*

The 5th Level of Leadership illuminated in the AQ Model represents the functional progression of an even more thoughtful and purposeful application of individual experience (Industrial Age), information and data gathering (Information Age), customization (Knowledge Age), and the connection of people's passion and purpose with work systems and processes (Understanding Age), through the balance of all of these as achieved in the *"Wisdom Age."* This balance is accomplished through a deeper understanding and experience with the fact that our internal environments are connected with the external environments, and that this interdependence can be seen and observed and engaged with over an unfolding timeline to create more sustainable results.

    Experience, if shared, leads to *Information* and Data, which if more closely examined, leads to *Knowledge*, which when connected to our purpose leads to *Understanding*, and when all of this is thoughtfully and purposefully applied within the *Awareness* of a connected, unfolding timeline, this leads to *Wisdom*. That's the progression here so far.

The Wisdom Age appreciates all of the efforts and outcomes of the previous Ages, and is obviously an outgrowth of them, and sees all of these Ages as a strong foundation with which to introduce even more impactful influences as an extraordinary Leader. There have most certainly been many examples throughout history of this level "Wisdom" applied to numerous challenges that have brought forth high levels of service to entire industries, cultures and civilizations. As discussed previously, all of the Ages have actually been expressed and represented in many areas of the planet and during many different time periods. And at this time, all of these Ages are actually overlapping each other and expressing themselves simultaneously!

Leadership Approach: *Servant Leadership*

Much has also been written over the past few decades about the concept of Servant Leadership, and it is a well-documented Leadership approach to achieving a number of additional benefits for our organizations and those we serve. Servant Leaders seek to "serve first," and their Leadership purpose is deeply grounded in this Mindset. What Servant Leaders do and how they do it is framed by this deep and genuine impulse to serve and support others (Meta-Mindset). So, we can read all of the books and articles, and attend seminars to learn all about the various traits of a Servant Leader, but if we don't have or we don't do our internal work to develop a Servant Leader mindset, then our efforts will fall short of the real potential of this approach. Just saying we are here to serve, and *deeply* and *genuinely* seeking to serve others whenever possible, are definitely not the same thing.

Servant Leaders endeavor to connect with and support others in a way that brings out our best effort and our best performance and our best version of ourselves, over a more sustainable time frame. In this type of Leadership environment, we have the potential to more fully express the best parts of ourselves, individually and as a team. And as a Servant Leader, we are positioned to very thoughtfully and consistently express the depth of our purpose, passion and heart, through our interactions over time, and especially during times of significant challenge.

Whereas Leadership Levels 1 and 2 are more transactional in nature, and many times based on a Leader's expression of their dominance over others, and Leadership Levels 3 and 4 tend to be focused on the motivation and inspiration of others to create personal, group and organizational transformation, Leadership Level 5 seeks to create and support a more lasting and sustainable transformation, as we continually monitor and adjust to the ever changing internal and external environment.

Predominant Leadership Characteristics: *Servant Leadership*

1. **Leadership through Clarity of Vision** is typically based on experience (Level 1); and information and data gathering (Level 2); on assessing and reorganizing information to customize it based on specific requirements of the team, business unit or organization (Level 3); on our purposeful *Awareness, Attention, Focus* and "Intent" regarding individual, departmental

and organizational transformation (Level 4); **and on direct perception and the functional application of emotion, information, knowledge and understanding for the benefit of all, over time.** At this Level of Leadership, we have developed the ability to clearly see and balance the efforts of the previous levels of Leadership, and to clearly see the impacts of these efforts over time, enabling us to facilitate even more significant, sustainable outcomes and results, and to adjust as needed over time.

2. **Grounded predominantly in both our internal and external environment**, we possess an experiential understanding of our connection within and between these two areas of our existence. Our internal environment includes our physical, mental, emotional, psychological and spiritual systems and processes, while the external environment includes other people, our organizational systems and processes, other organizations and how these are interconnected. It also includes the natural rhythms and cycles of various activities and events.

3. **Uses Understanding** as a tool to create even longer-term benefits for all things. Because of our practical connection between the internal and external environment at this level of Leadership, we can see the larger cycles and patterns of our teams, organizations, environments, and life to more directly and positively impact people and things.

4. **Typically, Long-Term Oriented** with the ability to understand the past, present, near and long-term

impacts, and the impact of our actions or that of a team or group. At this level of Leadership, we are positioned to move a group, team or organization confidently into the uncertain future.

5. **Focused on the ability to "see things" with increased clarity and from a holistic, BIG picture, interdependent perspective**, as we consistently exercise our ability to look at and perceive the whole of things and explore how things fit together and relate and support and impact each other over time.

6. **Problem Solving Method** usually involves moving from Opportunity to Research to Customization to Process and People Integration to Transformation to *Time Framing* to *Sustainability*. The added element of *Time-Framing* serves as a lens from which to view circumstances from various short and longer-term perspectives to enable us to see and work towards the genuine *Sustainability* of things.

7. **Common Leadership Statement** may be any version of *"How will this effort benefit and/or impact everyone involved along with the organization, the community and the planet, over time?"* Do we know of many organizations that take this type of long-term view? Some actually do.

8. **Common outcome of this Leadership approach** is frequently a more connected team and organization, as those involved accomplish the work in a way that they experience a sense of a broader connection (internal and external) and potential with their efforts, along with the positive impacts of this. Those in a work

group or team begin to feel that their efforts are actually contributing to something more permanent and sustainable as the work moves forward and gets done. This Leadership approach tends to establish a work environment where people may want to stay and are drawn to contribute in a more connected way towards each other and the goals of the group, creating even more optimal and sustainable results. This Leadership approach works to foster real connections between people and the far-reaching impacts of our efforts, while we develop greater levels of sustainability within given situations. This brings a deeper sense of purpose to a Servant Leader.

The Servant Leadership approach can't be chased, it must be embraced! Servant Leadership is not just about researching this topic and trying to identify what serving others consists of. It is more about connecting with and embracing our role and responsibility for supporting or serving others, and then as a result, nearly everything we do as a Leader can become an expression of this commitment to service. Service then becomes the context for all of our actions and interactions (content) as a Leader. And in order to accomplish this, we must first have or develop a deep desire to connect with and support others along this challenging journey, and to make a significant difference in our life and the lives of others. And then we must passionately and relentlessly follow our purpose.

The Servant Leadership approach incorporates the Leader's *Awareness, Attention, Focus* and *Intent* on our deep impulse to serve first and, through this approach, support and contribute to others in the process of moving forward to achieve the objectives of a group, team or organization. This Leader has as a part of our Meta-Mindset, the deep impulse to serve others to unleash their extra-ordinary effort towards a cause. A group or team in collaboration with a Servant Leader can achieve amazing things together as they learn and grow and create significant impacts through their interactions. The Servant Leadership approach represents a clear expression of extra-ordinary Leadership and everyone we interact with benefits from this, including ourselves. The Servant Leadership approach comes from deep within and moves from inside to out. Once this realization and commitment to service occurs, then the question of *"What are we here to do?"* goes away.

Servant Leadership clearly represents a level of Leadership that our teams and organizations crave on some level. Deep, or not so deep inside, many of us crave to serve and be served in an extra-ordinary way. We collectively sense that there is a way of *Being* and *Doing* that far exceeds the experiences that are so typical of our daily lives. We even see examples of it from time to time but may not yet have been able to establish this as a more consistent experience in our lives. However, this begins to change in the here and now as we establish ourselves and ground ourselves in Level 5, the Wisdom Age, Servant Leadership, where the opportunities to serve others and our organizations become so obvious to us that we can't help but respond to this call. *This is the Leadership Revolution that I am talking about!*

The Servant Leadership approach then serves as an excellent vantage point to more clearly see and explore even higher levels of Leadership performance. From this level, we can more freely access any of the more positive elements within the first four levels of Leadership while adding to them even more *Awareness* and understanding of all of the possibilities involved. The Servant Leadership approach further enhances the look and feel and experience and results of those involved.

The freedom we experience at this level of Leadership, and our ability to help others to access greater levels of freedom for themselves, brings everyone involved into much greater alignment with our purpose and passion as expressed through our work or task at hand.

And yet, there is still more available within the possibility of Leadership. There is more to share with and give to others, our organizations and ourselves. There remain still untapped reserves within ourselves and others that when understood and unleashed, can bring even further levels of results and even further degrees of growth and satisfaction experienced by those we serve and ourselves. The challenge of an extraordinary Leader at this point is to follow our impulse to serve, yet in a way that appropriately supports others with working through their own challenges and lessons for growth. This is a genuine service to others.

To take this a step further, the AQ Model represents a *Revolutionary*, exciting, innovative and functional *context* and approach for Leadership development. One that is quite valuable and relevant for the challenges we face in today's complex environment. But I make no claim that this model is some kind of "Universally Supreme Model" for Leadership development. And the reason for this is that because of the complex, multilayered, highly variable nature of our individual understanding and practice of Leadership within the multitude of environments that exist, there can be no singular approach or model for Leadership development that can address all of these possibilities. There is more than one right answer to the challenge of Leadership development. And in the end, it is always we who must take responsibility for discerning and developing our own way of Leadership, based on the specifics of our purpose, and the purpose of the those we serve.

There can be many ways to improve the specifics of our Leadership performance, based on whatever level we are operating from and what the needs are within our environment. What the AQ Model provides for us, however, is an overall understanding of this Leadership progression, along with a map of proven practices to support us in moving confidently forward, into the full possibilities of Leadership. What the AQ Model does add to the practice of Leadership development is that it provides us with the foundational "context" of Leadership, and an integrated progression of the broad journey of extraordinary Leadership. And it is shared in a way that is adaptable to our own specific situation, for those we serve. The AQ Model is an incredibly valuable Leadership development structure that even supports us with moving beyond this structure at some point.

This is one of the more unique and valuable aspects of the AQ Model. The AQ Model is not a cage, it is a springboard. It does not lock us into a particular way of Leadership *Being* and *Doing*; it frees us to determine our own best way, related to those we serve. One of the main goals of this book is that eventually we will no longer need this book or any other book to tell us what is real or true in our Leadership development. The goal of this journey is to support us and free us to the point that we eventually become our own primary source of learning in Leadership excellence through our own growing level of Leadership self-mastery! *This is the Leadership Revolution that I am talking about!*

Now, back to our progression here. To enable ourselves to move effectively beyond Level 5, Servant Leadership, let's explore the primary Level 5 Energetic Impediment that prevents us or impedes us in moving continuously forward with more ease on our Leadership Journey. At this point, we have explored much of the foundational work of the AQ Model and have moved quite a distance along on our extra-ordinary Leadership journey to plant ourselves firmly in Phase 2 of the Hero's Journey, The Initiation.

Up to this point in our exploration of the Leadership Levels, we have been exploring and expanding upon some of the more commonly known Leadership approaches out there and using some of the more ordinary terms. Well, that begins to shift as we move forward from here. As we move further along on our extra-ordinary Leadership journey, the approaches that we will explore and the terms we will use will also become a little more extra-ordinary. *This is where we start to really take off!*

5th Level Energetic Impediment:

Release the attachment *to what we think we know.* I am not referring here to what we know, just what we "think" we know. Think about that one. There is a big difference. Our programming around our opinions and assumptions, what we think we know, runs deep, especially in these complex and rapidly changing times. Our stream of opinions and assumptions just flows out of us, pretty much unchecked and unexamined. In order to *get in the way* of this flow, we must purposefully step into it, and look and listen and feel what is going on there.

We must step in and explore and examine this flow of opinions and assumptions that comes out of us and others. We must learn to distinguish between what we know, versus what we think we know, and resist the gravity of our programmed opinions and assumptions. We must remain strong and resolute in our commitment to serve others and our organizations at the highest levels, or the inertia of our own unexamined questions and assumptions will pull us back into suboptimal levels of Leadership performance. And back towards the status quo, away from our purpose as an extra-ordinary Leader.

What we think we know is not the same as what we know. What we know are things like the effect of gravity; if I touch the stove burner when it is on, I will get burned; 1 + 1 = 2 in most circumstances, and those kinds of things. What we think we know includes all of those things related to our social conventions, politics, culture and most all of the opinions and assumptions we possess. So, as we can see, there is a lot of stuff in our "what we think we know" category.

And for clarification, this does not mean that what we think we know is not valid or true or real on some level. What we think we know might very well be all of these things. Yet what is referred to here is releasing our attachment to what we think we know, not necessarily the thing itself that we think we know. This is an important distinction. We are working to release our attachment related to each of these energetic impediments, not necessarily the thing itself. When we release our attachment to a thing, we can feel much less of a need to defend it against anyone who sees things differently. When we release our attachment to a thing, it can free us up to genuinely consider other perspectives and ideas, and to freely move where needed. When we release our attachment to a thing, we are still able to connect with others who may have differing perspectives, even when they might be attached to the things they think they know.

This is a major issue in our organizations and in society everywhere. One of the outcomes of the Information Age is obviously that there is information everywhere. However, much of the information that most people are exposed to, comes in the form of information snippets or sound bites. These snippets and sound bites are not a bad place to start with our more thorough exploration of a subject but, in an of themselves, they are far too limited to give us a full picture of most topics. Yet too many Leaders, and people everywhere, do not commit to the additional exploration required to more deeply understand a topic. And even more problematic is the fact that many of us then formulate complete and unalterable opinions based on just these snippets of information. This goes on everywhere. It can be very interesting to watch and listen to someone express an obviously, only minimally examined opinion on either side of an issue with such fervent certainty. So many people seem to be so certain of what they think they know, and they are ready to defend it at all costs! This leads to so much unnecessary drama and dysfunction in the form of a lack of communication, a separation mentality, decreased collaboration and diminished connection as human beings. And in extremes, it can lead to a level of fear and hatred that serves no one.

It can be very challenging to have an open, exploratory dialogue these days since so many are so attached to what they think they know. There are numerous experts out there on every topic imaginable. This issue can be an interesting and worthy challenge for an extra-ordinary Leader. Information, in and of itself, does not represent knowledge or understanding, and certainly not wisdom. And yet, this is exactly what so many of us attempt to portray with these sound-bites of information. And there is no real reason for this. This approach serves no one except our ego. This approach is grounded in our unexamined attachments around what we think we know. And when we are questioned about these things, many of us will respond immediately with some form of defensiveness or anger of some kind (a Level 1 response), which further strengthens our commitment to our attachment here. But remember, this is going on, not because people are bad or dumb or less than anyone else. It is simply our programming and our attachments to this programming in action. It's not an IQ issue; it's an AQ and EQ issue. So yes, this common attachment to what we think we know can create significant dysfunction, and yet, it's also an incredible opportunity for an extra-ordinary Leader, committed in service to others.

This tendency or attachment to what we think we know, in all of its many forms, can create significant limitations to our true potential as a Leader. Therefore, we must address this one here and now. An extra-ordinary Leader, through our passion and clarity of purpose, understands the programming around what we and everyone else thinks they know, and continually looks inwardly and outwardly, to thoughtfully contribute to the most impactful outcome for everyone involved.

By working to release our attachments, we position ourselves to see other possibilities and to move through life and the challenges of Leadership a little more gracefully, and to support our teams with more flexibility and agility. Attachments lock us in to a specific perspective. Releasing attachments opens us up to additional options. This should make sense to us even from a straight business case.

As an extra-ordinary Leader, it is time to work through our programming around these issues with what we think we know, and to brave any resistance or ridicule that may come as a result of actively moving beyond the status quo. For on the other side of our questioning of the status quo, lies our freedom as a Leader to express what is really most important to us and to others. That is why we are here.

Once again, the first step in moving ourselves beyond this limited perspective is to become *Aware* of it, either on our own, through fearless self-reflection, or through the honest feedback from others, or by placing some level of provisional trust in another who is also committed to the journey of extra-ordinary

Leadership. There are others like us out there. We should continually seek each other out and share our perspectives and experiences to help to bolster our journeys, as we actively commit to replacing our more limited perspectives and habits and adopting a way of *Being* and *Doing* that is more expanded and supportive of others, our organizations and ourselves. And what could we replace this attachment with?

Develop the ability *to increase our level of acceptance of other possibilities to discover more of what may really be going on.* Remember way back in Chapter 1, where we were discussing *Consciousness, Awareness, Attention* and *Focus?* And we talked about how acceptance increases *Awareness, Attention* and *Focus,* while resistance decreases these? Well, attachments are a form of resistance. And anything that creates resistance limits our valuable *Awareness, Attention* and *Focus.* By now, it should be clear to us, that our journey of extra-ordinary Leadership depends on our growing *Awareness, or Awareness Quotient (AQ).*

Once again, there is no overly complex, sanctioned process for accomplishing this. We simply add to our expanding expression of our Leadership performance the consistent practice of relaxing our grip on what we think we know, even if only temporarily, to more openly explore where our efforts may lead. We can simply ask more exploratory questions from a place of genuine interest in other perspectives. This can be quite helpful in broadening our horizons. The next set of up-leveling steps can support us here. And we don't need to create this as a separate activity in addition to all that we are already doing as a Leader. At this point in our growth, we should be able to just layer activities like this over the things we are already doing. We can do these things at this point, simultaneously and very efficiently. What I am continuing to refer to is the expansion of our *Awareness*, and the concentration of our *Attention* and the refinement of our *Focus*. Through this process, we as extra-ordinary Leaders, on a Hero's Journey of service to others can develop astounding abilities related to our Leadership under-standing and performance on multiple levels simultaneously.

There could be quite a few other impediments or obstacles preventing a Leader from moving beyond Level 5, Servant Lead-ership. However, the attachment to *what we think we know* can be at the root of this issue. Although the right use of Wisdom can take us and our team on a more sustainable journey, any limitations to exploring other perspectives, other possibilities, can get in the way of creating and maintaining an environment where others can more consistently connect with their passion and purpose, to provide their best effort. It will take some level of *Awareness* and acknowledgement of this issue, and then a commitment to continued growth, for us to recognize our fur-ther potential and the further potential of our team. A Leader can be helped and supported through this growth and there are many approaches for this, but, ultimately, we must decide for ourselves to grow further.

As we explore these next two levels of Leadership that round-out Part 2 of this book and Phase 2 of the Hero's Jour-ney (The Initiation), it may appear that we are getting into some pretty lofty Leadership territory. The terminology may not be as familiar as the terminology of the previous levels of Leadership we have explored. Once again, this is to be expected as we continue this extra-ordinary Leadership journey further beyond where most Leaders have been compelled to explore. But be assured that despite the possibly unfamiliar terminology being used, these Leadership levels are equally grounded in the very real possibilities of Leadership and can bring us further significant value to the Leadership equation. We should not let the terminology distract us from what the terminology is attempting to point us towards.

I would also say at this point that we have definitely explored a lot of important territory so far. We have explored several key Leadership concepts along with the first five levels of Leadership in the AQ Model. And with just the material covered so far, a committed Leader would be well-positioned to serve others extra-ordinarily! If more of our Leaders were grounded in just the material covered so far, our organizational results and our experiences in our workplaces and in our teams and groups would improve significantly! The material explored so far could busy us for a lifetime with supporting and serving others and our organizations, as we continue to learn and grow and further refine our Leadership approach. And this would be a valid and valuable approach to our Leadership commitment.

As a matter of fact, as the AQ Model was emerging within the context of a very real and challenging Leadership journey, I thought for a time that these five Levels of Leadership were all that was needed. I thought that these first five Levels of the AQ Model represented a fairly comprehensive framework of Leadership development. I realized that there was a significant amount of very functional, high-value Leadership development material here for us to explore and apply. But a short time later, another level of Leadership became clear to me, and then another, and then three more. And I could not ignore the reality and the benefit of these additional emerging Leadership levels. So, that is just how it goes. There is always another step. There are always further explorations that await us, and I am quite confident that they are very much worth our time and effort.

Now let's move into the process of up-leveling ourselves and others from Level 5 (Wisdom Age, Servant Leadership) to Level 6 (Transcendent Age, Transcendental Leadership), as we step even further into our ability to serve others and our organizations exceptionally.

Up-leveling from Level 5, Servant Leadership, to Level 6, Transcendental Leadership

Up-leveling Ourselves:

Step 1 – Question our questions and explore our assumptions. We are typically very adept at questioning others' thoughts and motives but not nearly as adept when it comes to questioning our own thoughts, motives and assumptions. We are well programmed to question everything and everyone, while *our* paradigm and assumptions continue to run quietly and mostly unnoticed in the background of our minds. Have any of us ever experienced the impact of this? I most certainly have. Many times in the past, I have been very critical of others' thoughts and perspectives, while my own perspective went on pretty much unexamined. This gave me a false sense of superiority and limited my connection with myself and with others, while also limiting our subsequent experience and results. So, questioning our own questions and exploring our own assumptions goes directly against our programing in most cases, and can require quite a bit of personal *Awareness*, *Attention*, *Focus* and *Intent*, and fearless commitment to self-introspection.

This self-up-leveling step begins with literally questioning the questions we are asking, or the ones in our mind, and exploring the assumptions that we hold so dear. We start with questioning our questions because they are often much more important than the answers we seek. In fact, it is very often the right questions that lead us to the most appropriate experiences from which the answers emerge. The depth and breadth of our questions are also a reflection of the depth and breadth of our *Awareness*. And this is a key! Another and very powerful way of exploring and growing our *Awareness* is through the formulation and exploration of deep and meaningful questions. We should endeavor to ask ourselves and others more meaningful questions!

In step 1, we create a habit of quite literally asking ourselves why we asked or are thinking of asking a particular question. And why do we ask some of the same questions over and over again? What honestly may be behind the questions we are asking? What are we attempting to ascertain through the asking of this question? How will the answer to the question we are asking support others' growth and move things forward? How can we ask this question in a way that more thoroughly illuminates the key issues needed? There could be much more here that we could explore, but that should get us started with our questioning of our questions. Be creative!

If we were to really examine our own questions, along with those of others, we would see that often, our questions are nothing more than a tool to emphasize or exert our authority or control or our rightness. They can also function to maintain our assumptions or perspective on things. These types of unexamined questions that we often ask, come right out of our programming around maintaining our own programming. It's insidious! So, forcing ourselves to consider and formulate and ask deeper, more meaningful questions begins to re-program our programming into a much more productive version.

In step 1, we also create a habit of systematically exploring our assumptions. Now this can get even more interesting, since our assumptions can be even more challenging to identify than the questions that we have. Our questions can be easier to see and identify, as we think about them and voice them, while our assumptions sort of run more under our radar, on our stealth programming. This is the programming beneath the programming, so it can be much more challenging to see it. But, with just a little practice, identifying our assumptions can become fairly easy and kind of fun!

Our assumptions often express themselves through our opinions, and we have been sharing our opinions freely since we were kids. Most of the time, our opinions just flow from us, relatively unchecked and unexamined. Many of our opinions were formed long ago, based on our programming at that time. And even our most recently formed opinions and assumptions are still frequently based on a fairly weak vetting process and built upon much of our past programming. What I am getting at here is that our assumptions and opinions are often based on pretty flimsy criteria, and this is basically the same criteria we used as a small child. Because of this, these criteria may be based in some fear or some version of a reward or punishment scenario. Think about that one. Even those of us who have developed the ability to formulate opinions and assumptions in a more objective fashion, still quite often default back to our old programming when it is time for us to share our perspective, especially in a challenging situation. This can happen frequently!

In step 1, we quite literally question our questions and seek to formulate and express deeper more meaningful questions, while also identifying and looking at and examining our assumptions and opinions. This includes examining and refining our process for formulating our assumptions and opinions.

Assumptions and opinions are everywhere. Everyone has them. They have become such a part of us that we barely notice them. Take notice then! Many of the opinions we have may be based on an old set of rarely examined assumptions that may or may not be valid any longer, or relevant to the issue at hand.

When one of our many opinions flows through our mind or out of our mouth, we must develop the habit of noticing this, and tracking and examining where this opinion comes from and what it is based on. This process can lead to some interesting findings! And don't be surprised if what we discover is that we sometimes don't even know or can't remember what the basis was for a given opinion.

Just imagine how so much of what comes out of our mouths, and the mouths of others, is based in this baseless foundation. Such is the world we live in! Yet our responsibility as an extra-ordinary Leader requires us to go deeper into this thing, and to explore and create another possibility. This is valuable work! And fun work for an extra-ordinary Leader. And from a process standpoint, this work can be done on paper or in our head, if we can organize our thinking around this sufficiently.

Up-leveling Ourselves:

Step 2 – Look deeply into everything that is going on. So, step 1 involves questioning our own questions and exploring our own assumptions to gain deeper insight into what is going on in our own head, in our own programming, and noticing the outcome and impact of this, while step 2 extends this habit out into the world. In step 2, we develop the habit of examining what is going on around us, and what it is based on or driving it. The ability to gaze deeply into and examine something, or *purposeful observation,* is a valuable skill set that can be developed by an extra-ordinary Leader. This approach requires the thoughtful and purposeful exploration of our *Awareness, Attention* and *Focus.*

This is how we connect our internal processes of examination and growth to the external processes that we are part of. And when we make a habit of this, we gain many of the same types of insights about our external environment that we gained from our internal explorations. In these two steps, we are examining our thoughts and beliefs about our internal and external environment, and then determining the validity or reality of these thoughts and beliefs along with how they are serving us and others. And from this place, we are better positioned to keep, release or modify an existing thought pattern, belief or set of assumptions. From here, with our more refined *Awareness, Attention, Focus* and *Intent*, we can create entirely new patterns of thought and belief. As an extra-ordinary Leader, we can re-engineer or re-program our assumptions to better fit our unfolding reality to better serve our purpose and commitment. This can be high-value work for us as a Leader and for those we serve.

And we do this by just doing it. There are no complex or special instructions required. We can simply use the same tools (Problem Exploration tool, Sticky-Note tool, etc.) we have used in previous Leadership levels to break down our questions and assumptions to get to their root. Just pick a question or pick an assumption. That part should not be difficult for an extra-ordinary Leader. Yet if we are having trouble with this part, we can simply ask someone in our circle to give us some input on this. Reach out for support and insight from others. Remember, that is one of the reasons we are here for each other. And when we do reach out, I can pretty much guarantee that others will be able to provide us with very clear feedback on these issues. The things we pretend to not be able to see in ourselves, others can usually see very clearly.

So, in steps 1 and 2, we are identifying these internal and external questions and assumptions and thought patterns, and examining them for their validity, and then, as needed, re-programming them in the light of our present level of *Awareness*,

Attention, Focus and *Intent*. And then we can begin to operate from this new and improved, 2.0 programming perspective. It's time for an internal software update! We have been running on the same old operating system for far too long! Our operating system is represented by the programing beneath our programing. It is time for us to take responsibility for our own software upgrade. What core thoughts, beliefs and assumptions would serve us and others best at this point in our journey? What is our current reality telling us? Only we can answer these questions for ourselves. This is our work. *This is the Leadership Revolution that I am talking about!*

As in the previous level, this can be easier said than done at first, but it is not that hard! That is why we must have a rabid passion or burning desire to radically improve our leadership performance. Without this, we will not be able to overcome the energetic threshold or the inertia of our previous habits or programming required to step fully into a new and more productive way of *Being* and *Doing* as a Leader. Our desire to transform ourselves as a Leader must be stronger than our commitment to our previous habits or programming and the results we created. Our *Awareness, Attention, Focus* and *Intent* around this opportunity to truly serve as an extra-ordinary Leader must be sharp and keen and unwavering in these moments. This will always be the key to accomplishing this up-leveling process. And no matter how challenging we may find certain aspects of this process, we simply need to keep recommitting ourselves in thought, word and deed and we will succeed, no matter how many times it takes.

Up-leveling Others:

Step 1 – Question others' questions and explore their assumptions. This step 1 is very similar, as usual, to step 1 of up-leveling ourselves. It basically involves the systematic exploration of the "why" behind others' questions, assumptions, paradigm or thought processes. As a caveat, this exploration must be done from a supportive, nonjudgmental perspective. Remember, our groups and teams have been programmed for many years and by many Leaders who have often questioned them more punitively or in a way that exerts some form of dominance. So we should consider letting others know the purpose of our questions, to put them at ease and to free them up for the exploration at hand.

While in a group or team situation, we can just watch and listen for the typical types of questions and assumptions that come up, and then just insert a pause in the interaction, to explore the deeper underpinnings of the questions or assumptions on the table. We can simply explain to others that we are interested in exploring the issue a little further or a little deeper, to understand it more, and to potentially develop an even better plan. We can then simply add in a few well-thought-out and meaningful questions into the scenario such as: "Is XYZ really true or valid for this specific situation?" "Why do we think it is?" "Is it possible to look at this issue from a different perspective to understand it more deeply?" "Can we validate the assumptions that we are using in this scenario?" "How else might we approach and solve this issue?" This should get our creative questioning juices flowing around this process! Use any version of these or modify as needed. Just get some deeper dialogue going and adjust from there. And watch what comes of it!

Up-leveling Others:

Step 2 – Focus other's attention into the depth of every-thing that is going on. And once again, as in step 2 of up-leveling ourselves, we now turn the *Attention* and *Focus* of the group towards their *Awareness* of the depth of things going on around the periphery of the issue at hand. Once we have more deeply explored the group's questions and assumptions around the issue at hand in step 1, we are positioned for step 2, which involves this same exploration, focused outwardly and a little more broadly.

Guiding others' *Awareness*, *Attention* and *Focus* is more art than science. This involves a purposeful, facilitated, step-wise exploration and discussion of the deeper and deeper elements and connections within and surrounding a situation. And this is accomplished through the use of thoughtful, meaningful ques-tions, as we have been exploring in this section. So, we facilitate this dialogue through our questions, and then we watch atten-tively for what comes up, for what else we and others discover through this collaborative *experience*.

At this level of Leadership, our focus is more and more on facilitating and creating purposeful experiences for our groups and teams, in an effort to not only solve or address an issue, but to also bring out the individual and collective best of the group or team. And also, to begin to create a group dynamic or experi-ence that is extra-ordinary, and valuable and growth-filled and fun! *This is the Leadership Revolution that I am talking about!*

Additionally, this process should almost always be accom-plished through some sort of visible, documented process. If everyone cannot directly see the process as it unfolds, they will not be in the best position to contribute to the process in the most productive way. This process could be accomplished on a white board or with sticky-notes or with the use of any version of this process. We should also attempt to include or draw out everyone's perspective and input whenever possible.

So, before moving into full implementation of an effort, we facilitate a thoughtful, purposeful dialogue to orient other's *Awareness*, *Attention* and *Focus* towards this very real concept by simply reminding others of the importance of clarifying the validity of our questions and assumptions and perspectives, while engaging their thinking and perspective around this exploration (step 1). And then we facilitate a reflective, documented and visible process and exploration of the possible or potential deeper internal and external meanings and connections related to our effort (step 2).

Performing these two up-leveling steps automatically deepens everyone's *Awareness* and understanding of the pending action and in a way that can significantly inform the group's next steps. This process can help everyone to avoid many of the mistakes and unnecessary drama that we have created in the past through our programmed, unexamined approach to achieving objectives. These up-leveling steps automatically move us beyond the Level 5 Energetic Impediment and into higher levels of Leadership performance, while creating higher level experiences and higher levels of performance for those we interact with.

By pausing and paying *Attention* to the deeper meanings behind our questions and assumptions, in step 1, and by extending this exploration out into the deeper meanings behind the things going on around us or the process in question, in step 2, we and others are automatically up-leveled in higher levels of performance in real time. There is no drama or buy-in discussions needed. That's just how it works! Just *Be* and *Do* and repeat and repeat. This is a thread of simplicity that runs through the AQ Model. Just *Be* and *Do*. And these additional dialogues do not have to add significant amounts of time to the overall process, once we get the hang of it.

So now it's time to step more fully into our responsibility as extra-ordinary Leaders and serve others by supporting their growth through the gift of up-leveling. And once we have moved ourselves and then others beyond the more limited mindsets of Levels 1, 2, 3 and even Levels 4 and 5, there can be much more ease and growth and impactful results achieved through working with greater levels of *Awareness* within the challenges we all face. As a reminder, however, even under the best of circumstances, nothing is 100% as expected. We may need to finesse these approaches and tailor them for a specific person or situation, and we may need to repeat it multiple times to achieve the desired or needed impact. But more times than not, we can improve Leadership performance, the performance of others and everyone's overall experience in the workplace, consistently and in real time, especially when we have done our work first.

Everyone deserves an opportunity to step further into a level of Leadership performance that serves others more completely, as well as themselves. Everyone working with a Leader deserves the opportunity to work and contribute within an environment that inspires them towards their best effort and expression of their purpose. Let's do our part as an extra-ordinary Leader to give everyone a real chance for this, here and now. Let's help them and support them the very best that we can, as our very best continues to expand.

And now, with the support of our up-leveling practices, it is time to move to the next Level of Leadership, Level 6, the Transcendent Age, and "Transcendental Leadership." As valuable as Level 5, Servant Leadership is, it still has limitations that hold us back from a fuller expression of our passion and purpose, and the results that are possible.

As we move forward from this point, we may be exploring some slightly new, or maybe even entirely new terms and approaches to Leadership, based on our experience thus far. These next two levels of Leadership represent the much deeper possibilities of our Leadership expression, in service to others. These next two levels of Leadership represent another significant shift in our experience and perspective in Leadership, one that produces even more significant experiences and results for others and our organizations. These next two levels of Leadership also represent a significant and further expansion of our *Awareness, Attention, Focus* and *Intent,* and establish the solid foothold we need for our journey into yet even higher levels of Leadership understanding and expression, in Part 3 of this book.

There is one more brief point that I would like to make before moving on from here. Whereas the up-leveling steps in the previous levels of Leadership served as sort of a *springboard* for us to move into the next level of Leadership . . . the up-leveling steps we just explored here in level 5, the Wisdom Age, and Servant Leadership, serve us more like a *slingshot,* to launch us soaring into the next level of Leadership. So, prepare for take-off!

Level 5 Leadership Age & Approach	Predominant Leadership Characteristics	Up-Leveling Ourselves	Up-Leveling Others
		the thoughtful and purposeful process of improving our performance through an ongoing commitment to growing our awareness, attention and focus	helping others to improve their performance *"in real time,"* based on your growing awareness and your commitment to supportive, purposeful coaching
Wisdom Age: Servant Leadership	**1. Leadership through Clarity of Vision** – typically based on all the above, and onn direct perception and the functional application of emotion, information, knowledge and understanding for the benefit of all . . . over time. **2. Grounded** predominantly in both our internal and external environment. **3. Uses *Understanding*** as a tool to create more sustainable benefits **4. Is typically more Long-Term and Inclusively Oriented.** **5. Focused** on the ability to "see" trends, patterns and cycles with increased clarity and from a holistic, BIG picture, interdependent perspective. **6. Problem Solving Method** – Moves from "Opportunity" to "Research" to "Customization" to "P&P Integration" to "Transformation" to "Time Framing" to "Sustainability." **7. Common Quote** – *"How will this impact everyone involved, the organization, the community and the planet, over time?"* **8. Common Outcomes** – *Work gets accomplished in a way that employees experience a sense of a broader connection and sustainability with their efforts, along with all of the positive impacts of this.*	Moving from Level 5 to Level 6: 1. Question our questions and explore all of our assumptions. 2. Look more "deeply" into everything that is going on around us.	Moving from Level 5 to Level 6: 1. Explore other's questions and supportively explore their assumptions. 2. Focus other's attention into more of the depth of everything that is going on around them.

5th Level Energetic Impediment – Release the attachment to "what you think you know." **Develop** the ability to increase your level of "acceptance" of other possibilities, to discover more of what may really be going on.

CHAPTER 15

Level 6 Leadership
The Transcendent Age &
Transcendental Leadership

Leadership through Direct Insight . . .

Leadership Age: *Transcendent Age*

The 6th Level of Leadership illuminated in the AQ Model represents the functional progression of an even more thoughtful and purposeful application of individual experience (Industrial Age), information and data gathering (Information Age), customization (Knowledge Age), the connection of people's passion and purpose with work systems and processes (Understanding Age), balance and sustainability (Wisdom Age), through the more direct insight of the *"Transcendent Age."* *This more direct insight* is achieved through the purposeful habit of systematically questioning our assumptions, thought processes and paradigms, as well as the impact and outcomes created as people interact from differing perspectives. This level of deep and meaningful questioning can lead to more direct and valuable insights related to our Leadership performance, which can support us with determining the best course of action in the moment.

Experience, if shared, leads to *Information* and accumulating data, which if more closely examined, leads to *Knowledge*, which when connected to our purpose leads to *Understanding*, and when thoughtfully and purposefully applied within the *Awareness* of a connected, unfolding timeline, leads to *Wisdom*, which when questioned and explored more deeply, allows us to *Transcend* even our current level of extra-ordinary Leadership. That's the progression here, so far. The Transcendent Age raises the potential of creating experiences for our teams, our customers, our organizations and ourselves that are well beyond the norm of our typical workplaces.

The Transcendent Age appreciates all of the efforts and outcomes of the previous Ages and is obviously an outgrowth of them and sees all of these Ages as a strong foundation with which to introduce even more impactful influences as an extra-ordinary Leader. There have most certainly been many examples throughout history of this level of "Transcendent" Leadership and action, applied to numerous challenges that have brought forth high levels of service to entire industries, cultures and civilizations.

Leadership Approach: *Transcendental Leadership*

Transcendental Leadership may not be as familiar a term, or as familiar a Leadership approach to some of us. This is to be expected as we move into higher levels of Leadership. As I stated in earlier chapters, some of the material or terms in the AQ model will be familiar to us and some may not. Our focus here should be to explore what these terms are pointing us towards. The Transcendental Leadership approach, based on its inherent meaning, moves us well beyond the norm, beyond our typical experience. That does not mean that the norm is bad, it is just that it is not all that is possible from a Leadership perspective. Transcendental Leaders seek to explore the deeper meanings of things to "transcend" or move further beyond the current limits of our Leadership experience, for those we serve.

What we do as Transcendental Leaders, and how we do it, is framed by this genuine desire or impulse to understand the deeper drivers of our thoughts, words and deeds (Meta-Mindset). And this genuine desire is fueled by our growing experience in extra-ordinary Leadership. At some point on this extra-ordinary journey, the journey itself begins to provide all of the inspiration we need to fuel our ongoing commitment and effort. At some point on this extra-ordinary journey, books and other forms of information become merely supplements to our very real and grounded experience as a Leader.

Transcendental Leaders endeavor to connect with and support others in a way that brings out our best effort and our best performance and our best version of ourselves, as we more deeply explore and envision and manifest our potential together. In this type of Leadership environment, we have the potential to more fully express the best parts of ourselves, individually and as a team. As a Transcendental Leader, we are positioned to very thoughtfully and consistently express the depth of our purpose, passion and insight, through our interactions with others, especially during times of significant challenge. At this level of Leadership, we seek to explore beyond the normal boundaries or parameters or paradigms of the workplace, to help create extra-ordinary experiences for others and organizations.

Whereas Leadership Levels 1 and 2 are more transactional in nature, and often based on a Leader's expression of their dominance over others; and Leadership Levels 3 and 4 tend to be focused on the motivation and inspiration of others to create personal, group and organizational transformation; and Leadership Level 5 seeks to create and support a more lasting and sustainable transformation as we continually monitor and adjust to the ever changing internal and external environment; Level 6 seeks the deeper level of insight needed to explore and approach our potential.

Predominant Leadership Characteristics: *Transcendental Leadership*

1. **Leadership through Direct Insight** is typically based on all of the previous levels of Leadership, *and on a growing familiarity with "lucid reality."* Perceiving our circumstances with a high degree of refined *Attention* and concentrated *Focus* related to what is really going on in our field of *Awareness*, results in our experience in *Lucid Reality*. Leaders who intentionally and consistently practice purposeful observation, thoughtful reflection and honest validation, *expand our perception* to the point that we "*see*" more and know and understand things more directly, and have access to far greater levels of acceptance and choice.

2. **Grounded predominantly in the Meta-Mindset (AQ / EQ)**, we develop the ability to explore the "conditions of potentiality" through our growing *Awareness, Attention, Focus* and *Intent*. This exploration sets the stage for our ability to understand what is necessary for creating an extra-ordinary experience for

ourselves and others. At this level of Leadership, there is a focus on more deeply understanding ourselves, to create more of an impact beyond ourselves.

3. **Uses Wisdom** as the stage from which to explore the stuff that binds us all together. At this level, we begin to move beyond the norm and beyond our ego to help others to see a greater purpose in their work and the potential of our organizations, to align and bind us together with a shared path and vision, to more directly and positively impact people and things.

4. **Typically, Potential-Future Oriented**, with the ability to understand the past, present, near and long-term impacts of our actions and interactions, along with the ability to more directly see our potential future as an individual, team or group. At this level of Leadership, we are positioned to move a group, team or organization even more confidently towards our potential future.

5. **Focused on the ability to know the essence of things more directly**, and through the consistent and thoughtful exploration into the depth of things, we develop the ability to more clearly see and know the root or core or foundational elements involved.

6. **Problem Solving Method**, usually involves moving from *Potentiality* to Research to Customization to People and Process Integration to Transformation to Time Framing to Sustainability to *Expanded Perception* to *Discovery*. Starting with the mindset that we are exploring *Potentiality* (not a Problem or even an Opportunity), we can more easily step into and work with *Expanded* states of *Perception* to *Discover*

solutions that are beyond the access of more typical approaches to problem solving. The added element of *Expanded Perception* serves to support our ability to more directly see the potential of people and things, and our interactions and efforts.

7. **Common Leadership Statement** may be any version of *"How do we know what we think we know."* I would be quite surprised if more than just a few of us have heard any version of this statement uttered by a Leader we were interacting with.

8. **Common outcome of this Leadership approach** is frequently a more enthused team and organization, as those involved accomplish the work in a way that helps them to step into their deeper abilities and creativity, along with the many positive impacts of this. Those in a work group or team or organization begin to feel that their efforts are actually contributing to something well beyond the norm of most workplaces, something that will deeply impact the organization and its customers. This Leadership approach tends to establish a work environment where people want to stay as long as they can and are drawn to contribute in a more enthusiastic way towards each other and the goals of the group, creating even higher levels of potential with their results. This Leadership approach works to foster a real connection between people and the results of our efforts across environments, while we move towards the potentiality of a given situation. This brings a deep sense of joy to a Transcendental Leader.

The Transcendental Leadership approach can't be seen, but it can be felt! Transcendental Leadership, and most other higher levels of Leadership, are difficult to see or to pinpoint, since they can be so uncommon and so subtle. Yet the results can be quite powerful, and although most people may not be able to recognize what a Transcendental Leader is actually *Being* and *Doing*, they can definitely *feel* the results. When we commit to consistently exploring the deeper meanings of things, everything we look at or are involved in as a Leader appears to us in the context of an emerging potential. The natural expression of our Leadership then seeks to move ourselves and others towards this potential. And in order to accomplish this, we must first have or develop a deep desire to see and connect with and support others along this challenging journey, and to make a significant difference in our life and the lives of others. And then, we must passionately and relentlessly follow our purpose.

Let's do a little more exploration around the term "Lucid Reality" that was used in the above Predominant Leadership Characteristics. Many of us have probably heard about the concept of a *Lucid Dream*, and some may have even had this experience before. Anyway, when we are sleeping, there are dreams and then there are *Lucid Dreams*. In a Lucid Dream, we are able to sort of wake up, while still within our dream. Yes, really. And the result of this is that we are able to gain a much greater degree of understanding and control of our performance while within our dream scenario. Normally our dreams just kind of go where they go, just like our lives often do. But in a Lucid Dream, we can begin to take control our efforts and influence the direction of the scene. This can allow us to do all kinds of things within our dreamscape, such as fly or move through walls or access potentially important information, and many other interesting things.

Similarly, *Lucid Reality* is sort of like waking up while in our normal waking state. Yes, really. And the result of this is that we are able to gain a much greater degree of understanding and control of our performance while in our waking life. Normally, our lives and our workplaces just kind of go where they go, just like our dreams. But while in a state of *Lucid Reality*, we can begin to more deeply understand and control our efforts and influence the direction of our lives with a much greater degree of clarity and purpose. This can allow us to do all kinds of things within our waking lives, such as more purposefully choosing our thoughts, words and actions and applying them more productively, and accessing potentially important information, along with many other interesting things.

Lucid Reality is a very real state of *expanded perception* that we can access and purposefully use to serve others even more effectively. There are obviously degrees of wakefulness that we all experience each day, from our early morning, newly awakened, groggy state, to our mid-morning clarity, to our post lunch-time nappy feeling, and varying degrees of wakefulness beyond these. So, it should be clear to us that we all experience varying degrees of wakefulness or clarity related to our waking reality, and that our degree of wakefulness to reality has an impact on our understanding, perception and performance.

Through our purposeful *Attention* and *Focus*, we can access these higher degrees of wakefulness or *perception* and engage with the world much more thoughtfully and gracefully. Through our work at this level of Leadership, we can become more and more familiar with these more expanded states of wakefulness, or perception, or *Lucid Reality*. And we can choose whichever term works best for our situation, or we can develop our own term to reflect this concept. In either case, the concept itself is still real and valid and valuable and available to us, if we are willing to do our work and to drop any of our attachments and opinions and assumptions that may be creating resistance around this very real possibility for us as Leaders. *This is the Leadership Revolution that I am talking about!*

The Transcendental Leadership approach incorporates a Leader's *Awareness, Attention, Focus* and *Intent* on our commitment to discovering the deeper meanings and potential of things, and through this approach, supports and contributes to others in the process of moving forward to achieve the objectives of a group, team or organization. This Leader has as a part of our Meta-Mindset, the deep desire to understand our potential, and to present this to others in a way that helps them to unleash their extra-ordinary effort towards this vision.

A group or team in collaboration with a Transcendental Leader can achieve amazing things together while they learn and grow and create significant impacts through their interactions. The Transcendental Leadership approach represents a clear expression of extra-ordinary Leadership and everyone with whom we interact benefits from this, including ourselves. The Transcendental Leadership approach comes from deep within and moves from inside to out. Once this realization and commitment to discovering our potential occurs, then the question of *"Where are we going?"* goes away.

And yet there is still more available within the possibility of Leadership. More to share with and give to others, our organizations and ourselves. There remain still untapped reserves within ourselves and others that, when understood and unleashed, can bring even further levels of results and even further degrees of growth and satisfaction experienced by those we serve. The challenge of an extra-ordinary Leader at this point is in illuminating our collective potential to others and with helping them to experience the achievement of this potential.

Although a commitment to Leading through facilitating the potential of others can be incredibly impactful on this extra-ordinary journey, we can still be left with the clear knowing that there is more available to all of us on our journey as an extra-ordinary Leader. Transcendental Leadership represents a level of Leadership that our teams and organizations crave on some level. Deep inside, many of us crave to move towards our potential in an extra-ordinary way. We collectively sense that there is a way of *Being* and *Doing* that far exceeds the experiences that are so typical of our daily lives. We even see examples of it from time to time but have not yet been able to establish this as a more consistent experience in our lives.

However, this continues to change in the here and now as we establish ourselves and ground ourselves in Level 6, Transcendental Leadership. At this level, the opportunities to serve others and our organizations, and to move further towards our potential, becomes so obvious to us that we can't help but respond to this call.

The Transcendental Leadership approach then serves as an excellent vantage point to more clearly and committedly see and explore even higher levels of Leadership performance. From this level, we can more freely access any of the more positive elements within the first five levels of Leadership, while adding to them even more *Awareness* and understanding of all of the potentials involved. The Transcendental Leadership approach further enhances the look and feel and experience and results of those involved. The freedom we experience at this level of Leadership and our ability to help others to access greater levels of freedom for themselves brings everyone involved into much greater alignment with our purpose and passion as expressed through our work or task at hand. And yet there is more that awaits us as an extra-ordinary Leader.

And now it is time to move to the next Level of Leadership, Level 7, Mystic Age, "Leadership." But once again, in order to ground ourselves in this next level of Leadership, as opposed to just visiting there temporarily, we must understand and work through the attachments or programming that keep up grounded back in Level 6 Leadership. As valuable as Level 6, Transcendental Leadership is, it still has limitations that hold us and others back from a fuller expression of our passion and purpose and the results that are possible. As extra-ordinary Leaders, we must apply what we are discovering to ground ourselves in higher levels of performance, and to create the further benefits that are possible for our teams and organizations.

To enable us to move effectively beyond Level 6, Transcendental Leadership, let's explore the primary Level 6 Energetic Impediment that inhibits our ability to move forward more easily on our Leadership Journey.

6th Level Energetic Impediment:

Release the attachment *to the illusion of separation.* This is one of the biggies as far as attachments go, is it not? This one runs very deep in our programming and has been the subject of numerous philosophical, religious and spiritual writings and discussions throughout history. Are we separate from, or are we connected to, each other, nature, etc.? It's a fascinating exploration to take on, for sure. Our five senses may tell us that there appears to be lots of empty space between each of us and everything else, so the logical conclusion would be that yes, we are separate. But let's briefly explore.

The outcomes of this conclusion are the numerous and deep impacts to so many of our interactions with each other and our planet. Think about it! This perspective impacts us all very deeply, and so many of our challenges in society and in life may stem from this singular issue. Are we separate or are we connected? Let's pretend for a moment, that we could not prove this one way or another, and then let's ask a meaningful question. What are some of the results of believing or viewing our world as being separate from ourselves? I am separate from you and you are separate from me and they are separate from us. And everything in nature is most certainly separate from all of us.

Can we imagine what some of the results of this separation Mindset could be? Yes, exactly! It's not very hard, is it? So much of the unnecessary fear and drama and waste and hate and wars and pollution, and so much more, are the logical extension or outcome of a separation mentality. And how does a separation mentality impact us and everyone else in our workplaces? How does a separation mentality impact our workplace interactions and results? How much unnecessary fear and drama and waste and poor customer satisfaction and a lack of employee engagement, etc., is related to this separation mentality? This separation mentality is rampant in our world and our workplaces, and so are its results.

Now let's consider the opposite conclusion. I am connected to you, and you are connected to me, and they are connected to us, and everything in nature is most certainly connected to all of us. What are some of the results of believing or viewing our world as being connected to ourselves, a connection Mindset? Hmmm, are there any models that even reflect this position? Well, the good news is yes, there are many. And some are quite visible to us, if we know where to look and if we have an eye for connection. And in these examples of a connection Mindset, we also find some consistent impacts. People with a connection Mindset tend to appreciate and collaborate and support each other in much more interesting and productive ways. And our surrounding environment takes on much more importance and is seen as integral to our experience with a connection Mindset. We can do a little research on this and see what we see. We should prove this for ourselves.

My point here is to briefly explore some of the impacts within each of these perspectives, so that we can more deeply consider this issue. And then to ask a meaningful question or two. So first, what do we believe? And how do we express this belief within our groups and organizations, as it is here that our beliefs are compounded and magnified and then expressed through our group efforts, creating the results that we are all experiencing? The illusion of separation continues to create much of the unnecessary drama and dysfunction we experience, and it is time to come to a deeper, experiential understanding of the reality of this issue.

We could continue on with this exploration, as so many writings have already done, but now I would like to move further forward with this issue and get to the real point of exploring this attachment. The attachment to the illusion of separation has a *significantly* negative impact on our relationships, interactions, collaborations and many of our key efforts as a Leader. I can't say this any other way. We don't have the time anymore to dance around important issues like this or to justify concepts that are clearly limiting our experience and results. So, it is time for us on our extra-ordinary Leadership journey to take on this attachment. It is time to get clear about the answer to the question of "Are we separate or are we connected?" And we must come to know the answer to this question on a personal level, experientially, not through the logic of the five senses or based on someone else's opinion, including mine.

In order to get to this level of clarity about this attachment, we may have to do some work, some serious but interesting research and some deeper internal work. Yes, I know, this keeps getting more fun and inspiring! That is what extra-ordinary Leadership is all about! But, at this point, we should definitely be up for this level of work, and it is no longer "work" for us in the more traditional use of the word. This is simply why we are here, and we joyfully jump into explorations such as this. So, to begin to release this attachment to the illusion of separation, we must look directly at it, and explore it, and contemplate it, and think about it, and NOT think about it, and try to get a feel for it. It definitely has a feeling to it. If we immerse ourselves in it, we will typically perceive something. And based on that something, we can begin to develop more experientially-based conclusions and perspectives.

This tendency or attachment to the illusion of separation can create significant limitations to our true potential as a Leader. Therefore, we must address this here and now. As an extra-ordinary Leader, through our passion and clarity of purpose, we can come to understand the programming around the illusion of separation, and continually look both inwardly and outwardly to purposefully connect with and contribute to creating even higher, more productive expressions of Leadership, in service to others.

By working to release our attachments, we position ourselves to see other possibilities and to move through life and the challenges of Leadership a little more gracefully, and to support our teams with more flexibility and agility. Our attachments tend to lock us in to a specific perspective. Releasing our attachments can open us up to additional options. This should make sense to us on all levels at this point.

So, as an extra-ordinary Leader, it is time to work through our programming around this issue of the illusion of separation, and to brave any resistance or ridicule that may come as a result of actively moving beyond the status quo. For on the other side of our questioning of the status quo, lies our freedom as a Leader to express what is really most important to us and to others, even the ones poking fun at us. That is why we are here.

So, once again, the first step in moving ourselves beyond this limited perspective is to become aware of it, either on our own, through fearless self-reflection, or through honest feedback from others. There are others out there like us. We should continually seek each other out and share our perspectives and experiences to help to bolster our journeys, as we actively commit to replacing our more limited perspectives and habits and adopting a way of *Being* and *Doing* that is more expanded and supportive of others, our organizations and ourselves. And what could we replace this illusion of separation with?

Develop the ability *to connect more deeply with other people and the environment and with ourselves, to more effectively exercise our capacity for creating possibility from the seemingly impossible.* The process and experience of "connecting" is an ongoing progression in that the more we *Be* it and *Do* it, the more real it gets and the more impact it has on so many levels. But this must be experienced by us for it to be real. Reading about it is not enough.

And once again, there is no overly complex, sanctioned process for accomplishing this. We simply add to our expanding expression of our Leadership performance, the consistent practice of reaching out to others and our environment, and to explore where our efforts may lead. We can reach out and physically connect with others with a simple handshake. We can reach out and connect to others through our words, such as through our positive greetings and appreciation for the opportunity to get together and collaborate. We can reach out to others and connect through our thoughts of togetherness or collaboration or of being part of an extended family. We can reach out to others and connect from our hearts to their hearts.

All of these represent a very real way to establish a strong sense of connection. And we can do all of these at the same time! There are a thousand ways to connect and to experience this. We can just use our imaginations and explore away. It is time to reconnect with who we are and why we are here. It is time to reach out to others and our environment and to reconnect with our shared experience and our shared vision. No one is holding us back anymore, except ourselves! Let's take off our shackles and step out of the cage that was never locked to begin with! We are connected in some way to everyone and everything. And it is time for us to experience this for ourselves. There is no separation! *This is the Leadership Revolution that I am talking about!*

We don't need to create this as a separate step, in addition to all that we are already doing as a Leader. At this point in our growth, we may be able to layer activities like this over the things we are already doing. We can do these things at this point, simultaneously and very efficiently. What I am continuing to refer to is the expansion of our *Awareness*, and the concentration of our *Attention* and the refinement of our *Focus*. Through this process, we, as extra-ordinary Leaders, on a Hero's Journey, in service to others, can develop astounding abilities related to our Leadership understanding and performance on multiple levels, simultaneously.

There could be quite a few other impediments or obstacles preventing a Leader from moving beyond Level 6, Transcendental Leadership. However, the attachment to the illusion of separation can be at the root of this issue. Although Transcendental Leadership approaches can take us and our team on a more expanded journey, the lack of our ability to more fully connect with others and our environment can get in the way of creating and maintaining an atmosphere where others can more consistently connect with their passion and purpose, to provide their best effort. It will take some level of *Awareness* and acknowledgement of this issue and then a commitment to continued growth for us to recognize our further potential and the further potential of our team. A Leader can be helped and supported through this growth, and there are many approaches for this, but, ultimately, we must decide for ourselves to grow further.

Now, let's move into the process of up-leveling ourselves and others from Level 6 (Transcendent Age, Transcendental Leadership) to Level 7 (Mystic Age, "Leadership"), as we step even further into our ability to serve others and our organizations, exceptionally. The up-leveling processes help us and others to overcome the *Energetic Impediments* (our attachments) to our previous level of Leadership performance, while the *Predominant Leadership Characteristics* of the next level of Leadership serve as a model for us to focus on and ground ourselves. And once we are comfortable and confident in our Leadership understanding and expression at a given level of Leadership, it is then time for us to move to the next higher level.

Up-leveling from Level 6, Transcendental Leadership, to Level 7, Mystic Age, "Leadership"

Up-leveling Ourselves:

Step 1 – Engage our intent with "intent." This refers to engaging with and stepping into and more deeply aligning ourselves with our intent. This is not the same thing as hoping or wishing really, really hard. Stepping into our intent is more like identifying with it, or becoming it, to the point that our intent becomes indistinguishable from who we are, and it then gets expressed nearly effortlessly. "Our intent" is also not exactly the same thing as our purpose. Our purpose is more related to the question of "what are we here to do?" while our intent relates more to the question of "why are we here to do this?" Our purpose appears mostly in the "What" of our Leadership Purpose Statement and becomes part of our Mindset, while our intent manifests mostly in the "Why" of our Leadership Purpose Statement and emerges from our Meta-Mindset.

So, "our intent" refers to our deeper motivations or inspirations for doing what we do, and this is not always clear to us at the level of our *Awareness*. Most of us are not completely clear about our intent. Why we do what we do is often based on some form of programming or the opinions of others. Just ask someone why they do what they do and, in most cases, they will express some level of uncertainty or lack of clarity regarding the issue.

Now to clarify the second part of this step 1, where we refer to engaging our intent with "intent." This is a little more slippery to pin down. "Intent" could be viewed from multiple levels; however, for our exploration here, we could view "intent" as the energy and coherence related to "our intent." So, engaging "our intent" with "intent" could be viewed as aligning our deeper motivations and inspiration (our Intent), with the requisite energy and connectedness needed to enliven and fuel our efforts (Intent). The concept of "Intent" is another, very worthwhile area of further research and exploration for an extra-ordinary Leader. Check it out! It can take us deep!

Step 1 of up-leveling ourselves involves establishing a more expanded way of *Being* to position us to more genuinely implement what we will be *Doing* in step 2. In step 1, we once again purposefully exercise our *Attention* and *Focus* in the direction of our *intent*. We then align or enliven *our intent*, with *intent*. This is clearly an internal maneuver, an act of *Being* that can move powerfully from the inside to the outside, as we *Do* step 2.

Up-leveling Ourselves:

Step 2 – Purposefully engage in ambiguously challenging opportunities (the unknown), to directly experience our ability to transmute "lead to gold." Step 1 establishes our more expanded *Being*, while step 2 takes this expanded *Being* and applies it in real time and within the context of a host of purposefully sought out, ambiguous and challenging situations, or the unknown. These are the types of challenges in the workplace that most people, even seasoned Leaders, either ignore or run from. But instead, at this level of Leadership, we purposefully seek them out and step confidently into them. I know . . . crazy, right? Yet our confidence at this point is not based on some sort of false bravado, but on a very real experience in our growing *Awareness*. As we continue to explore and up-level ourselves and others on our extra-ordinary Leadership journey, and exercise our *Attention* and *Focus*, our *Awareness* also continues to grow.

This process helps us to see things in new and novel ways, and to also perceive things that were once invisible to us. This process helps us to gain real experience with working with the subtler, yet powerful elements of extra-ordinary Leadership. Our growing confidence comes from our very real and extra-ordinary experience as a Leader. And the more we exercise our *Awareness*, *Attention*, *Focus* and *Intent*, and purposefully engage our *Being* and *Doing* in the process of serving others and our organizations, the more effectively we all move forward on our journeys.

In step 2 of up-leveling ourselves to Level 7 Leadership, we purposefully seek out ambiguous, challenging situations (the unknown) to apply our Leadership in service to others. And it is not uncommon at this level for these types of challenging situations to seek us out! In either case, however, when we step into the unknown, with full *Awareness, Attention, Focus* and *Intent*, and then apply our purpose and passion to the tasks at hand while actively choosing to engage with the types of things that others either ignore or run from, we position ourselves and our teams to make the *seemingly impossible, possible*.

That's it! First, we establish a more expanded way of *Being* that involves engaging "our intent" with "intent." And then we consistently take our expanded *Being* into complex, real-world experiences, the kind that arise somewhat frequently in our complex workplaces and organizations these days. We then learn and grow and share and collaborate and plan and implement and course correct and repeat and repeat. When we make a habit of this level of *Being* and *Doing*, amazing things happen. And by performing these two up-leveling steps, we are automatically up-leveled into the next level of Leadership.

As we could probably guess by now, there are no special instructions required to accomplish these up-leveling approaches other than just *Doing* them and adjusting from there. In step 1, we can simply revisit our Leadership Purpose Statement, with some additional focus on the "Why" section, since this section is a reflection of our Meta-Mindset or "our intent." We can place our *Attention* and *Focus* here on a more consistent basis, and act from this perspective more purposefully. And then, we align our intent with "intent," which is an energy and coherence that we can align with to further enliven our efforts. And then, in step 2, we take this level of *Being* out into the unknown, or into those

BIG scary challenges that exist out there. And we connect with and collaborate with other inspired people, to work to move forward in these challenges. This is how we, together, can make the *seemingly impossible, possible.*

We don't have to analyze these steps any further before we do them. At this point, just apply some provisional trust to the process and to ourselves. If we have made it this far on our extra-ordinary Leadership journey and have experienced some positive results, then let's keep going. If we just *Be* and *Do* our best version of the up-leveling practices, we will continue to learn and grow as a Leader. We can become our own source of learning and growth, once we understand the map or the puzzle a little better. That is why we are here. This is our work. *This is the Leadership Revolution that I am talking about!*

And once again, we must have a rabid passion or burning desire to radically improve our Leadership performance. Without this, we will not be able to overcome the energetic threshold or the inertia of our previous habits or programming required to step fully into a new and more productive way of *Being* and *Doing* as a Leader. Our desire to transform ourselves as a Leader must be stronger than our commitment to our previous habits or programming and the results we created. Our *Awareness, Attention, Focus* and *Intent* around this opportunity to truly serve as an extra-ordinary Leader must be sharp and keen and unwavering in these moments. This will always be the key to accomplishing this up-leveling process. And no matter how challenging we may find certain aspects of this process, we simply need to keep recommitting ourselves in thought, word and deed and we will succeed, no matter how many times it takes.

Up-leveling Others:

Step 1 – Engage with others' intent, with clear intent. This step 1 is very similar, as usual, to step 1 of up-leveling ourselves. It basically involves purposefully connecting our intent with other's intent, "the why" of their purpose. This is why it can be very helpful at this point to do some version of the Leadership Purpose Statement exercise with our teams and groups. When we have some understanding of each other's deeper purpose, we are in a much better position to connect with and support each other. So, if we haven't done this exercise with our team by now, it is probably a good time to strongly consider it.

And we must do this with clear intent. In other words, we must be crystal clear about our motives when engaging with others at this deeper level, and our motives must be some version of genuinely serving and supporting our team. Otherwise, the impact of our effort or the feeling that our team will get from our efforts can have some negative implications. We cannot fake it here at these higher levels of Leadership. As we work with increasingly subtle approaches, our intent must be clear and benevolent and for the good of everyone involved. And when we are able to connect with others in this way, they are better positioned to then connect *their intent* with *intent*. They are then in a position to more deeply connect with the "why" of their purpose statement, to further enliven and fuel their extra-ordinary Leadership journey.

As a somewhat connected side-note here, this would be a good time to explore where Leadership traits such as "integrity" come from. As I mentioned earlier, we can't just act with integrity because we read in a Leadership article or book that this is a good thing to do as a Leader. Integrity and other Leadership traits come from somewhere. And this somewhere is actually our Meta-Mindset (*Awareness*), not our Mindset (*Attention*) as others would have us believe. The foundation of integrity flows out of our Meta-Mindset and then it can become anchored in our Mindset. We typically can't just contemplate these Leadership traits at the level of our mind and then expect sustainable results from this. If this were true, almost every Leader out there already would be displaying high levels of integrity and other productive Leadership traits, because we have all read these articles and books and thought about these things. But look around, this is clearly not the case! We must further explore these things if we are to truly embody these Leadership traits.

In order to affect the deeper growth and performance we seek as extra-ordinary Leaders, we must go deeper, we must explore further. We must experientially understand these very real concepts, such as the *Meta-Mindset* and *Intent*. We must step into these areas in a very real way and work from there. It is through our identification with and clarity with and development of our intent that we are able to more freely and more genuinely express higher levels of integrity and many other well-researched, positive Leadership traits. Therefore, we must commit to this level of work. It is our duty and responsibility as an extra-ordinary Leader, and also our privilege and our joy, to serve in this way. Step 1 involves *Being* crystal clear about our motives and our intent with supporting and connecting with others' intent, as we collaborate around an effort.

Up-leveling Others:

Step 2 – Facilitate more creative explorations and experimentation in challenging situations, to create more direct experiences for others regarding what's truly possible. This step 2 can be a very interesting endeavor. It is one thing to up-level our-selves and to make a habit of putting ourselves into ambiguously challenging situations (the unknown) and face our own uncer-tainties and insecurities while we move through a significant challenge. But it is quite another act of extra-ordinary Leadership to facilitate a group or a team through unknown territory, while managing the individual and collective uncertainties and insecu-rities of everyone involved. This is Leadership at its best! And it is totally doable, even by us mere mortals!

We can either push and drive others through these kinds of challenging situations, which is the more common approach to Leadership, or we can pull them along, and guide them along, and creatively and supportively question them along. We can purposefully facilitate experiences or phases of the work in such a way that those on the team directly experience more of their potential, more of their greatness together, as they make possi-ble what they once might have thought was impossible. Imagine what it would look like and feel like and smell like to facilitate such a team effort as an extra-ordinary Leader. Also imagine what it would look like and feel like and smell like to be part of a team, being led through the unknown by such a Leader.

Guiding others' *Awareness, Attention, Focus* and *Intent* is definitely more art than science. This involves a purposeful, agile, facilitated exploration and discussion of the deeper and deeper elements of an effort, and each other. And as an extra-ordinary Leader facilitating such a process, we must remain continually open to what the environment is communicating to us. We must stay connected with the work and the impacts of the work, and also to the people and how they are processing everything and interacting and performing and being impacted by everything else. This is most certainly a complex orchestra-tion and quite an interesting and rewarding dance.

At this level of Leadership, our focus is more and more on facilitating and creating purposeful experiences for our groups and teams, in an effort to not only solve or address an issue, but to also bring out the individual and collective best of the group or team. And also, to begin to create a group dynamic or experience that is extra-ordinary and valuable and growth-filled and fun! *This is the Leadership Revolution that I am talking about!*

Additionally, this process should almost always be accomplished through some sort of visible, documented process. If everyone cannot directly see the process as it unfolds, they will not be in the best position to contribute to the process in the most productive way. This process could be accomplished on a white board or with sticky-notes or with the use of any version of this process. We should also attempt to include or draw out everyone's perspective and input whenever possible. Before we move into full implementation of an effort, we facilitate a thoughtful, purposeful dialogue, to orient others' *Awareness, Attention, Focus* and *Intent* towards this very real concept of clarifying and connecting with our individual and group intent (step 1) to fuel us as we take on the seemingly impossible (step 2).

Performing these two steps automatically up-levels us into the next level of Leadership and deepens everyone's *Awareness* and understanding of the unfolding effort and in a way that can significantly contribute to the group's experience. This process can help everyone to gain the real confidence that we all need to continue to take on the increasing levels of complexity that will surely continue to come. These up-leveling steps automatically move us into higher levels of Leadership performance while creating higher level experiences and higher levels of performance for those we interact with, in real time! That's just how it works! Just *Be* and *Do* and repeat and repeat. This is a thread of simplicity that runs through the AQ Model. Just *Be* and *Do*. And these additional processes and dialogues do not have to add significant amounts of time to the overall process, once we jump fully into it.

It's now time to step more fully into our responsibility as extra-ordinary Leaders and serve others by supporting their growth through the gift of up-leveling. Once we have moved ourselves and then others beyond the more limited approaches of Levels 1, 2, 3 and even Levels 4, 5 and 6, there can be much more ease and growth and impactful results achieved through working with greater levels of *Awareness* within the challenges we all face. As a reminder, even under the best of circumstances, nothing is 100% as expected. We may need to finesse these approaches and tailor them for a specific person or situation, and we may need to repeat it multiple times to achieve the desired or needed impact. But more times than not, we can improve Leadership performance, the performance of others and everyone's overall experience in the workplace, consistently and in real time, especially when we have done our work first.

Everyone deserves an opportunity to step further into a level of Leadership performance that serves others more completely, as well as themselves. Everyone working with a Leader deserves the opportunity to work and contribute within an environment that inspires them towards their best effort and expression of their purpose. Let's do our part as an extra-ordinary Leader to give everyone a real chance for this, here and now. Let's help them and support them, the very best that we can, as our very best continues to expand.

There is one more level of Leadership that I would like to explore in Part 2 of this book. And remember, Part 2 of this book is also aligned with Phase 2 of our Hero's Journey (The Initiation). In Phase 2 of the Hero's Journey, we have made the clear decision to leave the status quo, the norm of Leadership, and to go on an extra-ordinary journey. A journey that is in alignment with the deeper elements of our Leadership purpose, in service to others. In Phase 2 of our Hero's Journey, we courageously take on the deeper work of Leadership, and brave the trials and tribulations that may come our way as a result, in an effort to establish the Meta-Mindset and Mindset necessary to fuel our commitment to developing the Skill Sets and Tool Sets required to consistently perform as an extra-ordinary Leader. And to position ourselves to begin to step confidently into a genuine expression of our Leadership Mastery. This next level of Leadership (level 7) completes, in a sense, the valuable, necessary, foundational work of our journey or "initiation" into extra-ordinary Leadership.

Level 6 — Leadership Age & Approach	Predominant Leadership Characteristics	Up-Leveling Ourselves	Up-Leveling Others
		the thoughtful and purposeful process of improving our performance through an ongoing commitment to growing our awareness, attention and focus	helping others to improve their performance *"in real time,"* based on your growing awareness and your commitment to supportive, purposeful coaching
Transcendent Age: Transcendental Leadership	1. **Leadership through Direct Insight** – typically based on all the above, and on a familiarity with *"lucid reality."* 2. Grounded predominantly in the meta-mindset (AQ & EQ). 3. *Uses Wisdom* as the stage from which to explore the stuff that "binds us and everything together." 4. Is "Potential – Future" Oriented 5. Focused on the ability to know the essence of things more directly. 6. Problem Solving Method – Moves from *"Potentiality"* to "Research" to "Customization" to "P&P Integration" to "Transformation" to "Time Framing" to "Sustainability" to "Expanded Perception" to *"Discovery."* 7. Common Quote – *"How do you know what you think you know?"* 8. Common Outcomes – **Work** unfolds in a way that helps others to "wake up" to their deeper abilities and creativity, along with the many positive impacts of this.	Moving from Level 6 to Level 7: 1. Engage our intent with "intent." 2. Purposefully engage in ambiguously challenging opportunities, to directly experience our ability transmute "lead to gold."	Moving from Level 6 to Level 7: 1. Engage with other's intent, with clear "intent." 2. Facilitate more "creative" explorations & experimentation in challenging situations to create more direct experiences for others regarding what's truly possible.
*6th Level Energetic Impediment – **Release** the attachment to the illusion of separation. **Develop** the ability to connect more deeply with other people and the environment and with ourselves, to more effectively exercise our capacity for creating possibility from the seemingly impossible.*			

Figure 10. (Level 6 Leadership)

CHAPTER 16

Level 7 Leadership
The Mystic Age & "Leadership"

*Leadership through the Facilitation
of Direct Experience . . .*

Leadership Age: *Mystic Age*

The 7th Level of Leadership illuminated in the AQ Model represents the functional progression of an even more thoughtful and purposeful application of individual experience (Industrial Age), information and data gathering (Information Age), customization (Knowledge Age), the connection of people's passion and purpose with work systems and processes (Understanding Age), balance and sustainability (Wisdom Age), more direct insight (Transcendent Age), and through the alchemy of possibility from the seemingly impossible, within the *"Mystic Age."*

The hallmark of the Mystic Age involves the ability to accomplish the seemingly impossible, and this is developed through the purposeful habit of systematically engaging our *Awareness*, *Attention*, *Focus* and *Intent*, while working in various ambiguous and challenging situations (the unknown). It is in these situations where we purposefully engage with our *intent*, in the context of

uncertainty, that we refine our practice with the alchemy of ourselves and our teams and the challenges we face. This level of deep
work can Lead to even more direct and valuable insights related
to our Leadership performance, which can support us with determining the best course of action in the moment.

Experience, if shared, leads to Information and accumulating data, which, if more closely examined, leads to Knowledge,
which when connected to our purpose, leads to Understanding, and when thoughtfully and purposefully applied within the
Awareness of a connected, unfolding timeline, leads to Wisdom,
which when questioned and explored more deeply, leads to
Transcendent experiences; and when we engage our intent and
apply it consistently within uncertainty, we can achieve what
others may perceive as impossible, connecting us to the Mystic.
That's the progression here, so far. The Mystic Age raises the
potential of creating experiences for our teams, our customers,
our organizations and ourselves that are far beyond the norm of
our typical workplaces.

And once again, let's not get too caught up in the terminology here. The term, "Mystic" has been around for thousands
of years and can mean different things to different people. The
Mystics of the past were many times revered for their perspective, and well-known for rocking the boat in their day; that is,
right up until some of them were burned at the stake or met
with some other unfortunate end. This term can have either
an "old age" or a "new age" connotation for some of us. So, let's
clarify our terms here. In this case, the term Mystic is meant to
point us toward some of the deeper mysteries of Leadership
that are actually hiding in plain sight! It is meant to point us
even more deeply towards our Leadership potential.

The Mystics of the past and present represent those who
have committed to the deeper internal work necessary to

understand ourselves, and therefore others and our surroundings in a way that helps us to serve even better. The term Mystic, in this case, is meant to connect us more deeply with reality, as opposed to the illusion of reality. And when we accept and embrace and deeply connect with and work more directly with reality, instead of denying it or arguing with it or fighting with it, sometimes what might seem impossible, becomes possible.

Leadership Approach: *"Leadership"*

The Leadership approach at this level is identified simply as "Leadership," since this level represents the ideal or standard for extra-ordinary Leadership. Whereas the preceding levels represent only some aspect of, or some of the key attributes of this level of genuine "Leadership." Therefore, this 7th level of Leadership is identified more directly as just, "Leadership." As an extra-ordinary Leader, this level represents one of the more adventurous goals that we should set for ourselves related to our Leadership Performance.

What we do at this level of Leadership, and how we do it, is framed by this genuine desire or impulse to perceive and to work directly with the subtler elements of ourselves and others and our environment, to more effectively serve. And this genuine desire is fueled by our growing experience in expanded *Awareness* and extra-ordinary Leadership. When I refer to the subtler elements of ourselves and others and our environment, I am referring to things like the foundation of our purpose, our typical thought patterns and programming challenges, our aspirations and talents, our skills and tools, etc. With regards to the environment, I am referring to the internal and external environment, the key systems and processes, key stakeholders, the areas of the environment that impact or are impacted by the effort, etc. These are some of the key *ingredients* necessary for creating possibility. And when we commit to deeply exploring these ingredients and understanding them and working with them by combining them and leveraging them in thoughtful, unique and situationally specific ways, we are able to create possibility from the seemingly impossible!

Leaders at this level endeavor to connect with and support others in a way that brings out our best effort, and our best performance, and our best version of ourselves, as we more deeply explore and envision and manifest our potential together. In this type of Leadership environment, we have the potential to more fully express the best parts of ourselves, individually and as a team. And as a Leader at this level, we are positioned to very thoughtfully and consistently express the depth of our purpose, passion, insight and transformative nature, through our interactions with others, especially during times of significant challenge. At this level of Leadership, we seek to explore beyond the normal boundaries or parameters or paradigms of the workplace, to help to create extra-ordinary experiences for others and organizations. At this point on our extra-ordinary journey, the journey itself provides all of the inspiration we need to fuel our ongoing commitment and effort.

Whereas Leadership Levels 1 and 2 are more transactional in nature, and many times based on a Leader's expression of their dominance over others; and Leadership Levels 3 and 4 tend to be focused on the motivation and inspiration of others to create personal, group and organizational transformation; and Leadership Level 5 seeks to create and support a more lasting and sustainable transformation as we continually monitor and adjust to the ever changing internal and external environment; and Level 6 Leaders seek the deeper level of insight needed to explore and approach our potential; Level 7 "Leadership" focuses on working directly with the subtle elements of ourselves and the environment to help us create possibility out of the seemingly impossible. This is the progression so far.

The up-leveling approaches that we performed in the previous level of Leadership serve to automatically usher us into this next level. However, in order to remain or ground ourselves here, we must begin to practice and to embody and express the Predominant Leadership Characteristics below.

Predominant Leadership Characteristics: *"Leadership"*

1. **Leadership through the Facilitation of Direct Experience** is typically based on all of the previous levels of Leadership, *and on the alchemy of possibility from the seemingly impossible.* The term "alchemy" refers to very purposefully working with both the subtle and gross elements of ourselves and our environment to create extra-ordinary outcomes. This represents the true art and science of Leadership.

2. **Grounded predominantly in extra-ordinary reality (expanded Awareness)**, we develop the ability to access perceptions, perspectives and experiences that are well beyond the norm of the workplace. "Extra-ordinary reality" is simply the experience of expanded *Awareness*, and refined *Attention*, and concentrated *Focus* and clear *Intent*. This exploration sets the stage for our ability to discern and to thoughtfully choose and to combine the ingredients necessary for creating an extra-ordinary experience for ourselves and others.

3. **Uses Transcendence** as our *slingshot* into the unknown (the mystery), to then return and to make it known. At this level, we make a habit of exploring the things that are unknown or unfamiliar, to illuminate them for the purpose of making use of these discoveries, to help others to see a greater possibility in our work and our organizations, to align with an experientially shared path and vision, and to more directly and positively impact people and things.

4. **Typically, "Possible-Future" Oriented**, with the ability to understand the past, present, near and long-term impacts of our actions and interactions, along with the ability to more directly contribute to our possible future as an individual, team or group. At this level of Leadership, we are positioned to move a group, team or organization confidently into what is possible for us.

5. **Focused on functioning with extreme agility within and across all Leadership levels with clarity of** *Awareness, Attention, Focus, Intent and Love*, through the consistent practice and commitment to extra-ordinary Leadership. At this level, we develop the ability to thoughtfully and compassionately create what is needed in the moment to move things forward, even if that means taking one step back to ultimately advance more productively from there.

6. **Problem Solving Method**, usually involves moving from *Possibility* to Research to Customization to Process and People Integration to Transformation to Time Framing to Sustainability to Expanded Perception to Discovery to *Transmutation*. Starting with the

mindset that we are exploring *Possibility* (not a "Problem," "Opportunity" or even our "Potential"), we can step into and work with expanded states of *Awareness* to create solutions that are beyond the access of typical approaches to problem solving. The added element of *Transmutation* acknowledges the utilization of the subtler elements of what has been *discovered* along the way, to explore the possibility of how these elements can be combined to create something that is *more than the sum of the parts.*

7. **Common Leadership Statement** may be any version of *"Just because we have never been able to do something before, does not mean that we can't do it now."* Versions of this are actually a little more common out there, with Leaders in highly innovative fields working to push the limits of what is possible. And some of these innovative Leaders are most certainly tapping into certain aspects of this level of Leadership. Have we heard or used any version of this statement lately?

8. **Common outcome of this Leadership approach** is frequently a more astounded team and organization, as those involved accomplish the work in a way that helps them to more directly experience our creative possibilities. Work then, becomes a near boundless creative exploration, along with the many positive impacts of this. Those in a work group or team or organization know that their efforts are actually creating something well beyond the norm of most workplaces. Something that will deeply impact the organization and all of its customers. This Leadership approach tends to establish a work environment where people want to

experience, as much as they can, the amazing results that are possible. This Leadership approach works to foster a real sense of belonging between people and a sense of awe with the results of our efforts. This brings a deep sense of wonder to a Leader.

The Mystic Age Leadership approach cannot be defined, but it can be experienced! Leadership and other higher levels can be difficult to define, since the actions here can be so subtle. Yet the results can be quite amazing, and although most people may not be able to recognize what this Leader is actually *Being* and *Doing*, they can appreciate the experience and the results. When we commit to consistently exploring the unknown, then everything we look at or are involved in as a Leader, appears to us in the context of an emerging possibility. The natural expression of our Leadership then seeks to move ourselves and others into this possibility. And in order to accomplish this, we must first have or develop a deep desire to see and connect with and support others along this challenging journey, and to make a significant difference in our life and the lives of others. And then we must passionately and relentlessly follow our purpose.

The Mystic Age Leadership approach incorporates our *Awareness, Attention, Focus, Intent* and *Love* with our commitment to creating something that is more than the sum of its parts. And through this approach, we support and contribute to others in the process of moving forward to achieve the objectives of a group, team or organization. This Leader has, as a part of our Meta-Mindset, the deep desire to experience possibility, and to present this to others in a way that helps them to unleash their extra-ordinary effort towards this vision.

A group or team in collaboration with a Mystic Age Leader can achieve amazing things together, while they learn and grow and create significant impacts through their interactions. This approach represents an experiential expression of extra-ordinary Leadership and everyone we interact with benefits from this, including ourselves. This Leadership approach also comes from deep within and moves from inside to out. Once this realization and commitment to creating possibility takes hold, then the question of *"How are we going to get there?"* goes away.

This might be a good time for another point of clarification. As I have stated previously, these expressions of Leadership described at each level of Leadership in the AQ Model have most certainly been expressed many times throughout our history, as well as in our present times. One key benefit of the AQ Model, however, is that it supports us as extra-ordinary Leaders with expressing these higher levels of Leadership in a more integrated and purposeful and consistent way. When we more deeply understand the progression of Leadership and how each level supports and builds on the others, and when we are crystal clear in our *Being* and *Doing*, through a refined level of *Awareness, Attention* and *Focus*, we are positioned to more intentionally express our Leadership purpose across all levels of Leadership, in the here and now.

Interestingly, it is somewhat common for even higher-performing Leaders to not be completely clear about their Leadership approach. Some Leaders just more naturally and easily express certain aspects of high-level Leadership or they have been part of the fortunate few who have actually had some extra-ordinary mentorship as a Leader. In either case, it is not uncommon for even higher-performing Leaders to not be clear enough about what they do and how they do it, for their approach to be reproducible in some way by other aspiring Leaders. However, through our explorations and efforts with the AQ Model, we can become crystal clear about *what* we are doing as a Leader, and why we are doing it, and *where* it is intended to take us, and also, *how* we are going to get there! Through this process, our Leadership no longer expresses itself *by accident* or based on the programming we received from another Leader. Through this process, we Lead on purpose! *This is the Leadership Revolution that I am talking about!*

And yet, there is still more available within the possibility of Leadership. More to share with and give to others, our organizations and ourselves. There remain still untapped reserves within ourselves and others, that when understood and unleashed, can bring even further levels of results and even further degrees of growth and satisfaction experienced by those we serve and ourselves. The challenge of an extra-ordinary Leader at this point is with choosing from the endless number of possibilities that surround us, as we move forward with others, into the unknown.

Although a commitment to Leading through manifesting possibility with others can be incredibly impactful and beautiful on this extra-ordinary journey, we can still be left with the clear knowing that there is more available to all of us on our journey as an extra-ordinary Leader. Mystic Age Leadership clearly represents a level of Leadership that our teams and organizations crave on some level. Deep inside, many of us crave to do the impossible in an extra-ordinary way. We collectively sense that there is a way of *Being* and *Doing* that far exceeds the experiences that are so typical of our daily lives. We even see examples of it from time to time, but have not yet been able to establish this as a more consistent experience in our lives.

The Mystic Age Leadership approach serves as an excellent vantage point to more clearly and committedly see and explore even higher levels of Leadership performance. From this level, we can more freely access any of the more positive elements within the first six levels of Leadership while adding to them, even more *Awareness* and understanding with all of the possibilities involved. The Mystic Age Leadership approach further enhances the look and feel and experience and results of those involved. The freedom we experience at this level of Leadership and our ability to help others to access greater levels of freedom for themselves, brings everyone involved into much greater alignment with our shared purpose and passion, as expressed through our work or the task at hand.

At this point we are going to depart temporarily from our standard pattern of first exploring a particular level of Leadership, and then its energetic impediment, and then ending the chapter by discussing the process of up-leveling ourselves and others to the very next level of Leadership. And the reason for this temporary departure is that this next set of up-leveling practices moves us into Part 3 of this book, or from Phase 2 of the Hero's Journey to Phase 3, "The Return." This is another key transition on our Leadership journey, and it is just as significant as was the transition from Phase 1 (The Separation) to Phase 2 (The Initiation) of the Hero's Journey, where we made the very real decision to step out of the status quo of Leadership by doing the work necessary to position and maintain ourselves on the path of an extra-ordinary Leader.

Through our commitment to the exploration and experimentation and work outlined in Part 2 of this book and Phase 2 of the Hero's Journey, we have begun to develop a genuine level of Leadership Mastery. And let's be clear about this term "Mastery." At this level, I am not claiming that we become "Masters of all things Leadership." I am using this term (Mastery) very purposefully to acknowledge the genuine, functional level of expertise, adaptability, agility and effectiveness that we can develop as a Leader though our work with the AQ Model. So, when I use the term "Leadership Mastery," I am referring to the very well-developed, consistent and purposeful expression of our individual Leadership performance that serves others and our organizations well beyond the norm or the status quo of Leadership. And our individual expressions of Leadership Mastery may look somewhat similar or very different, depending on the context and circumstances of our environment.

In this next transition into Part 3 of this book, we move into the exploration of Phase 3 of the Hero's Journey, and onto the last leg of this *extraordinary* Leadership journey, bringing us full circle with our efforts. On this last leg of our journey, we continue to explore, question, learn and grow as a Leader, while we, in a sense, connect back around to where we all started. In Phase 3 of our Leadership Hero's Journey, we begin to take our well-developed, individualized level of Leadership Mastery, and connect it back to the world of the status quo. At this stage of our journey, we step back into the world of the ordinary (status quo) with one foot, while keeping our other foot well planted in the world of the extraordinary. With one foot firmly planted in both worlds, we are now positioned to serve as a "bridge" for others travelling on their own Leadership adventure.

As a more fully initiated Leader at this point, we now move our *Awareness, Attention, Focus, Intent* and *Love* to the task of guiding or supporting Leaders of all levels, while connecting more deeply to where we all began. Otherwise, there is a chance that our ego, that sneaky, sometimes destructive part of ourselves, may at some point begin to whisper in our ear that we are now "The" Master of Leadership. This stance can then pull us away from one of the foundations of our Leadership purpose, which is service to others. So, coming full circle on our Leadership journey brings us back to where we all started, and reconnects us with all of the aspects of our Leadership growth. It connects us back to our own and everyone else's journey of Leadership. This positions us to move even deeper and more thoughtfully into our Leadership purpose, in service to others.

We have covered a significant amount of material by now and journeyed very deeply into extra-ordinary Leadership. We are now faced with the same choice that we have had in the beginning of this book, and at each step and level of our Journey. And that choice is to go back to the safety and security and familiarity of the status quo of Leadership, OR to continue forward on our journey into *extraordinary* Leadership. These choices are completely up to us. So, even though we have covered quite a bit of highly valuable Leadership material and explored and clarified quite a few of the key pieces of the Leadership puzzle, there is still more! And I would be negligent in another aspect of my Leadership purpose if we did not take this exploration *all the way*!

And one more important point related to the amount of material we are exploring: As we continue to explore these higher levels of Leadership and add still more to our journey, we should consider that at these levels, *more is actually less*. As we become *more* of who we really are and less of who we are not, it actually becomes easier to learn and grow and progress and to further express our commitment as an *extraordinary* Leader. At higher levels of Leadership, we step deeper into the flow of life and are carried along and supported by this energy. *More is less, at higher levels of Leadership. There is no work here. There is no struggle here. There is only the constantly emerging experience for us to explore, learn from, and dance with.* At this point on our journey, we can let go of many of the things that have held us back in the past. We can move into better alignment with the flow of our lives, and free up the energy and perspective we need to move our Leadership performance from extra-ordinary to *extraordinary*! It's now time to lighten our load and push on to the summit!

"The Return"

Integrating OUR Experiences and Sharing OUR Leadership Mastery (extraordinary Leadership in action)

Here we are, in Part 3 of this book, in Phase 3 of the Hero's Journey! And what a journey it has been so far! We have come very far at this point, and the BIG, complex puzzle of Leadership should be appearing much clearer to us by now. Part 2 of this book was designed to support our deeper exploration and *initiation* into extra-ordinary Leadership. In Part 2, we explored several key concepts such as "The Importance of Our Leadership Purpose," "The Drama Triangle" and "The Value of Others on our Journey." We also explored and journeyed deeply into five extra-ordinary levels of Leadership: Level 3, The Knowledge Age & Coaching Leadership; Level 4, The Understanding Age & Transformational Leadership; Level 5, The Wisdom Age & Servant Leadership; Level 6, The Transcendent Age & Transcendental Leadership; and Level 7, The Mystic Age & "Leadership." These concepts and levels of Leadership represent the real work and learning and growth required of our extra-ordinary journey of service.

We have explored many of the key aspects of extra-ordinary Leadership while also reviewing some fairly simple but effective approaches for creating very real and positive experiences and impacts for others and our organizations. In addition, our exploration established the foundation for us to more deeply understand this BIG, complex puzzle of extra-ordinary Leadership. And now that we have glimpsed it, and have more of an understanding of what it looks like, feels like and smells like, what do we do next? Well, my hope is that by now we are all feeling the strong pull and hearing the loud call for us to step more firmly on the path of *extraordinary* Leadership, our very best expression of ourselves in service to others and our organizations.

Part 1 of this book was shared for the primary purpose of inviting us all to step out of the status quo of Leadership, in a very real way. Through our explorations and journeys in Part 2 of this book, we were initiated onto the path of the extraordinary Leader, to step firmly and confidently into our unique expression of Leadership Mastery. And now in Part 3 of this book, we are invited to travel full-circle, to complete our journey as an *extraordinary* Leader, and to connect with where we all started. And only we as individuals can make this decision. Nobody can make this decision for us. Yet meanwhile, our teams, our organizations, our communities, our countries and even from within the depths of our own being, we continue to call out in need of something far greater from our Leaders.

In Part 3 of this book, we transition from Phase 2 of the Hero's Journey, *The Initiation*, to Phase 3 of The Hero's Journey, **The Return** (*to where we all started*), where we are continuing to learn and grow and further expand our Leadership perspective and performance, while we also come full-circle, in a sense, to where we all started, to serve as a bridge for others. This next phase of the Hero's Journey requires a clear, individual choice by us as Leaders, and it is a choice that must be continually made, each and every day. And during some of our more challenging days, this choice must consciously occur many times throughout. This is what the commitment to *extraordinary* Leadership and serving as a bridge for others is all about! *This is the Leadership Revolution that I am talking about!*

This book is our personal invitation to leave the ordinary world of Leadership and to go on an extraordinary journey for the benefit of ourselves, our organizations and everyone we interact with. It is also a map to support us on the journey with creating our expression of Leadership as an extraordinary work of art. This book is the invitation and the map, and now it is up to us as to how we proceed.

As we move into Part 3, we will be exploring and mapping out the key elements of extraordinary Leadership, so that we can confidently apply what we are exploring to the realities of our individual experiences, while beginning to develop our approach to sharing our level of Leadership Mastery through our moment-to-moment interactions and performance. Part 3 of this book, this exploration, this journey, is about continuing to courageously move forward in the here and now, with our very real expression of higher levels of Leadership performance.

As we explore these next, even higher levels of Leadership, it may become apparent that these practices are a little less concrete than the previous levels of Leadership. This is to be expected of course, as higher levels of Leadership are definitely subtler in nature, yet they are still quite powerful in their impact. Although these higher levels of Leadership are subtler in nature, they are clearly well grounded in the very real practice and results of Leadership. Make no mistake about it!

CHAPTER 17

Embracing the Totality of Our Leadership Performance

Stepping into and embracing the totality of our Leadership, is the act of an extraordinary Leader in service to others.

We have come so far, and yet there is still more on our extraordinary Leadership journey. The remaining material is extremely valuable in more fully clarifying and rounding out this BIG, complex puzzle of Leadership and the deeper possibilities of our individual Leadership performance. These next three Levels take us even higher and wider and deeper and further on our Leadership journey. I understand that this can feel like a lot to take on at this point on our Leadership journeys. But remember, one of the purposes of this book is to map out and to clarify the major elements of the whole thing, the entire framework of the Leadership context, so that we can better understand and navigate ourselves and others along the length and breadth and depth of its possibilities. And there are no rigid requirements attached to any of this. We are all free, in a sense, to take this in any direction we choose or to take it as far as we choose, and on a time-line that works best for ourselves and others.

So, the map or the BIG, complex puzzle of Leadership, just *is what it is*. My commitment is to reflect it more clearly and completely through the AQ Model, so that we can finally take some real and definitive steps towards elevating our Leadership performance in a way that more genuinely and more consistently serves others and our organizations, as we continue to learn and grow through our Leadership commitment. And there is no easy way or short-cut through this journey. Real, impactful Leadership transformation does not occur from simply reading one of those conveniently short books on the EZ-Steps to Great Leadership. It is a journey of consistent exploration, commitment, work, experimentation, understanding and self-reflection and making mistakes and course correcting and challenge and falling down and getting back up and excitement and sadness and joy and wonder and purpose and *Awareness* and *Attention* and *Focus* and *Intent* and *Love*! Real Leadership is a Hero's Journey!

The purpose of these next three levels of Leadership is to take us even deeper into ourselves as Leaders, so that we can impact those we serve on even deeper levels. They are also designed to support us in Phase 3 of the Hero's Journey, which involves us closing the circle on this journey and serving as a bridge for others, to and from the world of the ordinary and the extraordinary Leader. And again, don't get sidetracked with some of the terms related to these higher levels of Leadership. For some of us, words like "Transcendental" or "Mystic" or "Awakened" or "Integrated" or "Unified" can bring up some type of resistance. Remember, they are simply terms that attempt to reflect some of the key characteristics of these levels. Just dive in deep and explore. The name of the level of Leadership is not nearly as important as the level of understanding, performance and impact that the level is reflecting.

Another point that I would like to bring up at this time is that the AQ Model and its Leadership Levels, although also valuable as a Leadership assessment tool, are NOT meant to be used as some standardized methodology for assessing others in order to place a value judgement on their Leadership, or to pigeon-hole a Leader into one of the levels based on our determination. The assessment aspect of this model is meant to aid us in determining the most productive approach to supporting our own and others' performance and growth, in real time. Our explorations of the levels of Leadership and the recommended up-leveling approaches are meant to be utilized as a supportive methodology for more effectively improving Leadership performance and subsequently, the overall experience of others on our groups and teams and organizations. The AQ Model is not a labeling device, or a tool for Leaders to assert their superiority over others. The AQ Model is a guidebook, a field-guide for Leaders on an extraordinary journey!

It is even more important for us now, as extraordinary Leaders, to stay grounded in what we are actually *Being* and *Doing* and why we are *Being* it and *Doing* it and where this *Being* and *Doing* is intended to take us and those we serve, and also, how our *Being* and *Doing* is going to get us there. Otherwise, there is a chance that our extremely tricky egos may sneak in to attempt to hijack our Leadership Purpose back into a less productive expression and experience for others. That is not the purpose of this work.

The AQ Model is also not a "stick" or a "push strategy." It is primarily a "carrot" or a "pull strategy." It is a powerful, highly effective methodology for inviting and *pulling* ourselves and others into higher levels of performance, in real time. The approaches in the AQ Model also have a gravity to them that is hard to resist. And to be clear, this does not mean that as an extraordinary Leader, we may not have to have some "crucial conversations" with others from time to time, and to do some nudging in certain areas. These types of conversations and follow-up actions can still be a necessary part of the workplace reality for our groups, teams and organizations. A pull strategy does not mean weak or passive or irresponsible or ineffective in our Leadership. This type of pull strategy is quite the opposite. When done well, it is extremely efficient and effective with supporting the forward movement of people and objectives, while creating the opportunity for adding so much more to this experience.

In Part 3 of this book, we will explore the remaining levels of Leadership in the AQ Model, along with a few other important pieces of the puzzle. This is where we begin to step into and embrace the totality of our Leadership performance. This last section closes the circle in our extraordinary Leadership journey and connects our purpose and performance back to where it all started. Embracing the totality of our Leadership performance simultaneously connects us to all points along the Leadership journey. From this perspective, we are now in a position to express our Leadership purpose even more thoughtfully and more purposefully and more gracefully and more consistently and more naturally.

Stepping into and embracing the totality of our Leadership is the act of an extraordinary Leader in service to others. It leverages our entire Leadership journey, all of our experiences, learnings and growth, and brings them to bear on our moment-to-moment actions and interactions. It is an expression of true freedom, and an expression of our true purpose. It takes us far beyond Leadership approaches like "Management by Objective" and far beyond most approaches to Leadership that focus solely on strategic goals and objectives and budgets and profit margins. Stepping into the totality of our Leadership in this part of our Leadership journey includes all of these things and so much more! And at its core, it has one primary focus. And that is our service to others. *The journey of an extraordinary Leader is all about giving everything we have, in service to others. And in giving everything we have, we receive everything we need!* And the further growth we explore in Part 3 allows us to give even more! This is why we are here. *This is the Leadership Revolution that I am talking about!*

Let's now pick up where we left off in Chapter 16. There, we explored the fundamentals of Level 7, Mystic Age "Leadership" and explored the Predominant Leadership Characteristics of Level 7, but we held off on the exploration of the energetic impediment and up-leveling processes until we clarified some of the key elements of our transition here, into Part 3 or Phase 3 of the Hero's Journey. It is time to address the energetic impediment that can hold us back in level 7, and Phase 2 of the Hero's Journey, so that we can more easily move to the next Level of Leadership, Level 8, Awakened Leadership, and Phase 3 of the Hero's Journey.

Hear the alarm clock? It's time to wake up!

7th Level Energetic Impediment (to move beyond Level 7, Mystic Age "Leadership"):

Release the attachment *to expressing our life (our Being and Doing) as less than the extraordinary human being we are.* This is another one of the biggies, as far as attachments go. This one is very common, and also runs very deep in our programming. It too, has been the subject of numerous philosophical, religious and spiritual writings and discussions throughout history. Are we not good enough or do we not deserve to experience the best vision and version of ourselves? Are we unworthy of all that is possible for us? Or, are we extraordinary human beings, capable of creating a much better experience for ourselves and others? Much of the literature and TV, and much of our social programing emphasizes our inadequacies and our weaknesses and our frailty and our negativity and our unworthiness, etc. So, it should be of no surprise, that all of this programing impacts us as deeply as it does.

This programming has numerous and deep impacts on so many of our interactions with each other and our planet. Think about it! This perspective impacts us all very deeply, and so many of our challenges in society and in life, stem from some version of this issue. Are we inadequate or less than? Or, are we full of potential and possibility, capable of so much more? What are some of the results of believing or viewing ourselves from the perspective of *Being* inadequate. As in "I am not smart enough or skilled enough or good enough," etc.

We don't have to try too hard to imagine what some of the results of this "less than" Mindset could be. We all probably have the better part of a lifetime of experience with this Mindset, on some level. And as a result, we have created so much unnecessary fear and drama and waste and unmet potential and so much more. And how does a "less than" mentality impact us and everyone else in our workplaces. How does a "less than" mentality impact our workplace interactions and results? A "less than" Mindset causes us to default away from our potential, and what is possible for us. A "less than" Mindset can cause us to hold back to some degree with our very best effort. A "less than" Mindset can also spread across a group or team or organization, thus multiplying this dysfunctional perspective and compounding the sub-optimal results. A "less than" Mindset strangles or stifles our passion and purpose.

Now, let's consider the opposite perspective: that we are *extraordinary Beings*, capable of so much more. Really, so much more! I am not saying here that we can do anything we envision. We all have certain capabilities and limitations that impact the boundaries of what is possible for us. We are not talking about pretending to be able to defy the laws of gravity and that kind of thing. What we are talking about here is our very real ability to grow and improve in just about any area of our lives that we commit to. In some of these areas we may only be able to improve minimally, but, in other areas, we are capable of growing and performing in extraordinary ways!

Many of the limitations we have experienced in life have been self-imposed by us! We can, in many cases, however, move far beyond our preconceived limitations and the opinions of others. We are extraordinary *Beings*, capable of so much more! And from this perspective, we are positioned to more gracefully strive for our best efforts as a Leader, in service to others. We are also positioned to provide even better support, and to pull out the very best in others, because we so genuinely perceive others as extraordinary *Beings*. When we see ourselves and others as extraordinary *Beings*, so much more becomes possible. This very real and verifiable belief in ourselves and others has the potential to radically transform our performance and results. There are so many incredible stories out there of people overcoming incredible challenges and attaining high levels of performance. We have all seen these stories, and we may even know such a person. We may even *Be* one of these people.

We could continue with this exploration, as so many writings have already done, but now I would like to move further forward and get to the real point of exploring this attachment. The attachment to expressing our lives (our *Being* and *Doing*) as less than the extraordinary *Human Beings* we are, has a significantly negative impact on our relationships, interactions, collaborations and many of our key efforts as Leaders. And once again, I can't say this any other way. We don't have the time anymore to dance around or justify concepts that are clearly limiting our experience and results. It is time for us on our extraordinary Leadership journey to take on another significant attachment. It is time to get clear about the fact that we are *extraordinary Beings*. And we must come to know this reality on a personal level, experientially, not just through the logic of the five senses or based on someone else's opinion, including my opinion.

In order to get to this level of clarity about this attachment, we may have to do some work: Some serious but interesting research and some deeper internal work. Yes, I know, this keeps getting even more fun and inspiring! That is what extraordinary Leadership is all about! But at this point, we should definitely be up for this level of work, as it is no longer "work" for us in the more traditional use of the word. This is simply why we are here and we joyfully jump into explorations such as this. So, to begin to release this attachment to perceiving ourselves and others as "less than" the extraordinary *Human Beings* that we are, we must look directly at it, and explore it, and contemplate it, and think about it, and NOT think about it, and try to get a feel for it. It definitely has a feeling to it. If we immerse ourselves in it, we will typically perceive something. And based on that something, we can begin to develop more experientially-based conclusions and perspectives and actions.

By working to release our attachments, we position ourselves to see and experience other possibilities, and to move through life and the challenges of Leadership a little more gracefully, and to support our teams with more flexibility and agility. Attachments lock us in to a specific perspective. Releasing attachments opens us up to additional possibilities. This should be crystal clear to us by now.

This tendency or attachment to the "less than" Mindset can create significant limitations to our true possibility as a Leader. Therefore, we must address this here and now. As an extraordinary Leader, through our passion and clarity of purpose, we can understand the programming around the "less than" perspective, and continually look both inwardly and outwardly to purposefully connect with and contribute to our extraordinary nature. This is part of our deeper role as a Leader.

As an extraordinary Leader, it is time to work through our programming around this issue and to brave any resistance or ridicule that may come as a result of actively moving beyond the status quo. For on the other side of our questioning of the status quo, lies our freedom as a Leader to express what is really most important to us and to others. That is why we are here.

So, once again, the first step in moving ourselves beyond this limited perspective is to become Aware of it, either on our own, through fearless self-reflection, or through the honest feedback from others, or by placing some level of provisional trust in another who is also committed to the journey of extraordinary Leadership. There are others out there like us. We should continually seek each other out and share our perspectives and experiences to help to bolster our journeys, as we actively commit to replacing our more limited perspectives and habits and adopting a way of *Being* and *Doing* that is more expanded and supportive of others, our organizations and ourselves. And what could we replace this illusion of separation with?

Develop the ability *to deeply connect with and express the totality of our Leadership purpose to further inspire our Leadership* *journeys*. The process and experience of connecting with the totality of our Leadership purpose is an ongoing progression in that the more we *Be* it and *Do* it, the more real it gets and the more impact it has on so many levels. But this must be experienced by us for it to be real.

And yet, there is no overly complex, sanctioned process for accomplishing this. We simply add to our expanding expression of our Leadership performance, the consistent practice of deeply connecting with and expressing more and more of our Leadership purpose. We can more deeply connect with and express our Leadership purpose by consistently focusing on our Leadership purpose, and by acting from there. When we do this over time, and not that much time, we can find ourselves even more clear and even more grounded in our Leadership purpose. And acting from this level of clarity becomes easier and more natural. Through this level of *Being* and *Doing*, we actually become more of who we really are. This is one of the reasons it becomes easier for us to act from this place. It is actually much harder for us to be who we are not, to act out someone else's role, someone else's script. *Being* and *Doing* who we really are is easy and natural and graceful and fun and serves others in much more expanded ways.

I am not talking here about *Being* and *Doing* "who we think we are." I am talking about *Being* and *Doing* "who we really are!" There can be a big difference between the two. Many Leaders talk about how they are "just being themselves" or "just being real," when, in many cases, nothing could be further from this truth. Many of us are more accurately, just acting out our programing related to who we think we are. In these circumstances, we are typically not even aware of our programing and we mistake our programing for who we think we are. This is an understandable mistake, but a costly one. *Being* and *Doing* who we really are, emerges out of our ongoing commitment to our Leadership purpose, while immersed in the exploration and progression of our extraordinary Leadership journey. It flows almost effortlessly out of this experience.

Developing the ability to deeply connect with and express the totality of our Leadership purpose most certainly inspires our Leadership journeys in a profound way. By grounding ourselves in this perspective, we can actually see and experience our extraordinary nature and that of others. This is not about fueling our own ego. This is not about making some arbitrary choice to focus on acting one way versus another way, because we read that it would make us a better Leader. This is about consistently accessing and expressing the deeper and very real, extraordinary nature of ourselves, and looking for it and connecting with it in others. This is real! And we can all verify this for ourselves. All it takes is a genuine, ongoing commitment to extraordinary Leadership, and a good map to support us along the way.

We can use the AQ Model as a guide for our Leadership journey and explore away! It is our personal explorations and what we discover along the way that is most important for us and those we serve. This is where the real learning and growth occurs. This book, this map, is simply a *Tool Set*, a collection of information. Only when we use it and work with it to develop more productive Leadership *Skill Sets*, through the clarity of our *Mindset* (*Attention*), based in our *Awareness* (*Meta-Mindset*), do we experience real *Transformation* and real *Wisdom* and real *Transcendence* and real "*Leadership*," and a real *Awakening*. This is the Leadership Revolution that I am talking about!

We don't need to create this as a separate step, in addition to all that we are already doing as a Leader. At this point in our growth, we are better able to layer activities like this over the things we are already doing. We can do these things at this point, simultaneously and very efficiently, through the ongoing expansion of our *Awareness*, and the concentration of our *Attention* and the refinement of our *Focus* and the connection with our *Intent*, within the context of our *Love* for serving others. Through this process, we as extraordinary Leaders on a Hero's Journey, in service to others, can develop exceptional abilities related to our Leadership understanding and performance on multiple levels.

There could be many other impediments or obstacles preventing a Leader from moving beyond Mystic Age Leadership; however, the tendency to deny or shy away from our extraordinary nature is at the root of this issue. When we understand and accept that we are all truly incredible beings, we are in a position to share this truth with others, to support them in providing their best effort. It will take some level of *Awareness* and acknowledgement of this issue and then a commitment to continued growth, for a Leader to see their further potential and the further potential of their team. A Leader can be helped and supported through this growth, and there are many approaches for this but, ultimately, each of us must decide for ourselves to grow further.

As we begin to transition our exploration into the last three levels of Leadership in the AQ Model, it is important to point out that although there are a number of Leaders out there who are presently performing at these higher levels, they are still too few and far between. And the pathways into these levels of Leadership are rarely understood and even more rarely mapped out. So, let's bring some real clarity to these higher levels of Leadership, as we discover how even mere mortals like us can access and perform at these levels.

Let's move into the process of up-leveling ourselves and others from Level 7 (Mystic Age, Leadership) to Level 8 (Awakened

Leadership) as we step even further into our ability to serve others and our organizations, exceptionally. Each set of up-leveling approaches obviously contains both *Being* elements and *Doing* elements but the leaning thus far in our up-leveling approaches has been on *Doing*. At these higher levels of Leadership, that leaning or focus begins to shift towards our *Being*. Remember, we are typically involved simultaneously with both our *Being* and *Doing* on some level, and they are equally important. That is why I am using the term, "leaning." At this point and going forward, there is just a little more emphasis on our *Being*, while we are also *Doing*. The journey of the *extraordinary* Leader involves lots of *Being*. We can read every concept in this book or any other book, and understand these completely, but if we don't step more fully into our *Being*, very purposefully, then all we have accomplished is the gathering of more information and techniques.

Up-leveling from Level 7, Mystic Age, "Leadership," to Level 8, Awakened Leadership:

Up-leveling Ourselves:

Step 1 – Actively look for and identify other passionate Leaders and purposefully engage them in the *Leadership conversation*. This refers to our developing the habit of constantly scanning our environment for others that display or express a passion, or potential passion, for Leadership in its many forms. This is not the same thing as assessing others for their "Leadership Potential." This is also not meant to serve as a formal Leadership Succession program. What I am referring to here, is developing our eyes and ears and heart to the point where we can more deeply perceive other's passion for Leading in the broader sense, whether this is related to Leading themselves or in the more formal roles of Leading others. Various forms of Leadership are happening everywhere, and at this level, as an extraordinary Leader, our focus includes seeking out and identifying others' desire to move forward (our operating definition for Leadership) in any form and reaching out to them and connecting with their Leadership passion to grow and channel this in service to others.

Before we explore further, let's clarify the meaning of the term Leadership "passion." Leadership passion refers to the deep desire to explore, understand and apply ourselves to the path of serving others through Leadership. This passion comes out of and grows as a result of our experience in Leading from a more expanded and connected perspective. Leadership passion expresses itself as a deep appreciation for the privilege of serving others, and for the opportunity to more purposefully learn and grow and contribute to life. *It is our passion that transforms the work of Leadership into the joy of Leadership.*

So, in this up-leveling step, we are essentially developing and deploying our Leadership antenna, so that we can see or hear or feel or pick up on even the subtlest signs of Leadership passion. And as stated previously, nothing is 100%. Sometimes our Leadership antenna correctly identifies a passion for Leadership, while other times, upon further exploration, it turns out to be a "false-positive." Yet, even in this case, we just may be in the process of "planting seeds" for future Leadership. So, this is not an exact science. It is more art than anything. But the point is, as extraordinary Leaders, we are out there, constantly scanning the environment and purposefully engaging with other inspired Leaders, to serve by growing our group or team or family of Leaders. This is just one of the ways we give to and support others on our journeys.

And the next logical question might be, what does another's passion for Leadership look like and sound like and feel like? How do we recognize this? Well, on one level, and at this point, many times we just know. We just know Leadership passion when we see it, hear it or feel it. But if we were to tease out some of the expressions of Leadership passion, how might they show up? Let's explore this issue by first exploring how Leadership passion shows up in ourselves.

By now, we should be able to recognize even the subtlest signs of Leadership passion within ourselves. We should be clear about that feeling that we have inside, that feeling of excitement and wonder and purpose and commitment and joy, even when we are involved in challenging Leadership situations. We should be able to recognize the excitement in our voice as we collaborate with and support others during an effort. We should be able to identify with that little bounce in our step as we move into a challenge. Our Leadership passion can show up like any version of these examples, and more!

It is important to realize that as some of these signs show up in others, they might be extremely subtle, while other signs may be quite overt and easier to pick up on. Anyway, Leadership passion can show up in others much like it shows up in ourselves, as well as in ways that are not part of our experience. It can actually be quite interesting to pick up on someone else's Leadership passion, when their expression of this is different than what we are accustomed to experiencing within ourselves. Leadership passion has a diversity to it and it can show up in many ways. But once we know it and are clear about it within ourselves, we are in a better position to more readily recognize it in others, no matter in what form it expresses itself.

And once we perceive this passion for Leadership in another, our responsibility, our calling at this level, is to reach out and connect with these others and purposefully engage with them in the Leadership conversation. Now, notice that the up-leveling approach here is not broken up in two separate steps, such as step 1, recognize Leadership passion in others, and then step 2, reach out and purposefully engage with others in the Leadership conversation. There is no gap here between these two actions. In this up-leveling step, we recognize AND reach out to connect through the Leadership conversation. This is one movement or one act. We don't recognize, and then think about and analyze what we think we might have recognized, and then think about creating some sort of method to illuminate the secrets of Leadership to another. It is not that complicated. We simply recognize and connect with what we recognize. And we do this through the Leadership conversation.

Now let's explore the Leadership conversation. This conversation can occur in many different ways and on many different levels. The Leadership conversation is not some scripting approach, where if we notice someone who is passionate about Leadership, we step in and say X, Y and Z. The Leadership conversation is a way and a process of connecting with and engaging with someone for the purpose of sharing and exploring our passion for Leadership. This can be accomplished through a very casual and informal dialogue with someone, or through a more formal, structured approach. And it can also evolve in either direction. The Leadership conversation is also not limited to just the words we are using. As with any other conversation we have, much can be communicated through our body language, tone of voice and our attitude or mindset. This is where we bring everything, our entire Leadership purpose and commitment to the conversation.

This Leadership conversation is as fun as it gets for an extraordinary Leader! And the interesting thing is that, over time, we might begin to perceive some level of Leadership passion in pretty much everyone. At this point, nearly every discussion we are involved in is transformed into some form of a Leadership conversation, where our *Awareness, Attention* and *Focus, Intent* and *Love* and our Leadership antenna are operating at a very high level. We become extremely perceptive in engaging with others in a way that further supports our passion for Leadership. As an extraordinary Leader, we are here to serve and support others, and one of the most beneficial ways that we can do this is through our connection and encouragement and support of others on their Leadership journey, whether they know that they are on one or not.

So, up-leveling ourselves from level 7 to level 8 Leadership involves the combined actions of recognizing other's passion for Leadership AND reaching out to connect with them through the Leadership conversation, to focus and channel our desire to serve. This is one movement or one act. This act of *Doing* depends more on our *Being*, which is even more important with the higher levels of Leadership. This is mostly an internal maneuver, an act of *Being*, that can move powerfully from the inside to the outside as we *Do* this step.

We don't have to analyze this step any further before we just *Do* it. At this point, just apply some provisional trust to the process and to ourselves. If we have made it this far on our extraordinary Leadership journey and have experienced some positive results, then let's keep going. If we just *Be* and *Do* our best version of the up-leveling practices, we will continue to learn and grow as a Leader. We can become our own expression of the deeper possibilities of Leadership, once we understand the map or the puzzle a little better, and purposefully apply ourselves to it. That is why we are here. This is our work. *This is the Leadership Revolution that I am talking about!*

Up-leveling Others:

Step 1 – Encourage and support Leaders in identifying the Leadership passion in others and engaging them in the *Leadership conversation.* So, very similarly, as in the process of up-leveling ourselves, we are supporting and encouraging other Leaders who are on a similar journey as we, to develop the habit of constantly scanning their environment for people that display or express a passion or potential passion for Leadership in its many forms. In this step, we are supporting others with developing their eyes and ears and heart to the point where they can more deeply perceive others' passion for Leadership. Here, we are helping other committed Leaders to develop their Leadership antennas, so that they can also see or hear or feel or pick up on even the subtlest signs of inspired Leadership. Supporting others' development in this area exponentially increases the number of people out there involved in the Leadership conversation.

In order to encourage and support others with developing their Leadership antennae, we must first develop this to a degree in ourselves, and then share our explorations in this area with others. We can share what we have seen and heard and felt when scanning the environment for other passionate Leaders. We can share some of the Leadership conversations that we have had, and the results. We can talk about the importance of this activity, about how our groups and teams and organizations and communities and countries need, more than ever, higher performing Leadership. We can discuss our responsibility as extraordinary Leaders with sharing our Leadership purpose with others to expand and leverage the results of our growing group effort. We can genuinely speak about the joy and fun of connecting with other inspired Leaders, to share our challenging and rewarding journeys.

In this step of up-leveling others, we are essentially having a Leadership conversation about the Leadership conversation, with other *extra-ordinary* Leaders. Yes, we are having a multi-level Leadership conversation here, through the expression of our purpose and commitment at this level of Leadership. We are continuing to layer real and valuable Leadership *Being*s and *Doing*s into our expression of extraordinary Leadership. We are growing in our ability to work very purposefully and very effectively on multiple levels, simultaneously. At this point as a Leader, we are like the conductor of an orchestra, who skillfully layers in the musical elements of a composition to create a moving and memorable experience, a "masterpiece" of music, for the audience as well as the musicians.

So, through a Leadership conversation with other *extra-ordinary* Leaders about the Leadership conversation, we can help them to understand and point them towards their responsibility with this valuable and rewarding activity. We can also ask them if there is anyone in their circle who displays signs of Leadership passion. We can ask them how they might engage with this person and what they may say. We can ask them to follow up with us and let us know how things went. We can help to create some momentum and engagement around this activity. And once other extra-ordinary Leaders begin to engage in this way with even greater numbers of Leaders, we become part of the purposeful perpetuation and exponential growth of quite possibly one of the most important and needed contributions to society that we could be a part of. And that is the significant up-leveling of Leadership understanding and performance, in service to our groups, teams, organizations, communities, countries and the global community.

Let's explore an important and related topic here. The whole planet needs us now! Look around! Watch the news, if you can! Just read from the many sources of information out there! There are so many problems out there, while so many people, and pundits, and other experts continue to debate the various reasons and possible solutions for all of these problems. And yet, for some reason, most people continue to completely miss the root cause of many of our ongoing issues and, therefore, their solutions also miss the mark. They continue to focus on the symptoms and not the cause. They continue to blame ideas or plans or policies or actions. They continue to blame this person and that person, while that person blames them. This is not a process or personality issue! This is a Leadership issue! Ideas will not save us, although good ideas can certainly be helpful. Plans will not save us, yet a good plan can help to take us in a more productive direction. Policies will not save us either. And action in and of itself, will not save us.

If we were to do a more thoughtful root cause analysis with many of these issues we face, we might finally be able to see and understand the real issue at hand. And the real issue is Leadership! To be more specific, I am referring to Leadership performance that lacks the appropriate level of *Awareness*, *Attention* and *Focus* necessary to better support others with cultivating more thoughtful ideas; to better support others with developing more effective, customized plans; to engage others in the more purposeful, detailed work necessary to craft even more relevant policies; but most importantly, to genuinely connect with others and to inspire the energy, commitment and purpose of others to engage in even more productive, collaborative action. There is a vacuum of high-level Leadership out there! I didn't make this up. Look around. Do some research. This should be clear to us by now.

As a result of all this, we continue to get sidetracked with trying to address the symptoms of this issue and not the cause.

We have turned our discussions about Leadership into circu-
itous debates about individual personalities and their resultant
actions. Leadership is not a personality contest! Leadership
is also not a popularity contest, although too many Leaders
are put into their positions because of this. We say, "well, this
Leader does things like this, and this other Leader does things
like that, and that's what created the problem." This type of
dialogue completely misses the point of Leadership! Leadership is not simply about personalities or popularity or doing
this or that.

Our personalities are not Leadership. Our personalities
are simply our personalities. Our popularity is not Leadership.
And doing this or that to address a problem is not Leadership
either. Our personalities and popularity and doing this or that
can contribute to, or detract from, our Leadership approach,
but Leadership is much bigger than all of this. Leadership is
BIG, and complex, and it unfolds along a continuum or a progression, as we have been exploring. Leadership is a process of
thoughtful, purposeful and aligned *Being* and *Doing* that seeks
to genuinely serve others while moving things forward. But since
most people do not really understand this, because much of the
Leadership material out there does not speak more directly to
the reality of genuine Leadership, this is all we have. This is all
we have access to. And this has been a disservice to us all.

As an example, watch two Leaders in debate. Watch two
Leaders in discussion over a challenging situation. How often
do we see or hear real displays of higher levels of Leadership
understanding? What we usually see and hear, are various
expressions of Level 1 Leadership, or even lower. Yes, there are
even lower levels of Leadership than Level 1! Anyway, at best,
we may also see and hear some Level 2 Leadership mixed in
there, from time to time. All we usually see are various attempts

to control or outmaneuver the other party, or various attempts at proving how right one person or group or party is versus the other. This is the status quo of Leadership, playing itself out each and every day, over and over again!

And the commentary around these displays does not usually help to advance our understanding around this issue either. The commentary usually ends up simply highlighting or praising or criticizing certain aspects of these attempts at Leadership. Meanwhile, the same problems continue to show up, while the same types of personalities continue to step forward as Leaders to take a shot at them, and then the same commentaries recycle themselves once again. Our whole understanding, our whole dialogue, our whole conversation around Leadership needs to be up-leveled if we are to contribute in a more productive way to the Leadership Revolution we have been exploring. And to then position our groups and teams and organizations and communities and governments and nations to finally be able to more effectively address the issues we all face together.

And now to the point. This is why the Leadership conversation that we have been exploring here is so important. The Leadership conversation represents the conduit for our sharing and expressing the deeper realities of Leadership, in a way that others can begin to finally get this thing. So that others can finally see what Leadership really is and also what it isn't. So that others can understand what real Leadership looks like, and feels like, and smells like. Too much of what we see and experience out there has very little to do with higher levels of Leadership, the levels of Leadership that are needed for the complexities we face together. And the surrounding commentary around all of this is equally as unproductive. And even when someone does rightfully conclude that maybe there is some problem with the actual Leadership going on, they are typically unable to articulate an effective approach regarding what to do about it, and then they are eventually shouted down and pulled back into lower-level, non-productive conversations regarding Leadership.

So, this whole issue of the lack of higher-level Leadership performance out there and the lack of understanding of the continuum or progression of real Leadership is at the root of so many of the problems we continue to face, and this gets perpetuated through our organizations, communities and countries. This has been and is, a MASSIVE problem! And simultaneously, it has been and is an incredible opportunity for us as extraordinary Leaders to create another possibility while in service to others.

We now have an effective map of Leadership. We now have the key pieces of the puzzle AND the puzzle box with the picture of Leadership right on it, so that we now know what genuine Leadership looks like and feels like and smells like. Regarding so many of the problems we face, the root cause of the issue is, very often, inadequate Leadership. Therefore, the solution is . . . extraordinary Leadership! And through our ongoing commitment and expression of extraordinary Leadership and through our Leadership conversations, we can begin to pull others into a more expanded perspective and experience of what real Leadership is. We can now be a part of the up-leveling of the entire field of Leadership practice itself! We are truly on an extraordinary Leadership journey, truly on a Hero's Journey. *This is the Leadership Revolution that I am talking about!*

Now back to our up-leveling exploration. Performing this up-leveling step of engaging other inspired Leaders in the Leadership conversation, automatically up-levels us beyond the Level 7, Energetic Impediment, and into the next level of Leadership, and deepens everyone's *Awareness* and understanding regarding some of the deeper responsibilities and impacts of our Leadership. And this step multiplies the deeper Leadership purpose that many of us share across teams and organizations and communities and industries and cultures. This up-leveling step automatically moves us into higher levels of Leadership performance while creating higher-level experiences and higher levels of performance for those we interact with, in real time! That's just how it works! Just *Be* and *Do* and repeat and repeat. This is a thread of simplicity that runs through the AQ Model. Just *Be* and *Do*. And these additional processes and dialogues do not have to add significant amounts of time to the overall process, once we jump fully into it.

So now, it's time to step more fully into our responsibility as extraordinary Leaders and serve others by supporting their growth through the gift of up-leveling. And once we have moved ourselves and then others beyond the more limited mindsets of Levels 1, 2, 3 and even Levels 4, 5, 6 and 7, there can be much more ease and growth and impactful results achieved through working with greater levels of *Awareness* within the challenges we all face. As a reminder, however, even under the best of circumstances, nothing is 100% as expected. We may need to finesse these approaches and tailor them for a specific person or situation, and we may need to repeat it multiple times to achieve the desired or needed impact. But more times than not, we can improve Leadership performance, the performance of others and everyone's overall experience in the workplace, consistently and in real time, especially when we have done our work first.

Everyone deserves an opportunity to step further into a level of Leadership performance that serves others more completely, as well as themselves. Everyone working with a Leader deserves the opportunity to work and contribute within an environment that inspires them towards their best effort and expression of their purpose. Let's do our part as an extraordinary Leader to give everyone a real chance for this, here and now. Let's help them and support them, the very best that we can, as our very best continues to expand.

At this point, I hope we can all feel the energy, and the mass, and the momentum of our explorations, as they continue to build. This extraordinary Leadership journey we are on together, definitely has an energy, and mass and momentum to it that can help to carry us confidently forward on the next step of our journeys. Let it now carry us forward.

	Predominant Leadership Characteristics	**Up-Leveling Ourselves**	**Up-Leveling Others**
Level 7 Leadership Age & Approach		the thoughtful and purposeful process of improving our performance through an ongoing commitment to growing our awareness, attention and focus	helping others to improve their performance "*in real time*," based on your growing awareness and your commitment to supportive, purposeful coaching
Mystic **Age:** "Leadership"	1. **Leadership through the Facilitation of Direct Experience** – typically based on all the above, and on the alchemy of possibility from the seemingly impossible. 2. Grounded predominantly in extra-ordinary reality (expanded awareness). 3. Uses *Transcendence* as a springboard into the unknown (the mystery), to then return and to make it known. 4. Is Possible – Future Oriented 5. Focused on functioning with extreme agility within and across all Leadership Levels, and with clarity of awareness, attention, focus, and intent, purpose and love. 6. Problem Solving Method – Moves from "Possibility" to "Research" to "Customization" to "P&P Integration" to "Transformation" to "Time Framing" to "Sustainability" to "Expanded Perception" to "Discovery" to "*Transmutation*." 7. Common Quote – "*Just because we have never been able to do something before, does not mean that we can't do it now.*" 8. Common Outcomes – *Work* becomes a near boundless creative exploration, along with the many positive impacts of this.	Moving from Level 7 to Level 8: 1. Actively look for and identify the leadership passion in others and purposefully engage with them in the "*Leadership conversation.*"	Moving from Level 7 to Level 8: 1. Encourage and support others in identifying the Leadership passion in others while engaging them in the "*Leadership conversation.*"

7th Level Energetic Impediment – Release the attachment to expressing our life (our Being & Doing) as less than the extraordinary human being we are. Develop the ability to deeply connect with and express the totality of our Leadership purpose, to further inspire our Leadership journeys.

Figure 11. Level 7 Leadership

CHAPTER 18

Level 8 Leadership
The Awakened Age &
Awakened Leadership

Leadership through Leading Leaders . . .

Leadership Age: *Awakened Age*

The 8th Level of Leadership illuminated in the AQ Model represents the functional progression of an even more thoughtful and purposeful application of individual experience (Industrial Age), information and data gathering (Information Age), customization (Knowledge Age), the connection of people's passion and purpose with work systems and processes (Understanding Age), balance and sustainability (Wisdom Age), more direct insight (Transcendent Age), the alchemy of possibility from the seemingly impossible (Mystic Age), through the use of Leadership as a path to Awakening (Awakened Age). That's the progression here, so far. The Awakened Age raises the potential of creating experiences for our teams, our customers, our organizations and ourselves that reach even further beyond the norm of our typical workplaces.

The distinctive theme of the Awakened Age involves a focus on thoughtfully and purposefully Leading Leaders, and this is achieved through the commitment to our growth and learning through Leadership as a path to Awakening. This level of exploration can lead to still deeper levels of understanding, appreciation and application with the actions of our Leadership. This deep level of work can lead to more direct and valuable insights related to our Leadership performance and can support us with determining the best course of action in the moment.

The term "Awakening" has been around for thousands of years and can mean different things to different people. So, let's clarify our terms here. In this context, the term Awakening refers to the ongoing experience of our deepening perception and with gaining deeper insights into ourselves, others and our surroundings. Awakening further into these areas of our lives can help us to be of even greater service to others and to our organizations. The word Awakening is meant to point us even more deeply towards our Leadership responsibility. The Awakened Ones of the past and present represent those who have committed to the deeper internal work necessary to see and understand and appreciate ourselves, and therefore others and our surroundings. The Awakened, in this case, represent those with a significant depth of clarity related to the deeper purpose and functions of Leadership. This allows us to express and to articulate the complexities of Leadership with more ease, to make the more challenging concepts, principles and practices accessible to so many more.

Leadership Approach: *Awakened Leadership*

There are many paths to Awakening to the deeper truths of ourselves and our surroundings. And a committed journey on the path of genuine Leadership is one of them. And I say this because it is true! The path of Leadership includes many of the key elements that one finds on any other path that is genuinely focused on our deep personal growth. The path of extraordinary Leadership includes the requirement of ongoing, deep self-reflection, purposeful observation, inspired commitment to learning and growth, the reality-based validation of experiences, a deep respect, appreciation and compassion for others, a sense of awe and wonder for life and our place in it, a dedication to serving others working through life's challenges, and so much more. Real Leadership is not about bossing others around, and not about making more money. Real Leadership is a deep and never-ending path of service and inspired growth. It is about *Connection* and *Movement*. It is *Love in Action*! It is a genuine path to deeper Awakening!

What we do at this level of Awakened Leadership, and how we do it, is framed by this genuine desire or impulse to perceive and to engage directly with the Leadership passion of others, to more effectively serve. And this genuine desire to more effectively serve is fueled by our own passion and growing experience in extraordinary Leadership. Our Leadership passion seeks out the Leadership passion of others, to connect with and to inspire. Leaders at this level endeavor to connect with and to support others in a way that brings out our best effort and our best performance and our best version of ourselves, as we more deeply explore and envision and manifest our potential together.

In this type of Leadership environment, we have the potential to more fully express the best parts of ourselves, individually and as a team. As a Leader at this level, we are positioned to very thoughtfully and consistently express the depth of our purpose, passion, and transformative nature through our interactions with others, especially during times of significant challenge. At this level of Leadership, we seek to explore beyond the normal boundaries, parameters or paradigms of the workplace, helping to create extraordinary experiences for others and our organizations. At this point, the journey itself provides all of the inspiration we need to fuel our ongoing commitment and effort. At this point on our extraordinary journey, books and other forms of information become secondary to our very real and grounded experience as a Leader in service to others.

Leadership Levels 1 and 2 are more transactional in nature and often based on a Leader's expression of their dominance over others; Levels 3 and 4 tend to be focused on the motivation and inspiration of others to create personal, group and organizational transformation; Level 5 seeks to create and support a more lasting and sustainable transformation as we continually monitor and adjust to the ever changing internal and external environment; Level 6 seeks the deeper level of insight needed to explore and approach our potential; Level 7 focuses on working directly with the subtle elements of ourselves and the environment to help us create possibility out of the seemingly impossible; while Level 8 (Awakened Leadership) focuses our unfolding Leadership experience on the Leadership growth of others, to rouse them to their potential in service to others.

The up-leveling approaches that we performed in the previous level of Leadership automatically serve to usher us into this present level. However, in order to remain or ground ourselves here, we must begin to practice and to embody and express the Predominant Leadership Characteristics below.

Predominant Leadership Characteristics: *Awakened Leadership*

1. **Leadership through Leading Leaders** is typically based on all of the previous levels of Leadership and on *rousing Leaders to their purpose, potential and responsibility, through the commitment to Leadership as a path to awakening.* At this level, we focus our commitment on purposefully seeking out other Leaders who have also *shown up*, to support their further awakening to the real possibility of Leadership and their real possibility as Leaders and human beings.

2. **Grounded predominantly in** the commitment to growth, learning and awakening through the path of Leadership service. When Leadership is truly recognized and experienced as an effective, valuable and beautiful path to learning and growth, that brings significant benefits to the workplace and all other aspects of life, then it (Awakened Leadership) becomes the self-perpetuating, near continual state of our *Being* and *Doing*.

3. *Uses Mysticism (defined as – merging with reality)* as an experiential model to demonstrate just how ordinary and commonplace extraordinary Leadership can be. By consistently creating real experiences in higher levels of Leadership for others, we can support others in their ability to step confidently into these same levels.

4. **Sees the past, present and future** as an ongoing opportunity for awakening. At this level of Leadership,

our experience across time is focused on waking up to what each moment has to teach us, what each situation has in it to help us grow. From this perspective, we are positioned to better accept and understand the things of the past, present and future. And to share this perspective with others, especially those truly impassioned Leaders in our circle.

5. **Focused on** translating real Leadership into words, examples, actions, and models that others can readily connect with, understand, access and use. Through the process of making the complex, simple, and the simple, accessible, we can help other Leaders gain a more functional understanding and ability in applying higher level Leadership approaches, and with facilitating their further learning and growth along the path of Leadership. The Leadership puzzle is BIG and complex, yet when we truly understand this puzzle, experientially, we are in a position to articulate it and demonstrate it and translate it in a way that illuminates it and makes it more readily accessible to others.

6. **Problem Solving Method** involves awakening others to their ability to unleash the totality of their Leadership in the face of a challenge. At this level of Leadership, our focus is on rousing and stirring other inspired Leaders related to their commitment and purpose and responsibility as a Leader. We accomplish this through sharing our Leadership purpose, while helping others to connect more deeply with their Leadership purpose, to support them on their journey of learning and growth, while they step into the challenges that confront them.

7. **Common Leadership Statement** may be any version of *"If not you, then who . . . If not now, then when?"* Versions of this quote or statement have appeared across history. But have we heard or used any version of this statement in our workplaces, organizations or teams lately? As we ask this question of ourselves, I would also ask if anyone within our Leadership circle could benefit from hearing this statement from us at this time.

8. **Common outcome of this Leadership approach** is that our work, our organizations become a perfect tool and school for our ongoing learning and growth. This leads to a more Aware team and organization, as those involved accomplish the work in a way that helps them to more directly understand our creative possibilities. Work then becomes a near boundless creative exploration of learning and growth. Those in a work group or team or organization begin to know that their efforts are actually creating something well beyond the norm of most workplaces, something that will deeply impact the organization and all of its customers. This Leadership approach tends to establish an environment where people want to be part of the work experience, to learn and grow from the amazing results that are possible. This Leadership approach fosters a real sense of acknowledgement of the extraordinary efforts of people and the incredible results of our efforts. This brings an even deeper sense of commitment and connection to a Leader.

The Awakened Leadership approach cannot be grasped; it must be unleashed! Awakened Leadership can be difficult to understand intellectually, in a way that projects its true value. It must be genuinely expressed for it to be understood and experienced. Therefore, our *Attention, Focus, Intent* and *Love* in higher levels of Leadership is centered on creating real experiences in which others can participate and connect with. And although most people may not completely understand what an Awakened Leader is *Being* and *Doing* at this point, they know what they themselves have done, and they know what they have been a part of, and they know how all this makes them feel.

Moving through life and functioning as an Awakened Leader, allows us to perceive reality much more clearly and directly and to act and interact from this perspective. Too many Leaders are moving through life, as if still half-asleep. They are acting and reacting to one illusion after another. No wonder our results so often fall short of their potential! This more awakened state of Leadership is a very real and valuable experience and perspective that we can step into and act from, in service to others. Our clarity as a Leader can be expressed and shared with others and our organizations much more consistently and on a daily basis. This more constant Leadership experience can then help us all to wake up a little more. The *Leadership Revolution* requires us to wake up!

When we commit to the journey of Leadership as a path to awakening, everything we look at or are involved in as Leaders appears to us in the context of an emerging lesson, an emerging teaching, and an opportunity to engage our Leadership passion and purpose. The natural expression of our Leadership then seeks to move us and others further into our extraordinary nature. At this point we typically move through our days with much more grace and ease. We are no longer bound and controlled by fear or worry or control or our ego or the egos of others. We are free to creatively engage with others and to support them in working towards whatever challenges await us. This is real freedom. The freedom to purposefully choose our thoughts, words and actions, even within a challenging situation. Yes, this is freedom! And, in order to accomplish this, we must first possess or develop a deep desire to connect with and support others along this challenging journey and to make a significant difference in our lives and the lives of others. And then we must passionately and relentlessly follow our purpose.

The Awakened Leadership approach incorporates the Leader's *Awareness, Attention, Focus, Intent* and *Love* with our commitment to supporting others' growth and unleashing their Leadership purpose in the face of challenges, to achieve the objectives of a group, team or organization. This Leader has as a part of our Meta-Mindset, the deep desire to comprehend our extraordinary nature, and to present this to others in a way that helps them to step further into their Leadership purpose. Once this realization and commitment takes hold, then the question of *"How can we support other Leaders on our journey?"* goes away.

But before we travel further on our journey into these higher levels of Leadership, let's answer a question that might be coming up in some of our minds. In light of the terminology used for these higher levels, and the concepts that we are discussing in these higher levels, that question might be, are we getting into "Spiritual" territory here? And the answer is that it depends. It depends on our perspective. For some, the terminology and concepts of the higher levels of Leadership *do* remind us of Spiritual matters, and we are OK with this. For others, the terminology and concepts might create a little resistance in us, either because we feel that these matters should be kept separate or that we are just not into any of that Spiritual stuff. And still others may see no connection at all.

I would add as a reminder here that *there is no separation.* We explored the illusion of separation as we transitioned through the energetic impediment between Level 6 and Level 7 Leadership. So, to the specific question of whether the journey into higher levels of Leadership is related in some way to a Spiritual journey, based on the perspective that *there is no separation,* then yes, it is clearly related. As we explored earlier, the Leadership journey does align with many of the same elements found on personal growth or Spiritual paths, even though the path we are exploring here is focused on and grounded in our genuine Leadership service to others in our workplaces, groups, teams and organizations. And of course, we are all welcome to our own perspective on this issue. If at this point on our Leadership journey these terms and concepts appeal to us and create more alignment with the rest of our purpose and commitments in life, then we are free to incorporate the AQ Model as supportive to this aspect of our lives.

However, if at this point these terms and concepts create some form of resistance in us, or if we can't see them as connected in any way to Spirituality, well, then we are free to just focus on this material as it relates to our more formal Leadership role. In either case, by utilizing the AQ Model as a guide on our Leadership journey, we can position ourselves to serve others far beyond the status quo. There is one additional point to consider related to the types of issues that may create some form of conflict or resistance within us as we journey into higher levels of Leadership. *Interestingly, the path of Leadership is wide enough to accommodate all of our individual viewpoints, yet long enough to eventually grind them all down, until there is nothing left to impede us on our journey.*

And there is one more important point that we should explore here. There are clearly many paths to personal growth or spirituality out there. Yet, how much time are we able to devote to these kinds practices each week? A couple of hours a week, maybe? A weekend retreat here and there? Whatever it is, I am sure that it is time well spent. However, another question that I would ask is, as a result of these couple of hours a week of practice, how much or how well do the results of these practices typically carry over into the other parts of our life, especially the more challenging parts? For some people, I am sure these couple hours a week of practice do carry over to some degree into the rest of their lives, even during challenging situations. But I cannot even tell you how many times I have witnessed people, and especially Leaders, "lose it" during a challenging situation, and not even that big of one, while separately claiming to be committed to some kind of personal growth or spiritual practice. How interesting!

Now, consider this. What if we were able to study, explore and practice our chosen path to personal growth for 40 (plus) hours per week? What would that do for our level of growth and performance? How much more might this level of exploration and practice carry over into the rest of our lives, even into the more challenging parts? Think about it! Because this is exactly the opportunity that our workplaces and organizations present us with. *Our workplaces, our organizations and our Leadership practices are all genuine paths to personal growth and awakening!* Did we get that one? As previously stated, these paths to personal growth contain many of the same elements of any other more "recognized" path to our growth and awakening. AND, if we are able to see this, and step fully into this incredible opportunity, we are in a position to explore and practice this genuine path to awakening for 40 or more hours per week! Imagine practicing a path of personal growth for 40 (plus) hours a week, times 50-ish weeks per year, year after year! Or better yet, we don't have to imagine this. We can step into this reality and experience it for ourselves, in the here and now.

Our workplaces, organizations and our Leadership practice are genuine tools for transformation and growth! I also believe that our Leadership practice, in particular, places us in a unique position to learn and grow exponentially, if we are able to drop our resistance to it and awaken to its deeper possibilities. Think about it. Our Leadership role puts us into challenging interpersonal and process related situations on an almost daily basis. Our Leadership role causes us to frequently self-reflect on our own *Being* and *Doing* related to the numerous and varied situations we find ourselves in. And when we step into these situations with ever decreasing levels of resistance, as we do in Level 7 Leadership, and awaken to the greater possibilities of our path, as we do in Level 8, Awakened Leadership, our growth and performance and the subsequent experiences and results of others and our organizations are also transformed. Real Leadership IS a genuine, accelerated path to personal growth and awakening. A committed Leadership journey can put us on the fast-track to more expanded levels of perception and performance. *This is the Leadership Revolution that I am talking about!*

And yet, as far as we have come on this journey, there is still more available within the possibility of Leadership. More to share and give to others, our organizations and ourselves. There remain still untapped reserves within ourselves and others that, when understood and unleashed, can bring even further levels of results and even greater degrees of growth and satisfaction to those we serve, and ourselves. The challenge of an extraordinary Leader at this point is with describing and expressing higher levels of Leadership in ways that connect with and rouse other Leaders of varying levels or perspectives.

Now, to progress effectively beyond Level 8, Awakened Leadership, let's explore the Energetic Impediment that inhibits our ability to move forward from here. And let's explore how we might move beyond this attachment while simultaneously establishing a new, more expanded ability and the level of *Awareness*, *Attention* and *Focus* necessary to hold in place, these even more productive thoughts, beliefs, feelings and habits.

8th Level Energetic Impediment:

Release the attachment *to limitation as imposed by social constructs and the opinions of others*. The internal programming around this attachment is nearly completely invisible to most of us. The social constructs and the numerous opinions of others have been programmed so deeply into us that we hardly notice how they impact our perspective and mindset and attitude, and our overall paradigm, behavior and performance. This programming runs deep in our system and it is reinforced every day. Who is determining what we believe, and how we see the world? Is it ourselves, or someone else, or some other social mechanism? And how does all of this more specifically impact our typical workplace experiences and our Leadership approach?

Now, social constructs are not necessarily bad, and the opinions of others are not necessarily bad either. It's just that these things, if unexamined by us, can begin to dictate our worldview and establish unnecessary limitations on our life experience. And they may not provide us with the perspective we need to serve ourselves and each other to the degree that is possible or even necessary within our constantly changing environment. Most of our social constructs and many of the opinions of others are often quite slow to change. However, our businesses and our industries and many other elements of our cultures move and change and evolve much more quickly. And this can present quite a challenge for many Leaders, across industries. How do we move forward in a respectful and understanding manner, for those we serve?

We can see this challenge express itself everywhere. And unless we are *Aware* of it, we too can be impacted without even noticing. We may feel this challenge as some sort of cognitive dissonance, or resistance or confusion related to the reality of what we see and experience, versus what others are trying to convince us of. Until we can see these social constructs and the opinions of others, and look squarely at them and understand them, we may continue to be at their mercy. However, once seen and understood, these social constructs and the opinions of others begin to lose their uncontested power over us.

Again, I am not saying here that all social constructs and all of the opinions of others are completely dysfunctional. To the contrary, these elements can be quite supportive with our growth as a Leader. The issue is that we must examine and explore these things to determine their validity and their value to us and others, while respecting and appreciating where they may have come from. As an extraordinary Leader, we often must work within these social constructs and with the strong opinions of others, while still moving things forward within our rapidly changing environments. We must attempt to balance the contrast of some of the more stationary elements of the workplace culture with the more rapidly changing aspects of our environment.

If we are not clear about the impact of this energetic impediment, it can feel as if we are dragging an anchor behind us as we attempt to move forward. However, once Aware of it, we are in a position to more deeply explore these things and their impacts, and then to work more creatively and gracefully to address the challenges we face. Once *Aware* of it, we are better-positioned as an extraordinary Leader to apply the totality of our Leadership, even within the constraints inherent in many of our social constructs, and without necessarily making others feel bad or wrong about their perspectives. This is another aspect of high-level Leadership understanding.

But in order to accomplish this, we must first release our unconscious attachments to these social constructs and the varied opinions of others. That does not mean that we give them up or throw them away or ignore them. It just means that we release their control over us, and examine them for their validity, value and limitations. In doing this, we can work more creatively with them and through them, while respecting others' perspectives on these issues. We can live and work within these structures without being completely controlled by them, if we are clear about their nature.

These perspectives are constantly being reinforced in us and, if unexamined, we simply absorb them and accept them and, in many cases, are limited by them. We must see them for what they are. These perspectives represent ways of explaining and understanding things, or of feeling some level of safety and control in a chaotic world. There is nothing wrong with this and there is no need for us to argue or fight against this. It just is what it is. And as an extraordinary Leader, we can understand, embrace and work more creatively and compassionately with these things, once we have loosened our attachments to them.

In order to reach this level of clarity about this attachment, we may need do some work, some serious but interesting research, and some deeper internal work. Yes, I know, this continues to get even more fun and more inspiring! That is what extraordinary Leadership is all about! This is simply why we are here and we joyfully jump into explorations such as this. So, to begin to release this attachment to limitation as imposed by social constructs and the opinions of others, we must look directly at it, and explore it, and contemplate it, and think about it and NOT think about it, and try to get a feel for it. It definitely has a feeling to it. If we immerse ourselves in it, we will typically perceive something. And based on that something, we can begin to develop more experientially-based conclusions and perspectives and actions.

As an extraordinary Leader, it is time to work through our programming around this issue and to brave any resistance that may come as a result of actively moving beyond the status quo. For on the other side of our questioning of the status quo, lies our freedom as a Leader to express what is really most important to us and to others. That's why we are here.

So, once again, the first step in moving ourselves beyond this limited perspective is to become aware of it, either on our own, through fearless self-reflection, or through the honest feedback of others. There are others out there like us. We should continually seek each other out and share our perspectives and experiences to help to bolster our journeys, as we actively commit to replacing our more limited perspectives and habits and adopting a way of *Being* and *Doing* that is more expanded and supportive of others, our organizations and ourselves. And what could we replace this limitation as imposed by social constructs and the opinions of others with?

Develop the ability *to more deeply explore our internal and external reality to discern the larger truths in life.* "Truth" is an interesting thing. Many people would like to believe that truth is largely "black and white," and, in some cases, it actually is. Yet often there are shades of grey or multiple levels of truth. However, too many Leaders don't seem all that committed to doing the work necessary to discern these levels of truth. Too many Leaders do not take the time or do the work necessary to move beyond the superficial, the status quo. In order to move beyond our attachment to our social constructs and the various opinions of others, we must commit to developing our ability to more deeply explore the reality of our internal and external environments. We must develop the ability to more directly explore these deeper realities, to know the deeper truths hidden within.

And there is no overly complex, sanctioned process for accomplishing this. We simply add to our expanding expression of our Leadership performance, the consistent exercise of our chosen self-awareness practices, while working to apply them throughout our activities of daily living. When we do this over time, and not that much time, we can find ourselves even more clear and even more grounded in our Leadership purpose. Acting from this level of clarity becomes easier and more natural. Through this level of *Being* and *Doing*, we actually become even more of who we really are.

So, here we are at this point, working towards our transition into Level 9 Leadership, and suggesting the necessity of utilizing self-awareness practices to support our continued Leadership journey. It would be difficult to advance significantly on our extraordinary Leadership journey without these types of practices. At some point on our journey, they become a necessity for us. However, we most certainly do not need to wait to get to this point on our journey to apply these practices to our lives. As stated earlier, I have separated this Leadership model into these levels in this linear fashion in order for us to explore them more easily. In reality, there is much more overlap and interconnectedness related to the Leadership puzzle. My point here is that if we have not yet begun to purposefully incorporate self-awareness practices into our lives, then it is time to seriously consider this. However, I suspect that many of us have already done so. At this point, I would just add then, that we also *Focus* on bringing our practice into our activities of daily living on a more consistent basis, including our workplaces and organizations.

Developing the ability to more deeply explore our internal and external realities further inspires our Leadership journeys. By grounding ourselves in this perspective, we can actually see and experience the deeper truths of life while in service to others. This is not about making arbitrary decisions regarding what we choose to believe in an effort to make our life more convenient in some way. This is about consistently assessing and expressing the deeper truths in life, related to what is really going on and what the real impacts of our actions are. This is a much more valuable approach to Leadership and life than simply accepting things at face value. We can experience and verify this for ourselves, and we should. All it requires is a genuine, ongoing commitment to extraordinary Leadership and a good map to support us along the way.

There could be many other impediments or obstacles preventing a Leader from moving beyond Awakened Leadership. However, the tendency to structure our reality based on the numerous opinions of others or the many social constructs we have been exposed to, is frequently at the root of this issue. When we understand, experientially, who we really are and why we are really here, there is little left to hold us back from serving the world in a more extraordinary way.

As we now transition our exploration with up-leveling ourselves and others into the next level of Leadership, I would add one more point regarding Awakened Leadership. The Awakened Leadership approach fuels the fire within, within ourselves, and within other Leaders who are also passionate about learning and growing and serving others through extraordinary

Leadership. This growing fire also serves as the fuel we need to go even deeper on our journey. There is still more that awaits us! *The deeper we go, the deeper it gets!*

Let's now move into the process of up-leveling ourselves and others from Level 8 (Awakened Leadership) to Level 9 (Integrated Leadership), as we step even further into our ability to serve others and our organizations.

Up-leveling from Level 8, Awakened Leadership, to Level 9, Integrated Leadership:

Up-leveling Ourselves:

Step 1 – Saturate ourselves in self-awareness practices and take this *Awareness* out into the world. This refers to our developing a habit of consistently engaging ourselves in any of the numerous self-awareness practices available to us. Self-*Awareness* practices include the full range of practices from various forms of yoga, meditation, mindfulness practices, mantra, prayer, tai chi, and so many other traditional practices. I recommend whichever practices we are drawn to as individuals, but at this point I would also suggest we give consideration to some form of meditation practice. For many, practicing some form of meditation can more directly and more significantly support our growth and the deepening of our *Awareness*, *Attention*, *Focus*, *Intent* and *Love*, which is key to progressing further along on our Leadership journey. And there are so many types and forms of meditation to choose from that we can usually find one that meets our specific needs and perspective. But again, we should choose whichever self-awareness practices we are drawn to.

In addition to more traditional approaches, self-awareness practices can also come in many other forms, such as going for nature walks, or hanging out at the beach, or riding a bike, or fly fishing, or playing chess, or exercising, or visiting with friends and family, or working on a hobby, or washing dishes, or doing yardwork, or any number of activities. This is another key! Almost anything we do can be transformed into a self-awareness practice. With the right approach, which includes a purposefully *Aware, Attentive* and *Focused* approach aligned with our *Intent*, anything we do can help us to get deeper into the flow of life or deeper into ourselves and our surroundings. This is also how we take our yoga practice or mindfulness practice or meditation practice or fly-fishing practice out into the world. Without taking our practice out into the world, these self-awareness practices, both traditional and eclectic, are of only limited value beyond our own personal experiences with them.

To "saturate ourselves in self-awareness practices, and to take this *Awareness* out into the world" involves the consistent exercise of traditional or more eclectic self-awareness practices, while also taking the results of these practices out into the world through all of our various activities of daily living. It would be impossible for most of us to spend the majority of our waking hours doing yoga or in formal meditation. But it is possible for us, as extraordinary Leaders, to spend the bulk of our waking hours working and playing in more expanded levels of self-awareness, in service to others. It is certainly possible for us to ground ourselves in deepening levels of *Awareness, Attention, Focus, Intent* and *Love*. And the result of this from a Leadership perspective can be deeply impactful to others and our organizations.

And how do we know when we are sufficiently saturated in our self-awareness practices and acting in the world in way that brings more of our *Awareness* to all life? Well, on one level, we just know. We don't think we know, we just know. Remember that exploration from the 5th level energetic impediment (Attachment)? So, we just know. And this is a full-body knowing, applied to service through Leadership.

However, we may also notice that there is more ease to our thoughts, words, actions and interactions, despite the challenges in the moment. What we might notice at this point is that we are typically able to perceive at least one of the possible next right steps to take and are able to guide and support others in the deeper experience of the moment. This occurs, in part, because of the decreased level of resistance that we may be experiencing as a result of all of our work around our up-leveling practices and self-awareness practices, which serves to expand our Leadership perspective. At this point, we can move into near complete acceptance of the past, present and moment-to-moment, emerging reality. This gives us the freedom to engage with, and play and act and dance with, the flow of reality in a way that more completely serves all of life.

Now to be clear, "acceptance" of reality does not necessarily mean that we support or like whatever it is that we are accepting of. The act of acceptance is more specifically an act of acknowledgement of the reality of a situation. It does not serve us or anyone else to deny or resist reality. This inevitably creates even more challenge or dysfunction. By accepting or acknowledging reality, we are in a much better position to more clearly see it, and understand it and work with it, to either support it or challenge and transform it, or to enlarge our perspective around it. Denying or resisting or fighting with reality wastes energy and contracts our *Awareness*, *Attention* and *Focus*, and can add additional challenge to an already challenging situation. However, acceptance of reality frees our precious energy to respond to challenges more thoughtfully and purposefully, with more *Awareness, Attention, Focus, Intent* and *Love*.

In this up-leveling step, we are essentially *Focusing* more deeply into ourselves, to ground ourselves more completely in the totality of our *Being* and *Doing*, to even further enlarge our perspective, to understand and position ourselves to more effectively address the numerous gross and subtle variables inherent in the complexity of our worlds. Through this up-leveling step, we are positioning ourselves as extraordinary Leaders to serve even better everyone we come in contact with! There is no limit to how well we can serve others and ourselves. There is always one more step, if we are willing to take it!

And as stated numerous times here, nothing is 100%. Sometimes our Leadership *Awareness, Attention, Focus, Intent* and *Love* is fully engaged and aligned, and supports us in most appropriately identifying and acting on the variables in a given situation, while at other times, something comes into play to throw us off to a degree. This is not an exact science. It is an ongoing practice, an ongoing work in progress. It is more art than anything else. So, if we fall short in a given situation, there is no need to beat ourselves up. We just need to work to get back into alignment with ourselves as soon as we can, and then take ourselves back out into the world. This can take a day or so to recalibrate ourselves, or just a couple of hours. Or, as we continue with our growth, it can often be accomplished within a few seconds or less! The point is that, as extraordinary Leaders, we are out there, constantly bringing the best versions of ourselves to the people we serve and to the challenges we face. This is just one of the ways we can give back to life as a Leader.

So, up-leveling ourselves from Level 8 to Level 9 Leadership involves the combined actions of saturating ourselves in self-awareness practices AND taking this *Awareness* out into the world. This is one move or one act. This act or *Doing* depends more on our *Being*, which is even more important with the higher levels of Leadership. This is mostly an internal maneuver, an act of *Being* that can move powerfully from the inside to the outside as we *Do* this step.

We don't have to analyze this step any further before we just *Do* it. If we have made it this far on our extraordinary Leadership journey and have experienced some positive results, then let's keep going. If we just *Be* and *Do* our best version of the up-leveling practices, we will continue to learn and grow as Leaders. We can become our own expression of the deeper possibilities of Leadership once we understand the map or the puzzle a little better, and purposefully apply ourselves to it. That's why we are here. This is our work.

Up-leveling Others:

Step 1 – Introduce others to self-awareness practices, in a supportive way, to help them to experience and grow greater self-awareness. So, very similarly as with the process of up-leveling ourselves, we are supporting and encouraging other Leaders, who are on a similar journey, to develop the habit of saturating themselves in self-awareness practices. One of the keys here is that we are particularly sensitive to others' preferences and that we do not try to force our approaches onto others. There should be no dogma involved in these interactions. We should simply suggest options to others and allow their preferences to guide their choice of practice.

We can suggest options for these practices and check in from time to time related to how others are doing with their practices and how they are integrating them into their daily

Leadership activities. We can share our experiences with our own practice, along with the experience and impact of taking these results into our daily Leadership lives. This up-leveling step is no more complex than this. We simply introduce the value of this practice and encourage others in exploring this step through whichever approach they are drawn to. And then, we simply create a consistent Leadership conversation as a check-in around this practice. That's it.

Additionally, the opportunity may present itself within the structure and activities of our daily work environments, where we can also support others with bringing more of their *Awareness, Attention, Focus, Intent* and *Love* to the issue at hand. This can be done through a number of methods that include gently pulling others into greater levels of self-awareness and more directly into the Leadership flow during a challenge. We can accomplish this through our body language, tone of voice and word choice, as we express our own level of self-awareness and create a picture or an experience for others to step into. We can talk about self-awareness practices, and their value and benefits, and we can encourage others in this direction. We can also endeavor to create more direct experiences with others, with their own deeper levels of self-awareness. There is not much else for us to *Do* here in up-leveling others. At this point, it is our *Being* that does much of the work around up-leveling others. It is our *Being* that does a lot of the heavy lifting.

In this step, we are supporting others in developing deeper levels of *Awareness, Attentions, Focus, Intent* and *Love* for themselves, so that they are also in a position to express the best versions of themselves for the good of all involved. We are helping other committed Leaders with developing more expanded levels of self-awareness and stepping into and experiencing the Leadership flow, to further develop their Leadership performance. Supporting others' development in this area exponentially increases the number of people out there actively involved in higher levels of Leadership performance. At this point as a Leader, we are like a Choreographer, who collaboratively co-creates an evolving dance with other artists in an effort to share more grace and beauty and interconnectedness within the dynamics of our lives.

Performing this up-leveling step, automatically moves us beyond the Level 8, Energetic Impediment, and into the next level of Leadership. It further deepens our *Awareness, Attention, Focus, Intent* and *Love* regarding the deeper responsibilities and impacts of our Leadership. And this step multiplies the deeper Leadership purpose that many of us share across teams and organizations and communities and industries and cultures. This up-leveling step automatically moves us into higher levels of Leadership performance, while creating higher level experiences and higher levels of performance for those we interact with. That's just how it works! Just *Be* and *Do* and repeat and repeat. This is a thread of simplicity that runs through the AQ Model. Just *Be* and *Do* and jump into the flow of Leadership.

Everyone deserves an opportunity to step further into a level of Leadership performance that more completely serves others. Everyone working with a Leader deserves the opportunity to work and contribute within an environment that inspires them towards their best effort and best expression of their purpose. Let's do our part as extraordinary Leaders to give everyone a real chance for this, here and now. Let's help them and support them, in the very best ways we can, as our very best continues to expand. Let's integrate the whole of our Leadership purpose in this effort.

Level 8 Leadership Age & Approach	Predominant Leadership Characteristics	Up-Leveling Ourselves	Up-Leveling Others
		the thoughtful and purposeful process of improving our performance through an ongoing commitment to growing our awareness, attention and focus	helping others to improve their performance *"in real time,"* based on your growing awareness and your commitment to supportive, purposeful coaching
Awakened Age: Awakened Leadership	1. **Leadership through Leading Leaders** – typically based on all the above, and on *rousing* leaders to their purpose, potential and responsibility, through the commitment to Leadership as a path to awakening. 2. Grounded predominantly in the commitment to growth, learning and awakening through the path of leadership service. 3. *Uses Mysticism (defined as* – union with reality) as an experiential model to demonstrate just how ordinary, extraordinary leadership can be. 4. Sees the past, present & future as an ongoing opportunity for awakening. 5. Focused on translating real leadership into words, examples, actions, and models that others can readily connect with, understand, access and use. 6. Problem Solving Method – *Awakens others to the ability to unleash the totality of their Leadership in the face of a challenge.* 7. Common Quote – *"If not you, then who... If not now, then when?"* 8. Common Outcomes – *Work* becomes a perfect "tool and school" for our learning and growth, along with the many positive impacts of this.	Moving from Level 8 to Level 9: 1. Saturate ourselves in self-awareness practices and take this awareness out into the world.	Moving from Level 8 to Level 9: 1. Introduce others to self-awareness practices, in a supportive way, to help them to experience and grow greater self-awareness.

8th Level Impediment – Release the attachment to limitation as imposed by social constructs and the opinions of others. *Develop* the ability to more deeply explore our internal and external reality to discern the larger truths in life.

Figure 12. Level 8 Leadership

CHAPTER 19

Level 9 Leadership
The Integration Age and Integrated Leadership

Leadership through Actively Leading the Self . . .

Leadership Age: *Integration Age*

The 9th Level of Leadership illuminated in the AQ Model represents the functional progression of an even more thoughtful and purposeful application of individual experience (Industrial Age), information and data gathering (Information Age), customization (Knowledge Age), the connection of people's passion and purpose with work systems and processes (Understanding Age), balance and sustainability (Wisdom Age), more direct insight (Transcendent Age), the alchemy of possibility from the seemingly impossible (Mystic Age), the use of Leadership as a path to Awakening (Awakened Age), through more actively Leading ourselves (Integration Age).

The distinctive theme of the Integration Age involves a focus on more deeply understanding both our "light and shadow" selves, to the point where these key aspects of the self are known and accepted as aspects of us all. This provides us with the level of clarity and freedom necessary as an extraordinary Leader, to Lead ourselves with even more agility and purpose and effectiveness. This level of personal Integration is a key part of our Leadership journey and enables us to further expand our understanding and impact. This level of personal Integration opens us up to perceive the larger truths of life, more directly. This level of exploration can lead to even deeper levels of understanding, application and appreciation for the possibilities of Leadership. This level of deep work can lead to even more direct and valuable insights related to our Leadership performance, which can support us with determining the best course of action in the moment.

The term "Integration," in this case, refers to the ongoing experience of exploring and understanding the depth of the functionality of these connections with ourselves, others and our surroundings. This level of Integration can help us on all levels to be of even better service to others and our organizations. The word "Integration" is meant to point us even more deeply towards our duty and responsibility as an extraordinary Leader. The Integrated ones of the past, and present, represent those who have committed to the fearless self-reflection necessary to understand the deeper aspects of ourselves and therefore others, in a way that helps us to serve even better. This age is represented by those with a significant depth of clarity related to the light and shadow aspects of Leadership. This supports our ability to get out ahead of ourselves and to literally *lead ourselves* more effectively than is typically possible, which supports us in serving others exceptionally, especially during challenging situations.

Leadership Approach: *Integrated Leadership*

There are clearly many degrees of Integration available to us on our Leadership journey. And during our journey we are constantly working towards higher degrees of Integration, whether we are *Aware* of it or not. On our Leadership journey, we are nearly constantly exploring and practicing and getting feedback from our results and learning and growing from this and continuing to refine our understanding and approach. This is the Integration that I am referring to, and it happens automatically, to some degree, throughout our lives. Yet, when we begin to work more directly and purposefully on our ability to Integrate our Leadership experiences with the deeper realities we are exploring and experiencing, we can continue to improve our Leadership exponentially.

What we do at this level of Integrated Leadership, and how we do it, is framed by this genuine desire or impulse to perceive and to *merge* directly with the deeper parts of ourselves (light and shadow aspects) and, therefore, other Leaders, to more effectively serve. And this genuine desire is fueled by our own passion and growing depth as an extraordinary Leader. Our depth of Leadership seeks out the depth of other Leaders, to connect with and to inspire. Leaders at this Leadership level endeavor to connect with and support others in a way that brings out our best effort and our best performance and our best version of ourselves, as we more deeply explore and envision and manifest our potential together.

The up-leveling approaches that we performed in the previous level of Leadership serve to automatically usher us into this next level. However, in order to remain or ground ourselves here, we must begin to practice and to embody and express the Predominant Leadership Characteristics below.

Predominant Leadership Characteristics: *Integrated Leadership*

1. **Leadership through Actively Leading the Self** is typically based on all the previous levels of Leadership, and on *an ongoing, deep exploration of the self (both light and shadow aspects), creating the level of self-awareness and presence necessary to move beyond our own self-limiting programing.* This level of Leadership is focused on understanding and accepting ourselves and others, at a very deep level, to Lead extraordinarily, even in the most challenging of situations.

2. **Grounded predominantly in** the commitment to self-awareness and actively Leading (getting out and ahead of) ourselves. Because of this depth of presence to our authentic self, we are able to drop more of our attachments related to the illusions of ourselves and develop the ability to get out ahead of ourselves and discern the deeper truths of complex interpersonal interactions, to engage with them to move them towards more mutually beneficial outcomes. This level of presence helps us to more directly perceive reality *as it is emerging.* This is the active side of presence that helps us to get out ahead of ourselves, and to move out beyond our own programmed limitations and preconceptions.

3. *Uses Awakening* to further align our *Attention* and *Focus* with our growing *Awareness, Intent* and *Love.* By consistently working from deep presence, we develop a high level of agility with engaging with the emerging reality, as we more effectively support others on their Leadership journeys.

4. **Merges the past, present and future** into the now present moment. At this level of Leadership, our experience within time is focused on how the present moment creates and connects us to the past and future. From this perspective, we are positioned to better appreciate, accept and integrate our past, present and possible future. And, to engage with this perspective for the benefit of others.

5. **Focused on *Being*** present to the emerging reality and Leading ourselves into it. Through the process of consistently operating in deep presence, we can perceive reality as an emerging scene or experience. We can also more immediately perceive, accept and understand the emerging reality, and with this nanosecond of lead time, we can formulate and implement or intuit a Leadership approach to engaging with the scene, in a way that brings about the optimal outcome. This is another aspect of getting out ahead of and Leading ourselves.

6. **Problem Solving Method** involves moving through life as an expression of an Integrated Leader and human *Being*. When we are deeply present to our authentic self, that self that is beneath and beyond most of our programming and our biases, there is only the emerging experience of life to engage with in alignment with our purpose. And to share and connect and collaborate with others from this perspective, as we move through the challenges that face us.

7. **Common Leadership Statement** may be any version of *"Who am I BEING and what am I DOING in*

the here and now, to move forward in alignment with my purpose?" How often does any version of this get expressed in our workplaces, organizations and teams? This is one that we should ask ourselves frequently. And now might be a good time to start.

8. **Common outcome of this Leadership approach** is that *work* becomes an integral part of our journey through life, along with the many positive impacts of this. This leads to a more Integrated team and organization, as those involved accomplish the work in a way that helps them to more directly experience our deeper authenticity. Work then becomes a near boundless creative exploration of learning and growth. Those in a work group or team or organization know that their efforts are actually creating something well beyond the norm of most workplaces. Something that will deeply impact the organization and all of its customers, and something that is actually a part of us. This Leadership approach tends to establish an environment where people become a valuable part of the work experience, continually learning from and growing from the amazing results that are possible. This Leadership approach works to foster a real sense of wonder related to the extraordinary efforts of people and the incredible results of our efforts. This brings to a Leader, an even deeper sense of awe for the now present moment.

The Integrated Leadership approach can't be forced, it must be cultivated! Integrated Leadership cannot be actualized by just trying really hard. It must be deeply explored and developed over time, and not that much time, to be expressed and experienced. Therefore, our *Attention* and *Focus* in this level of Leadership is on developing these abilities within ourselves and creating real experiences for others to participate in and to explore and connect with. And although most people may not completely understand what an Integrated Leader is *Being* and *Doing* at this point, they know that they have been a part of something extraordinary, and they know how all this makes them feel.

Let's dive in a little deeper with this concept of *getting out ahead of our self or Leading ourselves or active presence*, as this is a key opportunity for us at this level of Leadership. The concept and practice of "presence" or "mindfulness," has been around for thousands of years and is quite popular these days, even in Leadership circles. Much of the application to Leadership and the workplace, centers around the concept of presence as being basically a more passive state of mind, whereby we can become calm and centered on the present moment, to filter out some of the more extraneous and irrelevant stimuli that may be a part of our typical decision-making processes. And this is most certainly true and quite valuable to our expression of Leadership. *Being* more present and centered most certainly does decrease the number of peripheral stimuli that might be overwhelming us, so that we can potentially make more focused and appropriate decisions.

As valuable to us as the passive side of presence is, there is so much more available to us here! There is an *active side* of presence that we can also access. Some also refer to this as the *flow state*. But remember, these are just terms. People have actually been doing this kind of stuff since the beginning of our history, long before these terms even existed. Active presence or flow states are actually ridiculously common, we just don't recognize them or refer to them in these terms. And then, some people step in as authorities on these concepts, and develop elaborate systems of teaching around them, often making these natural states more confusing and harder for us to access. Remember, part of our exploration of the predominant Leadership characteristics of an Awakened Leader (Level 8) involves using our words and our actions and various models to make the seemingly complex, *easier* for others to understand, access and utilize.

Let's consider some common, ordinary examples of active presence or flow states. They are everywhere! We can experience active presence during various sports activities, even while just watching. We can experience it while playing chess or any other board or tabletop game. We can experience it while riding a bike or watching a movie or reading a book or while fishing or playing with our children or visiting with a friend, or whenever we are fully absorbed in something. We could go on and on. We hear from high-level athletes how, when they are on the field, everything else (all their distractions and concerns and negative thoughts, etc.) disappears. And their experience is that of being totally present to the dynamics of the game. Some say that they can see the entire field in all directions, and that they can anticipate things before they happen, and that their performance increases exponentially. What? This makes athletes sound magical or supernatural! But there is nothing magical or supernatural about this! It is quite natural, as a matter of fact. We all do versions of this frequently within our own lives. We do it so often and so naturally that we don't even notice it!

But by **noticing it**, and purposefully placing our *Attention* and *Focus* here, we can create a more consistent habit of playing in or working at this level. And by *Doing* this over time, we can develop even more expanded skills with this, and serve others even better. I would imagine that we have all had experiences in our lives where, through our fixed *Attention* and steady

Focus, we have experienced a calmness and connection with what we were doing, and in a way that enhanced our perception and experience and performance during this activity. Have we ever had an experience while playing a game, where we were so into things that we made an amazing play or did something at a level that surprised even us? Have we ever been meeting with a friend, where the conversation just flowed and hours felt like minutes? Have we ever been driving in heavy traffic and were able to see what other drivers were going to do, before they did it? These are all very basic and very natural examples of our experiences in active presence or the flow state, and I could suggest many more.

Some of the signs of being in the Leadership flow will be extremely subtle while others may be quite overt and easier to pick up on. Anyway, this level of Integrated Leadership can show up in our lives occasionally *by accident*, but our goal is to make this experience a more consistent part of our lives, to do this *on purpose*. Integrated Leadership has an ease to it, a gracefulness to it, and it can show up in many ways. But once we know it and are clear about it within ourselves, we are in a position to more readily step into it in and serve others from this perspective.

Being and *Doing* while in the Leadership flow is also as fun as it gets for an extraordinary Leader! And the interesting thing is that, over time, we begin to more and more purposefully step into or find ourselves in the Leadership flow. At this point then, nearly every interaction we are involved in is transformed into some form of Leadership flow, where our *Awareness, Attention* and *Focus*, and our *Intent* and *Love* is *Being* expressed on purpose and at a very high level, as we are integrated with and fully absorbed by the now present moment. And we become extremely adept in engaging with others in a way that brings more ease and gracefulness to even complex situations. As an extraordinary Leader, we are here to serve and support others, and one of the most beneficial ways that we can do this is through our connection to the deeper parts of ourselves, and therefore the deeper aspects of others.

Picture one of us, or you, or me, moving through the chaos of our Leadership day with numerous distractions occurring simultaneously. But, just like in the examples we explored earlier, we maintain our *Attention* and *Focus* to the degree that we become *the calm in the middle of the storm*. We remain open to the input and feedback that the environment (people and processes) are sending us. We are in a state of non-resistance, and acceptance of reality as it is emerging. Our eyes and ears and hearts are wide open and our breathing is controlled and measured. And we are integrating all of the relevant information and perspective and emotion related to a challenge as we collaboratively discern the next possible right decision to move forward with, and then the next and the next.

This is Leading the self, as opposed to being Led by our programing or our default approaches, or the unexamined opinions of others, or by the effects of our environment. This is how we get *out ahead of* ourselves, beyond our habitual nature, to perceive the deeper, unbiased reality of a situation. So that we can make more insightful, collaborative decisions, and act and perform from higher levels of Leadership with more ease. These experiences are available to us all, in the here and now. We simply need to consistently put our *Attention* and *Focus* on this task. We simply need to establish this as a priority for ourselves, and use our energy, passion and commitment to light and fan our own internal fire to overcome the energetic threshold common in most workplaces, that allows us to perform at higher and higher levels of Leadership.

The same types of experiences that high-level athletes experience, the same types of experiences that so many of us have had in the many examples we covered, these same experiences are also available to us in the chaos and challenges of our workplaces. All we have to do is acknowledge this and apply ourselves in this way. *There is no separation between our work-life and our home life . . . there is only life.*

We are truly capable of so much more as Leaders. It's just that most of us did not know that this was possible or available to us, or we didn't think that we had the permission to step into the best version of ourselves in our workplaces, or we were afraid that others would tease us for this level of commitment because it might make them look bad. Well guess what? Now we know that all of this IS possible for us. Now we know that all of this IS available to us. And by stepping into this Leadership journey, we have given each other the permission to move into the best version of ourselves. And regarding those who will tease or poke fun at us or try to sabotage us because they think our level of commitment makes them look bad or feel bad in some way? Well, we can just take their comments as a form of acknowledgment of our transformational efforts, knowing that this is their way of working through their own resistance and programming, to eventually step into the best versions of their self. And so, we move confidently forward! *This is the Leadership Revolution that I am talking about!*

And when we commit to the journey of Leadership at this level of Integration, then everything we look at or are involved in as a Leader appears to us in the context of an emerging experience and an emerging opportunity to engage with and express our passion and purpose in the now present moment. The natural expression of our Leadership then seeks to move ourselves and others even further into our extraordinary nature. And in

order to accomplish this, we must first acknowledge and connect with our deeper purpose to serve and support others along
this challenging journey and to make a significant difference in
our life and the lives of others. And then we must passionately
and relentlessly follow our purpose.

The Integrated Leadership approach incorporates the
Leader's *Awareness, Attention, Focus, Intent* and *Love* with our
commitment to supporting others' growth and unleashing
their Leadership passion in the face of challenges, to achieve
the objectives of a group, team or organization. This Leader has
as a part of our Meta-Mindset, the deep desire to express our
extraordinary nature, and to present this to others in a way that
helps them to step further into their passion and purpose. A
group or team in collaboration with an Integrated Leader, can
achieve meaningful things together while they learn and grow
and create significant impacts through their interactions. Once
this realization and commitment to actively Leading ourselves
takes hold, then the question of *"What is the purpose of presence?"* goes away.

And yet, there is still more available within the possibility of
Leadership. More to share with and give to others, our organizations and ourselves. There remain still untapped reserves within
ourselves and others, that when understood and expressed, can
bring even further levels of results and even further degrees of
growth and satisfaction experienced by those we serve, and ourselves. The challenge of an extraordinary Leader at this point,
continues to be serving the number of people and contributing
to the number of inspiring efforts that are available to us in the
now present moment.

Although a commitment to Leading through active presence
can be incredibly impactful and beautiful on this extraordinary
journey, we can still be left with the clear knowing that there

is more available to all of us on our journey as a Leader. Integrated Leadership clearly represents a level of Leadership that our teams and organizations crave on some level. Deep inside, many of us hope to unite with an even more expanded experience of life. We collectively sense that there is a way of *Being* and *Doing* that far exceeds the experiences that are so typical of our daily lives.

Now, to enable ourselves to move effectively beyond Level 9 Leadership, let's explore the primary Level 9, Energetic Impediment, that inhibits our ability to move forward with more ease on our Leadership Journey. And let's explore how we might move beyond this attachment while simultaneously, establishing a new, more expanded ability and the level of *Awareness, Attention* and *Focus* necessary to hold in place these more expanded thoughts, beliefs, feelings and habits.

9th Level Energetic Impediment:

Release the attachment to attachment. Yes, the programming around our attachment to attachment is doubly invisible to most of us, as it speaks to the underlining programming of the attachment process itself. This process is such an integral part of how we learn and grow as humans, and it goes on mostly unexamined and unchecked during our lives. We are programmed to attach to or agree to things that appear to work for us. And when reinforced through repetition, these attachments become part of our habitual expression of ourselves.

Now, attachments or agreements are not bad, in and of themselves. They can actually serve us and others quite well, when examined and used thoughtfully and purposefully. It is just that if the process of more arbitrary attachment goes on unexamined and unchecked, then we can end up with quite a few unwanted and unnecessary limitations to our experience in life. So, since we are hardwired to create attachments, we should and can take a more thoughtful approach to participating in this process. We can systematically assess many of our attachments from the perspective of how they are they working for us. And then determine whether to keep them, modify them or drop them. And, just as importantly, we can also more thoughtfully determine which attachments we choose to incorporate into our lives.

To do this, it can help to first understand the basics of the attachment process itself and then, through our *Awareness, Attention* and *Focus* on this process, release or let go of, or step *in the way* of this automatic process. We can see this challenge express itself frequently. And unless we are *Aware* of it, we too are impacted without even noticing. Without our *Attention* and *Focus* on the process of attachment itself, we can quite easily find ourselves taking on and expressing perspectives that have not been fully examined by us. Yes, this actually happens quite automatically and frequently! It has happened to me on numerous occasions throughout my life, and it still challenges me to this day. We see and hear people express various perspectives as facts of life, all the time. And many times, these perspectives have gone through very little, if any, analysis regarding their basis in reality or their impact on ourselves and others. As I said, the programming around the process of attachment is hardwired and automatic. Just watch it play out.

That is why this attachment to attachment is doubly invisible and doubly challenging to identify and release. It takes a consistent, high-level of *Awareness, Attention* and *Focus* for us to see it and feel it and to more purposefully engage with this process. We can participate in this process much more purposefully and thoughtfully. And until we do, until we take on this attachment to attachment itself process, we might not be able to free up enough energy, and we might not be able to eliminate enough of our resistance, to move into even higher levels and expressions of Leadership.

Until we can see it and look at it squarely and understand it, we are at the mercy of it. Once seen and understood, however, the attachment process can lose some of its uncontested power over us. And again, I am not saying here that all unexamined attachments are dysfunctional. To the contrary, some of these attachments can be serving us quite well and can actually be quite supportive with our growth as a Leader. The issue is that we must examine and explore these things to determine their validity and their value to us and others, while respecting where they have come from. And as an extraordinary Leader, we must often work within situations where our or others' unexamined attachments are creating additional challenges. And, very thoughtfully and purposefully, we must still work to move things forward within our rapidly changing environments.

But in order to do any of this, we must first release our unconscious attachment to the process of attachment itself. This does not mean that we are now immune to this hardwired process. It just means that we are now better positioned to steer this process in a direction that is more productive for ourselves and others. We can live and work within these structures without being completely controlled by them, if we are clear about their nature. These perspectives are constantly being reinforced and, if unexamined, we simply absorb them and accept them and are possibly limited by them. We must see them for what they are. They are not something bad. They are simply part of the core process for how we take on different perspectives in an attempt to survive and thrive in our world. There is nothing wrong with this. It just is what it is. But as an extraordinary Leader, we can engage with this process much more thoughtfully and effectively.

In order to get to this level of clarity about this attachment, we may have to do some work, some serious but interesting research and some deeper internal work. Yes, I know, this never stops! Isn't is great? That is what extraordinary Leadership is all about! So, to begin to release this attachment to attachment, we must look directly at it, and explore it, and contemplate it, and think about it, and NOT think about it, and try to get a feel for it. It definitely has a feeling to it. If we immerse ourselves in it, we will typically perceive something. And based on that something, we can begin to develop more experientially-based conclusions and perspectives and actions.

By working to release our attachments, we position ourselves to see other possibilities and to move through life and the challenges of Leadership a little more gracefully, and to support our teams with more flexibility and agility. So, once again, the first step in moving ourselves beyond this limited perspective is to become *Aware* of it, either on our own, through fearless self-reflection or through the honest feedback from others. There are others out there like us. We should continually seek each other out and share our perspectives and experiences to help to bolster our journeys, as we actively commit to replacing our more limited perspectives and habits and adopting a way of *Being* and *Doing* that is more expanded and supportive of others, our organizations and ourselves. And what could we replace this attachment to attachment with?

Develop *the ability to accept the now present moment, and step impeccably into the whole of reality.* This ability involves our continuing journey into the depth of our purpose, the depth of our

Being, the depth of reality. It involves our growing experience in the interconnectedness of all things. It involves our ongoing work and experience with active presence or the flow-state. And, it involves our ongoing commitment to extraordinary Leadership service. It is through our deepening experiences in all of these areas that we are able to more completely accept the reality of the now present moment, and to stand in this reality to serve impeccably.

The term "impeccable" used here has multiple levels of meaning. It refers to an *Awareness* of the possibility of life; an *Attention* to the gross and subtle elements of life; a *Focus* on perceiving and engaging with reality; an unbending *Intent*; a *Love* for serving all of life; a high-level of freedom from the typical attachments and resistances; a precision and efficiency of thought, word and action; a depth of compassion, courage and commitment to our purpose; a sense of awe and wonder for our experience in life; and more. It's a big term, a big word! Suffice it to say that to step into Leadership, to step into life, impeccably, is the act of an extraordinary Leader.

And there is no overly complex, sanctioned process for accomplishing this. We simply add to our expanding expression of our Leadership performance, the consistent practice of applying the totality of our Leadership purpose to the now present moment, within the whole of the emerging reality. Yes, just that! And at this level of Leadership, it actually is just that. All we are talking about here is the passionately persistent, continuation of our thoughtful, focused commitment to the extraordinary journey of our Leadership purpose. Through this level of *Being* and *Doing*, we actually can become even more of who we really are within the context of why we are here.

So here we are, deep into the flow of our Leadership purpose. Developing the ability to accept the now present moment and step into the whole of reality with impeccability, most certainly further inspires our Leadership journeys in even more profound ways. By grounding ourselves in this perspective we can actually experience and express the deeper truths of life while in service to others. And yet, we must still continue to apply all of our *Awareness, Attention* and *Focus, Intent* and *Love* to our moment to moment Leadership expression. Nothing is free on our Leadership journey, our Hero's Journey. Each level of Leadership must be reclaimed each and every day, and on more challenging days, we may need to reground ourselves multiple times.

There could be many other impediments or obstacles preventing a Leader from moving beyond Integrated Leadership. However, the doubly invisible programing related to the process of attachment itself, is many times, at the root of this issue. When we understand, experientially, that we are fully responsible for our path and expression of extraordinary Leadership, then we can apply ourselves to the deeper attachments that continue to hold most of us back.

Now let's move into the process of up-leveling ourselves and others from Level 9 (Integrated Leadership) to Level 10 (Unified Leadership), as we step even further into our ability to serve others. Level 10 is the last level of Leadership illuminated in the AQ Model, at this time. As stated previously, early on in my Leadership explorations, I could only see the first five levels in the model, and I thought that this represented a fairly comprehensive approach to Leadership development. And it does! But then, another level came into view and eventually became clear. And then another, and another and still another, until all ten levels came into view to represent the composition of the model. It would be conceivable, however, that another level of Leadership might appear in the future. There is always another step, waiting to be discovered.

Up-leveling from Level 9, Integrated Leadership, to Level 10, Unified Leadership:

Up-leveling Ourselves:

Step 1 – Keep going and never stop! Go further! Go deeper! There is always another level or a next step for us! Now clearly, this step is more than a little vague, compared to many of the previous up-leveling steps. And this is on purpose. As stated several times in Part 3 of this book, as we become grounded in these higher levels of Leadership, we become more responsible for our own experiment in creating our Leadership expression, and our life, as a work of art. So, at this point, with all of our experience with thoughtful and purposeful up-leveling practices, and with grounding ourselves in higher levels of Leadership, and the work we accomplished with our energetic impediments (attachments), and the incorporation of the key concepts in the AQ Model, and any other relevant Leadership concepts that we as individuals have included in our specific journeys, it is time for us to discover and chart the direction of our own, individual next steps. It is time for us to step into the totality of our own expression of extraordinary Leadership, based on our own predilection for this journey of service.

This essentially means that in this next up-leveling step, it is our responsibility to determine or create our next up-leveling step(s). It is up to us at this point, to not only determine the specifics of the next level of expression of our extraordinary Leadership journey, but also the up-leveling steps to get us there. This is where we leverage the structure of the AQ Model, the structure that we have explored and tested and modified when needed and worked in and learned from and grown from. This is where we use this structure that has served us so well to this point, to move beyond this very structure itself! This represents the point where we step out into the world as fully responsible Leaders, fully responsible for all aspects of our Leadership approach and its impacts, and for the continued direction of our efforts.

Therefore, this next step involves us taking all of our experiences with the AQ Model, and any other Leadership development model or personal growth work, and sitting with these in some way, to seek more clarity regarding our possible next steps, and then engaging with them as they emerge into our *Awareness*. This process can take many forms, and I recommend whichever forms we are most drawn to. We could use some form of meditation for this process or contemplation or visualization. Or we could take a more concrete approach using our sticky-note process on a flip chart. We could even simply but very purposefully wait until something begins to come into our *Awareness*. There are many approaches we could use for this or we could make up our own. And it may take some time for our next steps to filter into our *Awareness* or we might become immediately *Aware* of our further direction. Our further Leadership journey becomes uniquely ours at this point, based on our predilection for this journey of service.

When I refer to "our predilection" for this journey of service, I am not referring to the concept of developing some sort of "Leadership style." What we have been exploring with the AQ Model goes far beyond the concept of Leadership styles. When we look at this concept of Leadership styles, we see various Leadership expressions presented as if they are distinct, comprehensive approaches to Leadership. And that as a Leader, our job is to research these various Leadership "styles," and then pick the one that is the best. Yet this approach rarely works that well for us over time.

That is not to say that there aren't many committed Leaders out there who are thoughtfully and purposefully researching and working to improve their Leadership approach, and the information related to Leadership styles can be helpful. But the concept of Leadership styles really comes down to an attempt at describing a very narrow aspect or group of associated Leadership traits, and in a way that most often does not provide the larger context or progression for this "style" or expression of Leadership. The result of this perspective on Leadership development has been the creation of a list or collection of Leadership styles that we get to supposedly choose from, without much direction or real understanding of the bigger picture of Leadership. Often, the Leadership style that we choose, has more to do with our programming than any real analysis of what is most needed by our organizations and those we serve.

So, although the information regarding various Leadership styles can be of some value to us in understanding and improving our Leadership performance to a degree, this approach is far too limited for the complex challenges we face, and for the needs of our organizations and people, and for the full expression of our Leadership passion and deeper purpose.

So, when I refer to determining *our own* next steps based on *our predilection* for this journey of service, what I am actually referring to is connecting even more deeply to our individual *Awareness, Attention, Focus, Intent* and *Love* and with our expression of extraordinary Leadership, and our individual growing Mindset and Skill Sets, and the direction of our individual *Being* and *Doing*, and the pull of the people and areas of interaction that we are drawn to in service, and in a way that best meets everyone's deeper needs. This is not about simply picking the Leadership style of the day or the one that sounds the coolest. This is about taking the very real and very deep and very purposeful and very powerful next step on our Leadership journey. *This is the Leadership Revolution that I am talking about!* This step in up-leveling ourselves into Level 10 Leadership involves us diving even deeper into the interconnectedness and interdependency of all life, through the further up-leveling practices that we are drawn to. Each step so far on our Leadership journey within the AQ Model has served to bring us a little deeper into this reality. And now, at this level of Leadership, this perspective has become a real experience and a real driver of our thoughts, words and actions.

Our extraordinary Leadership journey continues to become even more of an expression of this *oneness*, through our discernment of the next expression and opportunity for our extraordinary Leadership journey. And one of the key considerations in this next step involves the determining of the "What and Why and Where and How" of this expression of service to others. This next step involves us stepping into our Leadership purpose, commitment and passion with all that we are! Let's think about what that might look like and feel like for us and those we interact with.

The point of this next step is for us to now take complete responsibility for our Leadership expression. Yet to be clear, stepping into and grounding ourselves in Level 10 Leadership is still no guarantee for success. There are so many complex and interrelated variables within the Leadership context that we can rarely, if ever, achieve a perfect outcome. We are instead in this constant state of *becoming* the next best expression of our Leadership, while we continue to attempt to move things forward. There is no limit to how well we can serve others and ourselves. There is always one more step, if we are willing to take it!

And the next question might be: How do we know when we are sufficiently grounded in our *Awareness, Attention,* and

Focus, and aligned with our *Intent* and our *Love*, and acting in the world in way that is grounded in this level of Leadership? Well, at this point on our Leadership journey, I am not sure that we ever actually know the answer. And the reason for this is that at this point, this question itself is not even a consideration for us. At this point, the Leadership levels have all merged into one. At this point, our Leadership perspective has merged into oneness. And I am talking about this in a very real way. At this level, we step into and experience our Leadership and our life as an expression of connection and oneness with everything else. I am talking about the very real experience of seeing and feeling everything as part of the whole, and then acting from within this perspective. This is real and very possible for us.

From this perspective, we may notice that life, all of it, is infused with a different type of energy. An energy that is con-nected to and responsive to all of the other energies. And through our expression of Leadership and all of our interac-tions, this perspective informs our thoughts, words and deeds. This occurs in part because of our commitment to exploring and working in active presence. This gives us the freedom to play and engage and dance with reality in a way that serves others and all of life even more completely.

Being and *Doing* while in this level of Leadership flow is sublime for an extraordinary Leader! At the same time, it gives us the feeling that we are simply living out of and expressing our natural, authentic self. So, on one hand it is sublime, and on the other, it is simply the normal state of our authentic self. We are simply *Being* who we really are. And the interesting thing is that over time, we begin to more and more find that we are express-ing ourselves through our authentic *Being* and *Doing*. We finally experience the internal freedom we have been seeking, to fully express ourselves in service to others.

So, up-leveling ourselves from level 9 to level 10 Leadership involves the individualized process of continuing further and deeper on our Leadership journey, in a way that is best suited and most beneficial to us and those we serve. This is the very deep exploration of our *Being*, that translates directly into all of our *Doing*. This is a more balanced maneuver, where our depth of *Being* is balanced with the precision of our *Doing*. *This is the Leadership Revolution that I am talking about!*

We don't have to overanalyze this up-leveling step to perform it. As a matter of fact, this would be counterproductive. Because of our deep connection to our internal and external reality, all we need do is simply "follow our bliss," as Joseph Campbell would say. At this point, even the provisional trust we have explored all along, is no longer necessary. This way of *Being* and *Doing* has become our reality. Our reality just is what it is. When we no longer deny it, or argue with it or resist it, we are free to engage with it and flow with it in the most efficient and effective and graceful way possible for us.

If we have made it this far on our extraordinary Leadership journey and have experienced some positive results, then let's keep going. If we just *Be* and *Do* our best version of the up-leveling practices, we will continue to learn and grow as a Leader. And that is the real point of our work and the AQ Model. We can become our own expression of the deeper possibilities of Leadership once we understand the map or the puzzle a little better and purposefully apply ourselves to it. That is why we are here. This is our work. This is our joy, our *bliss*.

And once again, all that we need to attain this level of Leadership is a rabid passion or burning desire to radically improve our Leadership performance. Without this, we will not be able to overcome the energetic threshold or the inertia of our previous habits or programming required to step fully into a new and more productive and inspiring way of *Being* and *Doing* as a Leader. Our desire to *Revolutionize* ourselves as a Leader must be stronger than our commitment to our previous habits or programming, and the results we created. Our *Awareness, Attention* and *Focus* and *Intent* and *Love* around this opportunity to truly serve as an extraordinary Leader must be sharp and keen and unwavering. This will always be the key to accomplishing this up-leveling process. And no matter how challenging we may find certain aspects of this process, we simply need to keep recommitting ourselves in thought, word and deed and we will succeed, no matter how many times it takes.

Up-leveling Others:

Step 1 – Support others to keep going and never stop! Support others with going deeper! There is always another level or a next step! Very similarly, as with the process of up-leveling ourselves, we are supporting and encouraging other Leaders who are on a similar journey, to keep going and never stop. We support them through our *Being* and *Doing* and our connection and interactions with them, to continue to explore even more deeply, and to follow their *bliss*, to go in the direction that they are drawn to serve. At this point, our role in this up-leveling process is usually that of a sounding board, or a mirror, reflecting back to someone what they already know. Through the *Leadership conversation*, we are reflecting back what they already know to be true and real for them, as they work through whatever remaining energetic impediments or attachments they have that are continuing to limit their next, best expression of extraordinary Leadership.

One of the keys here is that we are particularly sensitive to others' purpose and passion and preferences and that we do not try to influence them through our perspective. We should simply reflect what we are seeing in others and allow them to guide themselves in the most appropriate direction. This can be done through a number of methods that first include our own *Being* and *Doing* of this level, and then through a version of the Leadership conversation, gently pulling others deeper into themselves. We can accomplish this through our body language, tone of voice and word choice, as we create a clear picture or an experience for others to step further into.

In this step, we are supporting others with developing deeper levels of *Awareness, Attentions, Focus, Intent* and *Love* for themselves, so that they are also in a position to express the best versions of themselves for the good of all involved. We are helping other committed Leaders with stepping into and experiencing deeper aspects and talents that they possess, to further develop their Leadership expression, so that they can also see or hear or feel or pick up on even the subtlest signs of resistance that may be limiting ourselves or others. Supporting other's development in this area exponentially increases the number of people out there actively involved in higher levels of Leadership performance.

In order to encourage and support other Leaders with further developing their sense of oneness, we must obviously first develop this to a degree in ourselves, and then share our explorations in this area with others. We can share what we have seen and heard and felt while in this Leadership flow. We can share some of our up-leveling practices and our experiences while in the Leadership flow, along with their results. We can talk about the importance of this activity, about how our groups and teams and organizations and communities and countries need, more than ever, higher performing Leadership. We can discuss our responsibility as extraordinary Leaders with stepping into the fullness of our expression of Leadership, in service to others. We can genuinely speak about the joy and fun of sharing and connecting with other extraordinary Leaders, while stepping into the Leadership flow to move more gracefully through our challenging and inspiring journeys. And we can ask for ongoing feedback from others regarding their experiences in creating their personal expression of extraordinary Leadership. This is how we build on all of our experiences in higher levels of Leadership service.

In this step of up-leveling others, we are essentially having a Leadership conversation about the full responsibility and expression of Leadership with other extraordinary Leaders, while we are simultaneously *Being* and *Doing* our best expression of extraordinary Leadership. We are continuing to layer real and valuable Leadership *Beings* and *Doings* into our expression of extraordinary Leadership, in real time. We are growing in our ability to work very purposefully and very effectively at multiple levels simultaneously.

At this point, we are much like the Director or Lead Actor in an improvisational theatre group committed to this most pure form of collaborative expression, who masterfully co-creates an experience with others. Using purposefully creative versions of the "yes and" approach, we seek only to advance the scene forward while supporting the best expression of the other actors (Leaders and Followers) to create the most inspiring experience possible for the audience (our groups, teams, organizations, customers and stakeholders). This is a high-level Leadership art form, where everyone we are involved with and the environment we operate in, becomes a unified part of the "act," the "play," the "composition." *This is the Leadership Revolution that I am talking about!*

Through our Leadership **dance** with other extraordinary Leaders, we can support them and point them towards their full responsibility with this valuable and rewarding Leadership approach. We can also, at this point, engage with them and explore with them how they might engage others in their own Leadership circles to further expand this expression of Leadership. We can also ask them to follow up with us and let us know how their play is unfolding. We can help to create some momentum and engagement around this activity. And, as other extraordinary Leaders begin to engage themselves in this way with even greater numbers of Leaders, we become a key part of the purposeful perpetuation and exponential growth of, quite possibly, one of the most important and needed contributions to society that we could be a part of. And that is the significant up-leveling of Leadership understanding and performance, in service to our groups, teams, organizations, communities, countries and the global community.

Performing this up-leveling step automatically up-levels others into the next level of Leadership and further deepens our *Awareness, Attention, Focus, Intent* and *Love* regarding the deeper responsibilities and impacts of our Leadership. And this step multiplies the deeper Leadership purpose that many of us share, across teams and organizations and communities and industries and cultures. This up-leveling step automatically moves us into higher levels of Leadership performance while creating higher level experiences and higher levels of performance for those we interact with, in real time! That's just how it works! Just *Be* and *Do* and repeat and repeat. This is a thread of simplicity that runs through the AQ Model. Just *Be* and *Do* and jump into the experience of Leadership.

And now with the support of our personal up-leveling practices, it is time to move to the next Level of Leadership, Level 10, the Unification Age, and Unified Leadership. As valuable as Level 9, Integrated Leadership is, it still has limitations that hold us and others back from a fuller expression of our purpose, and the results that are possible.

As we now transition our exploration into Level 10 Leadership, I would make the point here on our Hero's Journey that we are not coming to the end of our journey with the AQ Model. We are actually coming back around to the beginning, where it all started. We are returning home in a sense. Phase 3 of the Hero's Journey, *The Return*, involves crossing the threshold back into the world of the ordinary while keeping one foot in each world (the world of the ordinary and the world of the extraordinary), to serve as a bridge between each world, and as an effective guide for others travelling in both directions. At Level 10 Leadership, we do not become more distant to those operating at lower levels of Leadership. We do not become more aloof or above everyone else. To the contrary, we actually become more connected to everyone else. At Level 10 Leadership, our perspective, based on our very real experience is that we are all one!

Level 9 Leadership Age & Approach	Predominant Leadership Characteristics	Up-Leveling Ourselves	Up-Leveling Others
Integration Age: Integrated Leadership	1. **Leadership through Actively Leading the Self** – typically based on all the above, and on an ongoing, deep exploration of the self (both light & shadow aspects) to the point where key aspects of the self are "known & accepted" as aspects of us all. 2. Grounded predominantly in the commitment to understanding and "actively leading" (*def.* – getting out and ahead of) the "self." 3. Uses *Awakening* to further align *attention* and *focus* with one's growing awareness and intent. 4. Merges the past, present and future into the "now present moment." 5. Focused on being *"present"* to the *"emerging reality"* and leading the self into it. 6. Problem Solving Method – *Moves through life as an expression of an integrated leader and human being.* 7. Common Quote – *"Who am I BEING and what am I DOING in the here and now, to move forward in alignment with my purpose."* 8. Common Outcomes – *Work becomes an integral part of our journey through life, along with the many positive impacts of this.*	the thoughtful and purposeful process of improving our performance through an ongoing commitment to growing our awareness, attention and focus Moving from Level 9 to Level 10: 1. Keep going and never stop! Go further! Go deeper! There is always another level or a next step.	helping others to improve their performance *"in real time,"* based on your growing awareness and your commitment to supportive, purposeful coaching Moving from Level 9 to Level 10: 1. Support others to keep going and never stop! Support others with going further and deeper! There is always another level or a next step.

*9th Level Impediment – **Release** the attachment to attachment. **Develop** the ability to accept the now present moment and step impeccably, into the whole of reality.*

Figure 13. Level 9 Leadership

CHAPTER 20

Level 10 Leadership
The Unification Age &
Unified Leadership

Leadership through a Consistent
Expression of the Whole of Life . . .

Leadership Age: *Unification Age*

The 10th Level of Leadership illuminated in the AQ Model represents the functional progression of an even more thoughtful and purposeful application of individual experience (Industrial Age), information and data gathering (Information Age), customization (Knowledge Age), the connection of people's passion and purpose with work systems and processes (Understanding Age), balance and sustainability (Wisdom Age), more direct insight (Transcendent Age), the alchemy of possibility from the seemingly impossible (Mystic Age), the use of Leadership as a path to Awakening (Awakened Age), by actively Leading ourselves (Integration Age) through an unwavering expression, in thought, word and deed, of the interconnectedness, interdependency and *oneness* of all things (Unification Age).

The distinctive theme of the Unification Age involves the perception and experience of the oneness that we are all a part of. This perspective and experience provides the freedom necessary for an extraordinary Leader to live and act and serve others even more deeply. This level of Unification is a key part of our Leadership journey and enables us to even further expand our understanding and impact. This level of Unification opens us up to perceive and experience and express the larger truths of life, more directly. This level of exploration can Lead to even deeper levels of understanding, appreciation for and application of the possibilities of Leadership. This level of deep work can lead to even more direct and valuable insights related to our Leadership performance, which can support us with determining the best course of action in the moment.

The term "Unification," in this case, refers to the ongoing experience of "oneness" with everyone and everything. This perspective takes the concept of connectedness even farther and deeper. Our sense of oneness involves not only the perspective that we are connected, but also, that we are *whole* within the whole of existence. The Unified ones of the past and present, represent those who have committed to the ongoing depth of exploration and practice necessary to understand the *whole* of ourselves, and therefore, others, in a way that helps us to serve even better. This age is represented by those with a significant depth of clarity related to the *whole picture* of Leadership. This supports us in more *wholeheartedly* Leading, especially during challenging situations.

Leadership Approach: *Unified Leadership*

There are clearly many aspects and expressions and levels of Unification available to us on our Leadership journey. And during our journey, we are constantly working towards higher degrees of Unification, whether we are *Aware* of it or not. On our Leadership journey, we are nearly constantly exploring and practicing and merging with the feedback from our interactions and results, and learning and growing from this, and continuing to refine our understanding and approach, and seeing and experiencing our connection and our place within this exploration. These are aspects of Unified Leadership, and they can be experienced to some degree, automatically, throughout our lives. Yet when we begin to work more directly on our ability to Unify our Leadership approach with the deeper realities we are exploring and experiencing, we can continue to enlarge our Leadership perspective and impact, exponentially.

As I have stated multiple times, the Leadership levels mapped out in the AQ Model, are not actually separate from each other, they are one. I have separated them out and arranged them in their typical progression, so that we could more clearly explore them and understand them. But, in reality, all of these levels of Leadership are overlapping and intermingled and interconnected with each other, like a complex, three-dimensional puzzle! And at times, we can experience and express elements of each of these levels, to some degree or another. This concept can be a little challenging to connect with, but this is the reality of the complexity of Leadership. The purpose of the AQ Model then, is to support us in understanding and performing more consistently and more purposefully in these higher levels of Leadership.

What we do at this level of Unified Leadership and how we do it is framed by a genuine predilection to perceive and to work directly with the deeper parts of ourselves and other Leaders within the oneness of reality, where we serve. And this genuine predilection is fueled by our own passion, purpose and growing depth as an extraordinary Leader. Our depth of Leadership is a reflection of the depth in all people and all things we serve, interact with, and grow from. Leaders at this level endeavor to connect with and support others in a way that brings out our best effort and our best performance and our best version of ourselves, as we more deeply explore and envision and manifest our vision together.

The up-leveling approaches that we developed and implemented specifically for ourselves in the previous level of Leadership, serve to automatically usher us into this next level. However, in order to remain or ground ourselves here, we must begin to practice and to embody and express the Predominant Leadership Characteristics below.

Predominant Leadership Characteristics: *Unified Leadership*

1. **Leadership through a Consistent Expression of the Whole of Life** is based on all of the previous levels and on *an unwavering expression in thought, word and deed, of the interconnectedness, interdependency and "oneness" of all things.* This level of Leadership is focused on the very real expression of "wholeness" at a very deep level, to Lead extraordinarily, even in the most challenging situations.

2. **Grounded predominantly in** an expanded understanding and acceptance of whatever life is presenting us in the moment. Because of this depth of presence to reality, we can develop the ability to discern the deeper elements of complexity, to engage

with it and to move towards more beneficial outcomes.
This level of presence helps us to more directly work
within reality *as it is emerging*, before the present
moment is gone. This is the creative aspect of presence
that we can directly merge with, in service to others.

3. *Uses Integration* as a catalyst to merge into the
whole of life. By consistently working within the
emerging reality, we develop a high level of agility
with co-creating experiences and efforts, as we more
effectively serve others.

4. **Sees the past, present and potential future** in the
now present moment. At this level of Leadership,
our experience within time is more fluid, yet it is
only reflected in the now present moment. From this
perspective, we are positioned to better appreciate,
accept, integrate and work with our past, present and
potential future, and to share this perspective and
experience with others.

5. **Focused on *Being*** present IN the emerging reality and dancing with it to create life as a work of art.
Through the process of consistently operating in deep
presence, we can experience reality as an emerging
scene or foundational structure, and from this position, we can purposefully and actively improvise the
Leadership approach most appropriate to engaging
with the present scene, and in a way that brings about
the optimal learning and growth for all involved.

6. **Problem Solving Method** involves approaching all
phenomenon as part of the flow of life. When we
are deeply present within the emerging reality, the

foundation of creativity, there is only this emerging
experience of life, to engage with impeccably, and to
share with others from this perspective as we move
through the challenges that face us.

7. **Common Leadership Statement** may be any version
of *"There is only the now present moment, and there
is much we can do here!"* Think about that one. Who
among us has ever heard that one in our workplace?
If any of us has ever heard or used any version of this,
well, very nicely done!

8. **Common outcome of this Leadership approach** is
that the concept of "work" ceases to exist. At this point,
all activity is perceived as an opportunity for learning,
growth, co-creation and service. From this Leadership perspective, "all the world's a stage," and wherever
we find ourselves, the opportunity exists to creatively
express our purpose, in service to others and all of life.
This is why we are here.

*The Unified Leadership approach cannot be completely con-
ceptualized, but it can be actualized!* It can be discussed and
deliberated but this discussion cannot begin to approach the
depth of understanding and precision and versatility and agility and complexity and purpose *Being* expressed by a Leader
at this level. It is the purposeful act of an extraordinary Leader
who has achieved a level of *personal Leadership mastery*. And
although most people may not completely understand what
a Unified Leader is *Being* and *Doing* at this point, they know
that they are in the presence of an extraordinary experience,
and that this presence supports them with moving deeper
into their own purpose. This is the essence of a Unified

Leader's impact on others, to directly and indirectly support our expanded *Awareness* and real experience with deeper levels of our purpose.

By its very name, "Unified Leadership," and based on the fact that it is the last and 10th level of Leadership illuminated in the AQ Model (at this time), some might think that this is a level of Leadership that is unattainable by us mere mortals. And there has been some truth to that, historically. And that is mostly because there was not a clear and readily available *map* of how to get us there. The AQ Model has changed that, however! Now we have the map and all of the key pieces of the puzzle needed to understand the map! It's a new day for committed Leaders everywhere! So, yes, Unified Leadership is definitely attainable, even by us mere mortals! More than at any time before, we can achieve this high-level of Leadership self-mastery, in service to others. We can very thoughtfully express a level of Leadership service that represents the very best version of our personal Leadership purpose, and in a way that exceptionally supports others and our organizations.

And, let's get even clearer about what this level of Leadership looks like in expression. Although there is no fixed model of a Unified Leader, or any other level of Leadership for that matter, we can explore some generalities to help us to get our arms around this expression of Leadership. Level 10, Unified Leaders, are at times represented by those who have stepped off of any formal employment relationship within a singular organization. In this case, these Leaders are often operating on a larger or more diverse scale, endeavoring to impact others and systems more broadly. Unified Leaders often position themselves much more broadly, to create larger impacts than would be possible if they were only focusing their efforts on the specific details within a narrower area of impact.

Unified Leaders, due to our core purpose and area of inter-action (deep presence), are often found interacting with various groups and individuals, across industries and across other areas of human interaction. Unified Leaders are here for the good of us all, and very often work towards serving greater and greater numbers of people. They sometimes do this very publicly, attracting some level of notoriety, while in other examples, a Unified Leader may work completely behind the scenes. That all depends on the predilection of the Leader, as well as the needs of those the Leader serves. Although Unified Leaders are typi-cally committed to serving larger numbers of people at a very deep level, they are still quite approachable and quite grounded as Leaders and human beings.

A Unified Leader may choose to work in a model that serves various groups or organizations, and in other situations they will work for periods of time within a single group or industry, lending their perspective to both larger scale and more indi-vidualized efforts. These Leaders may also be found serving in any area of white-collar or blue-collar business sectors, science, politics, education, human services, the environment, music, theatre and other arts, religion and other spiritual groups, in indigenous or native cultures, working in the home raising a family, and any other area of human interaction. They may be found within the ranks of those Leaders who teach or write books or deliver training workshops. They may even develop their own unique model or approach for serving others. Or they may choose to work more quietly, one-on-one, with those they serve. There are no limitations related to our expression of Leadership, as a Unified Leader.

Yet, as a Unified Leader, no matter what form of service we choose to express ourselves through, those involved know on multiple levels that there is something extraordinary about the interactions and perspective of this Leader. Most people know that there is something of high value that this Leader is reflecting back to them. And that there is much depth to what this Leadership is sharing. And most people can't help but realize that they would like to learn more, much more, about what this Leader is *Being* and *Doing* and expressing. I am not talking about the experience of observing a "motivational speaker" here, although Unified Leaders can be very motivating and inspiring. I am talking about the very real and genuine experience of us, merging with other's purpose through the process of Leadership. And by the way, Level 10 Leaders do not pretend to stand above anyone else. The circular nature of the journey of a Unified Leader positions us side-be-side with everyone else on the path.

No matter what form of service a Unified Leader chooses to express ourselves through, those involved are typically impacted very deeply. The interesting thing however, is that depending on the level of *Awareness* of the individual interacting with a Unified Leader, some people may actually come away with a very strong, negative reaction to this Leader. They may consider the experience to be "nonsense," or a "waste of time." Such is the variability of the nature of our perspective and programming. Everyone is welcome to their own viewpoint. We are all on our own journeys. However, the key question for us to answer is: What was our experience like with this Leader, and more importantly, what is our next step on our Leadership journey, and what are we going to *Be* and *Do* in the here and now to move forward in service to others?

And here is a key point to highlight again. Even at this level of Leadership, there are still no guarantees. Our Leadership presence and contributions are only one piece of a larger, complex dynamic of action and interaction. As we have explored throughout the AQ Model, our Leadership can be a critical component in supporting the betterment of many types of processes and systems, and the experience and growth of the people involved. Yet there can be other *energies* at play, other *forces* with their own programmed or hidden or more explicit agendas. And sometimes, these forces and agendas can thwart the efforts of even high performing Leaders and the committed people they serve.

As stated several times already, the context in which Leadership occurs is incredibly complex and nuanced. There are numerous elements within this context that can either support or hinder an optimal outcome. And although there are never any guarantees, high-level Leadership often does provide for the best potential for success within the complexities that we are faced with, and so much more. Additionally and very importantly, at this level of Leadership, the goals or the objectives of an effort are actually secondary to the genuine interactions with others within the oneness of our experience together. *Other people and energies can come in to thwart the achievement of our goals, but they cannot thwart our experience in oneness!*

I have also mentioned at each Leadership level, how there have been many examples of each level throughout history and even today. With that said, what might a Level 10, Unified Leader look like from our past or in our present day? Who might we consider in this category? Based on what we know now, we could most certainly put together a list of possible Leaders for this category, but how about if we do this instead: What if we were to identify for ourselves, one potential Leader that we consider in this category? What if we were to do some level of research on this Leader, to get to know them as much as we can? We could read about them or read their books or view their other works, if these are available. We could do an internet search to understand their perspective and approach more deeply. We could inquire with others who may have known them, to get a feel for what it is like to work directly with this Leader. And if we are really fortunate, we may be able to reach out to this Leader and work more directly with them in some way. What if we were to familiarize ourselves with this Level of Leadership to the point that it serves as sort of an *anchor point* to pull us towards this possibility, as we continue on our journey of Leadership growth?

We could even use some version of this type of activity, as part of our personal up-leveling approach into this level of extraordinary Leadership. The point I am trying to make here is that Unified Leadership is most certainly accessible to us, and the world would benefit tremendously from our efforts towards this goal. The number of Unified Leaders out there is not that large yet, but that is all changing quickly. More and more of us are getting clear about this possibility and moving in this direction as best we can. And now we have a map that can help to get us there more directly. Our groups and clubs and teams and families need us! Our organizations need us! Our local, state and federal governments need us! The world needs us! And it is time for us to answer this call! *This is the Leadership Revolution that I am talking about!*

We are truly capable of so much more as Leaders. It's just that most of us have not been clear enough about what is possible or available to us. And now we are clear about what is possible for us. Now we are clear about what is available to us. And so, we can move confidently forward! And when we commit to the journey of Leadership at this level of Unification, then everything we look at or are involved in as a Leader appears to us in the context of an emerging expression of oneness within the whole of existence, and as an emerging opportunity to engage with and express our passion and purpose. The natural expression of our Leadership seeks to move ourselves and others even further into our extraordinary nature.

In order to accomplish this, we must first acknowledge and connect with our deeper purpose to serve and support others along this challenging journey, and to make a significant difference in our life and the lives of others. We must passionately and relentlessly follow our purpose. And once this realization and commitment to expressing, in thought, word and deed, the interconnectedness, interdependency and oneness of all things takes hold, then, *the questions themselves become the answers we seek.*

And even with all of this, there is still more available within the possibility of Leadership. More to share with and give to others, our organizations and ourselves. There remain still untapped reserves within ourselves and others, that when understood and expressed, can bring even further levels of results and even further degrees of growth and satisfaction experienced by those we serve and ourselves. The Unified Leadership approach serves as an incredible vantage point to more clearly and committedly see the *whole picture* of Leadership and all of its impacts. From this level, we can more freely access any of the more positive elements within all of Leadership, while adding to them, even more *Awareness, Attention, Focus, Intent* and *Love in Action.*

The Unified Leadership approach further enhances the look and feel and experience and results of those involved. The freedom we experience at this level of Leadership, and our ability to help others to access greater levels of freedom for themselves, brings those involved into much greater alignment with their purpose and passion as expressed through our work or the task at hand. And yet, even at this level, there is more that awaits us as an extraordinary Leader. There is always another step, waiting to be discovered.

And how might we continue to move further and deeper at this level of Leadership? At this point on our Leadership journey, any further up-leveling approaches can be determined based on the needs of the whole. We can borrow, adapt, create or improvise these as needed, based on the situations we are involved in and the growth needs of others. Similarly, we can also approach the energetic impediments or attachments that we will most certainly continue to be dealing with at this level. We can determine which of these attachments is most beneficial for us to explore and address, as we develop the most appropriate new habits to move beyond them. As we continue with a commitment to our deeper explorations in Leadership Awareness, and continue to exercise our *Awareness, Attention, Focus, Intent* and *Love* in service to others, additional perceptions and perspectives will most certainly emerge to fuel and inspire our ongoing learning and growth.

It could be said at this level of Leadership, that we actually get to create our own way or approach through life, but that would not be totally accurate. At this level, anything we choose to create or any approach we decide to use, is directly based on our interaction and interconnectedness with the whole, our experience and service in oneness. At this point, there is no more individual "I" that creates. At this point, we have been pulled by the path itself into the oneness of co-creation. At this point, we are simply a part of the creative process of the whole of life itself. *At this point, we are co-creators with all that is . . . oneness.*

Level 10 Leadership Age & Approach	Predominant Leadership Characteristics	Up-Leveling Ourselves	Up-Leveling Others
		the thoughtful and purposeful process of improving our performance through an ongoing commitment to growing our awareness, attention and focus	helping others to improve their performance *"in real time,"* based on your growing awareness and your commitment to supportive, purposeful coaching
Unification Age: Unified Leadership	1. **Leadership through a Consistent Expression of the Whole of Life** – typically based on all the above, and on an unwavering expression, in thought, word and deed, of the interconnectedness, interdependency and "oneness" of all things. 2. Grounded predominantly in an expanded understanding and acceptance of whatever life is presenting us with, in the moment. 3. *Uses Integration as catalyst to merge into the whole of life.* 4. Sees the past, present and potential future in the now present moment. 5. Focused on being *"present"* IN the *"emerging reality"* and dancing with it to create life as a work of art. 6. Problem Solving Method – *Approaches all phenomenon as part of the flow of life.* 7. Common Quote – *"There is only the now present moment, and there is much we can do here!"* 8. Common Outcomes – The concept of work ceases to exist.	1. To be determined by us, based on the needs of those we serve and the environments we serve in.	1. To be determined by us, based on the needs of those we serve and the environments we serve in.

10th Level Energetic Impediment – 10th Level Energetic Impediment – To be determined by us, based on the needs of those we serve and the environments we serve in.

Figure 14. Level 10 Leadership

CHAPTER 21

The BIG Complex
Puzzle of Leadership

*. . . But unless we step into this puzzle and
explore it experientially, we may never be able to
catch a glimpse of what it really looks like, and
feels like, and sounds like, and smells like.*

Throughout our Leadership journey, we have been talking about and clarifying elements of the BIG, complex puzzle of Leadership. This is a critical effort for us to be able to see and understand, and then to be able to apply our Leadership to the real challenges we face as Leaders. So, let's now take a moment to look specifically at the BIG, complex puzzle of Leadership, from the perspective of all we have learned on our journey so far. Let's further clarify the picture of this puzzle so that we can more clearly see what this thing looks like and how it is connected in the AQ Model, so that we can utilize it most effectively.

The foundation of the BIG, complex puzzle of Leadership is based in our growing *Awareness*, *Attention* and *Focus*. Everything flows from here. As we grow in these areas, we have access to more expanded perspectives and more and better choices in the face of a challenge. The deeper root cause of our global problems with Leadership are to be found right here, with the misguided or inadequate level or degree of *Awareness, Attention* and *Focus* expressed by far too many Leaders. In contrast, the solution for our global Leadership problems is also to be found right here, with those of us who are also committed to growing our *Awareness, Attention* and *Focus,* to express the best versions of ourselves, in service to others. To be clear, the AQ Model, this Leadership path, is intended to facilitate the direct, experiential exploration of our growth in Awareness, Attention, Focus, Intent and Love.

From this growing foundation emerges our understanding of the deeper meanings of Leadership, which includes *Love in Action,* or *Connection* and *Movement,* or *Support* and *Growth.* And it is through our growing *Awareness, Attention* and *Focus* as a Leader, that we are able to understand and connect with and express these deeper meanings *of who we are in service to others.*

A couple of additional pieces of the puzzle that we explored on Part 1 of our journey are the complimentary, core elements within the meaning of Leadership, our *Being* and *Doing.* Our *Being* flows out of our growing *Awareness* and is expressed as a function of our *Meta-Mindset* as it coalesces in our *Mindset,* through our refined *Attention* within our more expanded perspective here. Our *Being* is represented by our consistent attitude, beliefs and how we show up in life, and also our depth and expression of *Love.* Our *Doing* flows out of our purposeful, concentrated and aligned *Focus* as expressed through our well-developed *Skill Sets* with our thoughtfully chosen *Tool Sets.* Our *Doing* is represented by our consistent formal and informal approach to moving things forward and getting things done in our increasingly complex work environment and in life, and also represents the complementary *Action* component of the meaning of Leadership (*Love in Action*).

At this point, our BIG, complex puzzle of Leadership includes and connects the foundational components of our *Awareness, Attention* and *Focus*; our understanding of the meaning of Leadership, *Love in Action*; and its associated core elements of *Being and Doing*; along with how all of these are connected to and expressed through our *Meta-Mindset, Mindset, Skill Sets* and *Tool Sets*. It's all connected!

It is these foundational elements of our BIG, complex puzzle of Leadership that position us to gather the mass and energy and inertia needed to move beyond the *Energetic Threshold* of our daily workplaces, organizations and institutions. The *Energetic Threshold* in any environment is represented by the amount of desire and commitment (*energy*) required to move beyond the boundary (*threshold*) that holds us back from expressing our continuous best effort. We must light our own fires first, to move ourselves beyond the *Energetic Threshold*, to consistently give our best. And then, purposefully and consistently support our coworkers and teams and friends and families in raising their energy, desire and commitment above the *Energetic Threshold* required for them to give their best. Anything less will not generate the level of energy and momentum necessary to break out of the status quo, to move further on our Leadership journey, *our Hero's Journey*.

These foundational elements of our BIG, complex puzzle of Leadership also position us to see and understand the limitations of the most predominant expressions of Leadership on the planet, or the status quo of Leadership, which is represented by Level 1 (*Authoritarian Leadership*) and Level 2 (*Evidence-Based Leadership*). These foundational elements, these key Leadership concepts, also help us to establish the sufficient understanding, perspective and energy needed to effectively work to move beyond the status quo of Leadership, and into higher levels of genuine Leadership performance.

The other pieces of the BIG, complex puzzle of Leadership in Part 1 include the two levels of Leadership covered, the *Authoritarian* and *Evidence-Based Leadership* approaches. And each of these levels of Leadership (puzzle pieces) are presented through a description of the *Leadership Age* that they come out of; a description of the *Leadership Level* itself; the *Predominant Leadership Characteristics* of the level; the *Energetic Impediment* (*Attachment*) associated with this level; and the recommended *Up-leveling steps* for moving beyond the *Energetic Impediment* and into the next level of Leadership. This cluster of associated pieces of the BIG, complex puzzle of Leadership represent a unique and innovative approach to Leadership development and create the consistent pattern of functional progression characteristic of each level of the AQ Model of Leadership development.

These first two levels, these two key pieces of the BIG, complex puzzle of Leadership, although representative of the status quo of Leadership, provide us with a clear picture of the predominant Leadership approaches out there today, to help us to understand them more deeply, and bring our *Awareness* to how we may be defaulting to these sub-optimal approaches, especially in more challenging situations. These first two levels represent key pieces of the BIG, complex puzzle of Leadership necessary for us to more thoughtfully and purposefully move beyond them. These first two levels of Leadership are like stepping stones for us, or like the first steps of a ladder, leading us upwards.

Taken all together, this initial exploration of the BIG, complex puzzle of Leadership in Part 1 of our journey positions us to more deeply see our current state of Leadership, and to hear and feel *the call* to move ourselves beyond these limited expressions of Leadership. Part 1 of this book represents the 1st Phase of the Hero's Journey, *The Separation* (from the status quo). That's the picture of the BIG, complex puzzle of Leadership, so far.

Now, let's weave into our BIG, complex puzzle of Leadership, the key components of Part 2 of our exploration, or Phase 2 of our Hero's Journey (*The Initiation*). In Part 2 of our exploration we weave into the BIG, complex puzzle of Leadership the key components needed to solidly establish ourselves on the path of extra-ordinary Leadership. This starts with the critical element of developing our own *Leadership Purpose Statement*, the *What, Why, Where and How* of our extra-ordinary Leadership expression. This is a critical piece of the BIG, complex puzzle of Leadership.

Our *Leadership Purpose* is our compass, our anchor, and the source of inexhaustible energy that can keep us going through the ups and downs and challenges of our Leadership journey, and life. The *"Why"* of our *Purpose Statement* is connected to and comes out of our *Meta-Mindset* (*our Awareness*). While, the *"What"* of our *Purpose Statement* is connected to and comes out of our *Mindset* (*our Attention*). The *"Where"* of our *Purpose Statement* is also related to and flows out of our *Mindset* (*Attention*) and represents a natural extension out into the future, of the *"What"* of our *Purpose Statement*. And the *"How"* of our *Purpose Statement* is related to and flows out of our developed *Skill Sets* and chosen *Tool Sets* (*our Focus*).

Our *Leadership Purpose* is also a critical piece of the BIG, complex puzzle of Leadership necessary for us to understand and to step off of the *Drama Triangle*. The *Drama Triangle* and its associated dysfunctional roles of the *Victim, Persecutor* and *Rescuer* sit in and overlay *Leadership levels 1 and 2* and help to keep us trapped in unnecessary drama and dysfunction. Through the consistent application of our *Leadership Purpose*, along with our understanding of the *Drama Triangle*, we are positioned to step out of these dysfunctional roles and into the opposite, more supportive, productive roles of the *Co-Creator, Catalyst* and *Coach*. These roles sit in and overlay Leadership *Levels 3 and 4*. So, stepping off of the *Drama Triangle* is a key component of moving into higher levels of Leadership performance.

The next piece of the BIG, complex puzzle of Leadership is the key component of our *connection to others* and the value of developing deeper, more productive relationships with those we interact with. And when we actually see the inherent value of others, I mean all others, every interaction can both inform and transform our journey. Everyone and every situation, *especially* the challenging ones, then becomes our own personal mentor and coach. This critical piece of the BIG, complex puzzle of Leadership actually overlays and is connected to every part, every piece, every step of our Leadership journey. *People are important* and they are a critical piece of the BIG, complex puzzle of Leadership.

The remaining key pieces of the BIG, complex puzzle of Leadership in Part 2 of our exploration, include the *Leadership Levels 3 through 7*. Each level of Leadership, each piece of this part of the puzzle, is presented identically to the first two levels of Leadership. The progression within each level of Leadership follows the same pattern to reinforce the understanding and integration of the information presented. The pattern and repetition of this structure supports the development of our own "mental map" of the territory or puzzle we are exploring.

Each level of Leadership is connected to and comes out of its previous level of Leadership. Leadership Levels 1 and 2 are more Transactional in nature and, many times, are based on a

Leader's expression of their dominance over others; and Leadership Levels 3 (*Coaching Leadership*) and 4 (*Transformational Leadership*) tend to be focused on the motivation and inspiration of others to create personal, group and organizational Transformation; and Leadership Level 5 (*Servant Leadership*) seeks to create and support a more lasting and sustainable transformation as we continually monitor and adjust to the ever-changing internal and external environment; and Level 6 (*Transcendental Leadership*) seeks the deeper level of insight needed to explore and approach our potential; while Level 7 *"Leadership"* focuses on working directly with the subtle elements of ourselves and the environment to help us create *possibility* out of the *seemingly impossible*. These are the key connections and interrelationships of the pieces of the BIG, complex puzzle of Leadership. This is the progression so far.

And these pieces of the puzzle in Part 2 of our exploration connect with and flow out of and build on the pieces of the puzzle we put together in Part 1 of our exploration. The pieces of the puzzle in Part 2 of our exploration, build on those we explored in Part 1, and help to establish us solidly in Phase 2 of the Hero's Journey, *The Initiation*. The *Separation* from the status quo in Part 1 leads to our *Initiation* into an extra-ordinary journey of Leadership expression in Part 2. And all of this prepares us for Part 3 of our exploration, Phase 3 of our Hero's Journey, *The Return*, to where we all started.

And now, to complete, in a sense, the BIG, complex puzzle of Leadership we have been exploring and building, let's weave into our puzzle, the Part 3 components of our exploration. In Part 3, *The Return*, we connect more deeply with and build on the previous pieces of our puzzle of Leadership, to move even further along on our journey into *extraordinary* Leadership performance. And at the same time, we circle back around to reconnect with where we all started on our Leadership journey. Part 3 of our Leadership exploration closes the circle and, through our experience, simultaneously connects us with everyone at every part of the Leadership journey.

The key pieces of the BIG, complex puzzle of Leadership in Part 3 of our exploration include embracing the *Totality of our Leadership* through the practice of Leadership Levels 8, 9 and 10. Level 8, *Awakened Leadership*, connects with other inspired Leaders out there, while Level 9, *Integrated Leadership*, connects us more deeply with ourselves, including our light and shadow aspects. And Level 10, *Unified Leadership*, merges us with everyone and everything and connects us back to where we all started, and to every other Leader and Follower out there. And to our foundation of *Awareness, Attention* and *Focus*, we add our *Intent* and *Love*. Our *Intent* relates to the deeper *"Why"* of our *Purpose Statement* and comes out of our *Meta-Mindset* (our *Awareness*) and relates more to the question of "why we are here?" And *Love*, is obviously a key element of our *meaning of Leadership* and is a key driver of our deeper *connection as human beings, and the deeper desire to serve and support each other.*

These last key pieces of the puzzle, in Part 3, serve to fill in the picture of Leadership that we have been exploring and building. These last pieces of the puzzle add significant depth and gracefulness and purpose and gratitude and effectiveness to the BIG, complex puzzle of Leadership, and connect everything together, giving all of the elements of the puzzle even more meaning and value.

This is not called the BIG, complex puzzle of Leadership for nothing. As we can all see, all of the elements of our exploration in the AQ Model of Leadership development come together in a very dynamic way to build on and support all of the other elements. That is why the entirety of the AQ Model cannot be depicted in a simple diagram, like some of the more basic Leadership development models out there. The whole of the AQ Model cannot be captured in some kind of geometric or circular diagram in a way that would do it justice. We can diagram certain elements of the model to illuminate and simplify some of the details, and this can be very helpful to clarifying specific elements of the model, but we cannot capture the whole of it in a simple diagram.

The BIG, complex puzzle of Leadership is actually built piece-by-piece and held together by our ongoing growth and expansion in Awareness, Attention, Focus, Intent and Love. Our Awareness Quotient, which represents the depth and breadth of our perception and experience, is then the key to our purposeful and effective growth in Leadership service. Our Awareness Quotient reflects the measure or impact of our efforts and progress as a Leader, and it also represents the glue that connects and holds our growing perspective on Leadership together. And the name of this Leadership development model, the AQ (Awareness Quotient) Model, is reflective of this process. Remember, our experience in Leadership, and in life, all starts and ends with our Awareness. That is why the AQ Model starts and ends with this (Awareness).

To start to get the full picture of the BIG complex puzzle of Leadership, we must frequently look at it and explore all of the pieces and how they fit together. But, unless we step into this puzzle and explore it experientially, we may never be able to catch a glimpse of what it really looks like, and feels like, and sounds like, and smells like. When we do commit to the journey of extraordinary Leadership however, and study it, and practice it, and live it, then the full picture of the BIG, complex puzzle of Leadership will take shape for us, *and then we find that we are also a key piece of this Leadership puzzle. This is the Leadership Revolution that I am talking about!*

CHAPTER 22

Closing the Circle
on Our Hero's Journey

By closing the circle here, we now position ourselves,
as extraordinary Leaders, at every point on
the Leadership journey, simultaneously.

So, are we there yet? Are we done? Have we completed our Leadership journey, our Hero's Journey? Well, in a word, No. We are never done on our Leadership journey, our Hero's Journey. There is always more. By the way, I would hope that by now that it is abundantly clear why our Leadership journey is considered to be an expression of *the Hero's Journey*. The exploration that we are moving through is undoubtedly inspiring, yet not for the faint of heart. This level of commitment to serving others through extraordinary Leadership takes a serious level of desire and purpose and courage, and so much more. There are many challenges and traps and potential disappointments that await us.

And along the way, we will continue to come face-to-face with our most worthy adversary, which is *ourselves*. We will get the opportunity to confront many of the aspects of ourselves that have been holding us back, that we have been resisting or in denial of. We are our chief challenge in life, and the Leadership Journey, the Hero's Journey, is primarily focused on understanding and addressing this very challenge. And although this exploration has focused mostly on the impact of our efforts as applied to our organizations and workplaces, I want to add one more consideration to this journey. It would not be possible to commit to this level of expanded Leadership development, through our focus on the growth and refinement of our *Awareness, Attention, Focus, Intent* and *Love* without it having a similar impact on our perspective and performance in all other areas of our lives. It's all connected! A genuine path of Leadership development will also help us to become a more *Aware* and better spouse and sibling and friend and citizen and human *Being* (and *Doing*). What a gift.

So many challenges await us on this journey that we have chosen to undertake. But, so do countless joys and learnings and growth opportunities and deeper relationships and new relationships and more positive results and more ease and grace and more expanded *Awareness, Attention, Focus, Intent* and *Love.* The challenges that we have thoughtfully chosen to put ourselves through, will most certainly, exponentially, give back to us and others, through our more purposeful collaborations in the face of the challenges that we are confronted with. And we can assure this through our ongoing commitment to our deepening Leadership purpose, along with our passion for serving others.

This is the point in our journey where we *close the circle.* In other words, we return, in a sense, to where we started. We return to where we all start. And this return home helps to keep us connected to the whole of the journey itself. This return home provides us with the ongoing opportunity to serve all of life, at all levels. This return home keeps us connected with our entire Leadership family, and the entire Leadership journey. By taking this journey from the beginning, and out into the possibility of Leadership, and then all the way around and back to where we all started, we are experientially connected with the entire Leadership journey and everyone on it. By closing the circle here, in oneness, we now position ourselves as extraordinary Leaders, at every point on the Leadership journey, simultaneously. Through this experience, the *ordinary* becomes *extraordinary*. And through our continuing efforts, the *extraordinary* then becomes simply *ordinary*. It is from this perspective that we are in a position to serve all of life in the most balanced way possible. *This is the Leadership Revolution that I am talking about!*

Yet, our journey continues! Our service continues! Another cycle of learning and growth, another Hero's Journey is sure to present itself again, to call us into further action. This is why we are here. Enjoy the journey!

CHAPTER 23

The Full Application of the AQ Model (how to really do it)

. . . in order to really do this thing, we must
very thoughtfully and purposefully apply
our very best, every step of the way.

We have explored our way through a significant amount of Leadership material and the key pieces of the BIG, complex puzzle of Leadership through the AQ Model. We have illuminated multiple Leadership levels and explored the expanding progression of Leadership. We have also explored some of the major energetic impediments that we face on our Leadership journey, those attachments that further prevent us from grounding ourselves in these higher levels of Leadership. We have explored the key up-leveling strategies that can support us in moving from one Leadership level to the next. And along the way, we also explored several other key concepts and important perspectives within genuine Leadership. We have journeyed far beyond the status quo, the norm of Leadership, and back around again to where we all started. We have taken this Leadership journey all the way!

The AQ Model is designed in such a way that it can be used as a straight-forward, step-by-step exploration or progression for our Leadership growth and development. There is also plenty of room in the model to finesse or modify our Leadership approach, based on our individual and group circumstances. But since the Leadership puzzle is actually quite BIG and quite complex, and a little challenging to get our arms around, some of us may still be asking ourselves, "But how do we really do this? What should we do next?" So, let's review a few key points for further consideration.

In order to really do this thing, we must first, *really do this*. I know that sounds like common sense. But unfortunately, common sense does not always carry over into common practice. So, in order to really do this thing, we must very thoughtfully and purposefully apply our very best, every step of the way. Just do our best! Half-hearted attempts will only take us so far and eventually stall our progression. This issue of not giving our best, actually stalls numerous growth efforts. And then we end up typically blaming the model or methodology or process itself. So, in order to really do this, we need to really do this. And if we really do any version of this, we will progress on our Leadership journey, in service to others.

We must stand in the full *Awareness* of our responsibility as a Leader and we must *pay Attention* to our Leadership purpose and the needs of our teams and organizations. And we must use our concentrated *Focus* on the things that matter on our Leadership journey. These are the key, foundational elements of effectively accomplishing anything. It all starts and ends here! That is why they are illuminated right from the beginning in Chapter 1 and carried forward throughout this exploration. The up-leveling steps of the AQ Model also serve to directly cultivate and grow our *Awareness, Attention* and *Focus*. Therefore, in order to really do this, we must start here. We must work with these and exercise our capability and capacity here. We must exercise our *Attention* and *Focus* on our Leadership purpose. How long can we maintain our *Attention* and *Focus* here each day. If only for a minute, that's a good start. Tomorrow, try for two minutes and keep expanding from there. *We should start from wherever we are, and courageously go forward from there.*

That brings up the next reminder. Our Leadership Purpose is critical to our progression and our journey. If we are not clear about the What, the Why, the Where, and the How of our deeper Leadership purpose, we may not be able to gather and maintain the energy and direction we need to navigate this path over the long haul. We must clarify and re-clarify our Leadership Purpose over time. Our Leadership Purpose is our compass, our anchor, and the source of *inexhaustible energy* that can keep us going through the ups and downs and challenges of our Leadership journey and life. So, in order to really do this thing, we must do the work necessary to clarify and anchor ourselves to our Leadership Purpose, especially the "why" of our purpose. And if we really do any version of this thing, we will progress on our Leadership journey, in service to others.

The above issues are key for us to really do this thing. Coincidently, these issues are the same keys that can help us to progress in any endeavor we choose. If we are going to really do something, we need to make the decision and put in the ongoing effort needed to really do it. We need to apply our *Awareness, Attention* and *Focus* to the process itself. This is where our growing insight and perspective and experience will come from and be shared from. And the key support structure for this decision process and for fueling our effort along the way is our clarity of purpose. These are the basic and critical keys to really doing this thing on an epic, Hero's Journey scale. On a scale that everyone we serve, deserves.

This extraordinary Leadership journey has been mapped out in enough detail for us to simply follow along step-by-step, and to thoughtfully modify it as needed. We can re-read and re-explore any section that we are drawn to. Study the figures at the end of most chapters that summarize the information in the chapter. Write some notes to clarify things or create personal reminders of key points. Start back at the beginning and work up through the levels of Leadership until we genuinely feel that we are not yet grounded in the particular level that we are re-reading. And then dive into the work (play) necessary to ground there, and to prepare to move beyond that level. Just follow the recommendations and/or modify as appropriate. We can also choose one of the chapters related to a key Leadership concept, and spend some time exploring this concept to more deeply understand its application and impact.

And eventually, we should even consider developing our own Leadership model, our own map, based on our own discoveries along the way. That is what we are actually doing on this journey anyway! The AQ Model serves to support us in moving further and further into our authentic Leadership-self, each step of the way. On this journey, we are all becoming more and more of the best version of ourselves as a Leader, in service to others. All of our Leadership journeys serve as a mirror, reflecting our efforts and our impacts and our *Being* and *Doing*, in every direction, for us all to benefit from. There is no singular expression of extraordinary Leadership. The word "extraordinary" actually means "astonishing" and simultaneously, "unusual." So, all of our expressions of extraordinary Leadership are unique, to us.

And lastly, remember to seek feedback and interaction with others. Don't make this into some top-secret project. We should be transparent about our Leadership Purpose and *Intent* and share this liberally. And just keep moving through the levels at the pace that works best for us. Consider creating a small group to work through the material together. There can be much benefit with this. Other people are so important, and so essential to our Leadership journeys. Use this book, this tool that has been presented. Use it in any way that helps on our Leadership journey. Through our purposeful *Being* and *Doing* of any version of this effort, further insights will come to us, and further growth opportunities will present themselves. That is just how this journey works. *Be* the journey!

CHAPTER 24

The Revolutionary Leadership Opportunity

It is now time for us to make our stand for those we serve, for those who need us so much.

The *Leadership Revolution* is obviously not based on shifting our understanding and performance with any one aspect of Leadership. The *Leadership Revolution* involves a nearly complete up-leveling of our software, our paradigms, our assumptions and agreements regarding Leadership. And the purpose of this book has been to reveal and illuminate these key elements of the *Leadership Revolution*, the key pieces of the BIG, complex puzzle of Leadership, for us to explore and to step further into. With this level of clarity comes the opportunity and the responsibility to align our Leadership purpose and passion. The AQ Model is designed to directly support our commitment toward higher levels of Leadership performance, in the here and now of our journeys.

There should be no question at this point regarding the extent of the need for extraordinary Leadership, and no question regarding the value that extraordinary Leaders can bring to any group, team or organization. Every area of human endeavor, from business to politics, struggles unnecessarily to some degree, due to the limitations placed upon them by inadequate or underperforming Leadership. In most cases, it is not because these Leaders are bad people. In most cases, it is because of the pervasive lack of clarity and depth of understanding regarding what real Leadership is, and how to really *Be* it and *Do* it. And this lack of clarity gets perpetuated across our organizations everywhere.

So, now that we clear about the cause of our Leadership dilemma, we should be equally clear about the solution to this Leadership opportunity. And that is to provide committed, inspired Leaders everywhere with a proven map and a functional progression for the journey into extraordinary Leadership. Our responsibility now is to step into this map, this BIG, complex puzzle of Leadership, and to express our Leadership purpose, in service to others. It's a new day in the field of Leadership development. All of the key pieces of the Leadership puzzle, that to this point, have been unavailable or incomplete to most of us, are now readily accessible to us. The AQ Model has illuminated this for us in clear detail.

The only question left for us to answer as individual Leaders is: Now that we know what we know; now that we are clear about the significant limitations of the status quo of Leadership; now that we are clear about the potential and possibilities and the depth of service and impact on individuals and organizations that truly extraordinary Leadership can bring; and now that we know about the joy and grace and freedom that can come from stepping deeply into our Leadership purpose, stepping deeply into our authentic self; now that we know all of this, what will our next decisive step be? There is no time for further rumination on this issue. It is time to act! People everywhere need us, and now. It is time for us to finally do something definitive. It is time for us to step forward in a way that is best for those we serve. Our journey starts right now for us, no matter which direction we choose to follow.

It should be clear to us, what it would mean to choose to remain in the status quo of Leadership. It should be clear to us, what it would mean to choose to do nothing at this point. It should also be clear to us that we are being offered a possibility here, and that we are being provided with the keys to get us there. We can no longer be held back by a lack of knowledge regarding the possibilities of Leadership. Now, we can see it and know it and feel it and step right into it. It is now time for us to make our stand for those we serve, for those that need us so much. This is why we are here! *This is the Leadership Revolution that I am talking about!*

As we bring this phase of our exploration together to a close, I would like to say that I have so much enjoyed our journey together. And I so much look forward to the possibility of our paths crossing on our future journeys! But just knowing that we are all out there somewhere, really doing some version of this thing, to the best of our abilities, and learning and growing, and sharing, and making mistakes, and picking ourselves back up again, and getting back in the game, and really going for it, and getting into the depth of reality, and connecting with others, and serving, serving, serving, provides me with a feeling of incredible joy and an extraordinary sense of awe and gratitude. I want to thank everyone in advance for your commitment to extraordinary Leadership and your service to others, and for the waves of inspired people and exceptional results that will surely follow!

In Service,
Brian

21991928R00270

Made in the USA
San Bernardino, CA
13 January 2019